D1032704

The Forms of Things Unknown

PABLO PICASSO: Minotauromachy. Etching, 1935
(*The Museum of Modern Art, New York*)

THE FORMS OF THINGS UNKNOWN

Essays towards an Aesthetic Philosophy

by

HERBERT READE

Man can embody truth
but he cannot know it.
W. B. Yeats

Meridian Books

THE WORLD PUBLISHING COMPANY

CLEVELAND AND NEW YORK

A MERIDIAN BOOK

Published by The World Publishing Company
2231 West 110th Street, Cleveland 2, Ohio
First Meridian printing December 1963.

Reprinted by arrangement with Horizon Press.
Library of Congress Catalog Card Number: 60-14683
Printed in the United States of America. MWP1263

Contents

PART I

PART II

PART III

PART IV

Illustrations

And as imagination bodies forth
The forms of things unknown, the poet's pen
Turns them to shapes, and gives to airy nothing
A local habitation and a name.

A MIDSUMMER NIGHT'S DREAM, V.i.

Preface

This book is concerned with the nature of the creative mind and with the part it plays in the maintenance of those values that in the past have been inseparable from the idea of a civilization. I believe that such values are threatened by the developments, variously known as industrialization, mechanization, automation and mass communication, that together constitute the technological revolution of our time. This revolution has been accompanied by the rise of a scientific philosophy which is obviously in harmony with it. The arts, too, are in a stage of transition that can only be called revolutionary, and in the general confusion it is very necessary to reaffirm, not so much the values of the past, which understandably have no appeal to people already committed to technology and all the power and wealth that goes with it, but certain psychological facts about the mind and its formative functions.

This, however, is not a scientific treatise. It is a collection of essays, most of which were originally delivered as successive lectures to a select audience of philosophers and psychologists. They may therefore be assumed to have a certain measure of continuity, and apart from two introductory lectures which are concerned with necessary definitions and qualifications, they are all preoccupied with the nature of the artistic activity, and with its social and biological functions. Though I can hardly dare to hope that yet another book of mine on such a subject will be received with sympathy, nevertheless the problem is not only important but also urgent. The forces that give momentum to the technological revolution are powerful, and power does indeed seem to be the only solution for the many social and economic problems of our troubled world. But the human agents of these forces are often insensitive and blind—insensitive to aesthetic values and blind to the consequences of ignoring the subtle springs of creation, on which science itself no less than art depends for its vital continuance.

The subject is as difficult as it is important, and I cannot hope to have reduced it to a clear outline. I write as a poet rather than as a scientist, but I must ask the reader to believe that the importance I attach to such factors as image, symbol, myth and icon is not due to any initial prejudice, but rather to an objective realization of the controlling influence of these factors in the development of human culture. If I thought that the world could be saved and the happiness of mankind guaranteed by the sacrifice of aesthetic sensibility, I would not hesitate to accept that sacrifice. But my belief is just the contrary. It is because I see everywhere the threatening shadow of the catastrophe that overtakes a people without vision that I strive to reanimate the only philosophy that can save us.

The audience I have referred to above is that which gathers every year on the shores of Lake Maggiore—the Eranos Tagung. There are no formal discussions at these meetings, but a sympathetic contact of minds takes place, with an interflow of very various cultural traditions. I have greatly benefited from this experience, and would like to express my gratitude to Olga Fröbe-Kapteyn, the gracious lady who brought Eranos into being and gave it shelter, and whose devotion to spiritual values has kept its proceedings vital for more than twenty-five years. I would also like to thank the Trustees of the Bollingen Foundation in New York, who own the copyright in the lectures first published in the *Eranos Jahrbuch*,[1] for their kind permission to include chapters 3, 4, 7–14 in this volume.

HERBERT READ

[1] Published by the Rhein Verlag, Zürich.

PART I

CHAPTER 1

The Limitations of a Scientific Philosophy[1]

Objectivity is a perception
EVERETT KNIGHT

A distinction which runs through the whole development of human thought has become blurred during the past two hundred years. Implicit in all ancient philosophy, acknowledged by medieval scholastics and the natural philosophers of the Renaissance, and even by Locke and Newton, is a difference of kind, if not of value, between *wisdom* and *understanding*. By wisdom was meant an intuitive apprehension of truth, and the attitude involved was receptive or contemplative. *Intellectus* was the name given to this faculty in the Middle Ages. Understanding, on the other hand, was always a practical or constructive activity, and *ratio* was its name—the power by means of which we perceive, know, remember and judge sensible phenomena. Philosophy was conceived as an endeavour to perfect this constructive power of the mind as an aid to wisdom. To clarify perception, excluding all distortions due to emotion and prejudice; to analyse statements so that our knowledge is consistent; to establish facts, so that our memory is consolidated; to bring the inquiring will into harmony with the intuitive intellect, so that our judgment is true and constant—such have been the aims of all who called themselves philosophers.

[1] This chapter contains the substance of the first Annual Institute of Education Lecture, delivered in Birmingham on 10th October 1957. It was first printed in *Educational Review*, Vol. 10, No. 2, Feb. 1958, pp. 92–107.

I do not propose to review the great debate which we associate with the names of Descartes, Locke, Hume, Leibniz and Kant. That argument, which is essentially an inquiry into the meaning of existence, still goes on in the works of Husserl, Heidegger and Sartre. But at some point in the development of human understanding—and it was certainly not before the time of Kant—a tendency to radical empiricism developed. One might also call it a tendency to radical scepticism, for it was based on a determination not to ask questions that cannot be answered without indulging in speculation—the only acceptable answers are those which are based on empirical observations, and which can be checked or proved by repeating the same empirical observations. Human understanding was redefined in this restrictive sense, and wisdom disappeared from the philosopher's vocabulary. Since the Lord was no longer feared, one might say, wisdom could have no beginning.

The determination of scientists not to ask questions that cannot be answered empirically, and proved logically, has led to a drastic shrinkage of philosophical territory: philosophy is now identified with logic, deductive and inductive, and it is the claim of the scientific philosophers that no other mental activity deserves the name of philosophy. Logical formulas have taken the place of what the scientist calls 'the picture language of speculative systems', and on a diet of such dry dog biscuits modern man is asked to undertake his spiritual Odyssey.

One may observe that concurrently with this development science itself, in the representative field of physics, has retreated farther and farther from a direct reliance on sense data, and though rigorously maintaining its principle of verifiability, constructs an invisible world of atoms as remote from normal experience as the unseen stars. It is possible to maintain, paradoxically, that science has become speculative, and art empirical, for truth, as Saint-Exupéry said in a brilliant aphorism, is not what we discover, but what we create.

We may admit, with the logical scientist, that it is an illusion to assume that the human mind can have any direct access to truth—truth in Plato's sense of a pre-established harmony waiting for our intuitive understanding. But what we must not admit is that knowledge is only knowledge when it is based on those elements of perception that can be reduced to measurements and verified in a laboratory—so-called functional knowledge. Science functions within the limits of its sign-system—that is to say, it must confine itself to the cognitive content of its particular kind of language; but beyond this scientific sign-system, quite apart from it, is the symbolic system of art, which is also a particular kind of language with a cognitive content.

I am not writing for philosophers and, indeed, I do not claim to be a philosopher myself. As I proceed, therefore, I must make clear in what sense I am using terms that have a technical philosophic connotation—this phrase 'cognitive content', for example. When in doubt I run to a dictionary to confirm that my use of the word has some justification in general usage; and there I find cognition defined as knowledge in its widest sense, including (*a*) non-propositional apprehension (perception, memory, introspection, etc.—note that etcetera); as well as (*b*) propositions or judgments expressive of such apprehension.[1] What in this jargon is called non-propositional apprehension would include among its 'cetera' the intuitions of the artist—of the poet, the painter, the sculptor, the architect and the musician—and may I make it clear that I shall be using the words 'art' and 'artists' indifferently for any of the arts?

Could anyone for a moment doubt that the artist, in his acts of apprehension, is making a statement with a cognitive content? The answer is yes—the scientific philosopher usually makes precisely this assumption. He assumes that his own propositions or judgments are the only statements with a cognitive content—that all other propositions or judgments are either pseudo-statements (his favourite term for the statements of idealist or rational philosophy), or are a picture-language expressing subjective desires, and therefore not propositions or statements of any kind. A different school of thought to which I myself belong, a school entirely ignored by the scientific philosopher, maintains on the contrary, in the words of one of its few representatives, that 'the artistic impulse is an impulse of cognition; artistic activity, an operation of the power of achieving cognition; the artistic result, a sequel of cognition'.[2]

I am going to take as a representative of scientific philosophy the famous logical empiricist Hans Reichenbach—I do not think his

[1] Runes, D. D. (ed.), *The Dictionary of Philosophy*, London, Routledge, 1944.

[2] Fiedler, C., *On Judging Works of Visual Art*, trans. Schaeffer-Simmern, H., and Mood, F., University of California Press, 1949, p. 76.

representative standing would be challenged by the scientists. I take him for the practical reason that in his last work, *The Rise of a Scientific Philosophy*,[1] he has given us a clear summary of the claims of a scientific philosophy.

That phrase is not so innocent as it sounds. By a scientific philosophy is not now meant a grammar of science, such as, in my youth, writers like Karl Pearson provided. The phrase means what it says—a philosophy that bases itself on scientific method, just as physics bases itself on scientific method. Gone is the idea that philosophy is in some way a generalization of scientific knowledge; and gone, of course, the Kantian claim that philosophy is knowledge based on independent powers of reasoning—powers independent, that is to say, of sense observation, powers of insight or intuition. The basic assumption of a scientific philosophy is that philosophy is the product of the power of abstraction, and must be confined to abstract statements that have been verified by logical analysis. Such a philosophy, says Reichenbach, 'does not offer the persuasive solutions of systems that talk picture language and appeal to aesthetic desires. It presents answers understandable only to a mind trained in abstract thought; it requires that its disciples study every item with the precision of the engineer and the scrutiny of the mathematician. But to those who are willing to submit to these requirements it offers the reward of an intellectual insight of amazing proportions.'[2]

We must not expect truth or certainty from such a philosophy. Fundamentally the scientific philosopher does not believe that a comprehensive truth is possible. Truth is a predicate of statements, he says; certainty is inseparable from emptiness; there can be no synthetic *a priori*. The speculative philosophy of the past, says Reichenbach, 'is characterized by a *transcendental* conception of knowledge, according to which knowledge transcends the observable things and depends upon the use of other sources than sense perception'. Scientific philosophy (on the other hand) rejects such a conception of knowledge in its entirety and constructs instead 'a *functional* conception of knowledge, which regards knowledge as an instrument of prediction and for which sense observation is the

[1] References are to the paper-bound edition, University of California Press, 1956.

[2] Op. cit., p. 121. It is not clear why the word 'insight' is used in the last sentence: it does not belong to the vocabulary of the scientific philosopher.

only admissible criterion of non-empty truth'. Not even mathematics will satisfy this conception of knowledge—'it is self-deception to believe the human mind to have a direct access to any kind of truth other than that of empty logical relations'. Verifiability is the only ideal of the scientific philosopher, who 'must learn that probable knowledge is a basis solid enough to answer all questions that can reasonably be asked'.

Scientific philosophy, then, is a philosophy of logical formulas, and all the rest, metaphysics and ethics, is to be dismissed as the picture-language of speculative systems. The scientific philosopher does not even bother to discuss such systems: he dismisses speculation as such, as a pretension to knowledge which cannot be verified: sense perception is the only basis of knowledge, and every statement of an observed fact must have a logical meaning and must be capable of being checked by further observation. 'A sentence,' says Reichenbach, 'the truth of which cannot be determined from possible observations is meaningless. Although rationalists have believed that there are meanings in themselves, empiricists at all times have insisted that meaning hinges on verifiability. Modern science is a documentation of this point of view.'

What, in this context, is meant by an observation, or an empirical fact? Possibly the whole of my criticism of scientific philosophy turns on this point.

A scientist in his laboratory examines natural phenomena—it may be a frog's leg or the eye of a beetle; it may be a spiral nebula as seen in a 200-inch telescope or the X-ray diffraction pattern of uranium. He makes thousands of observations of this kind, classifies them, and when a verifiable sequence of events begins to emerge from this classification, he *abstracts* a meaning. This meaning is not an assertion of fact: the only facts are the discrete observations he has made, the data provided by his instruments. But he dignifies his abstracted meaning, his guess, with the name of philosophy. 'Philosophy,' Reichenbach says, 'is no longer the story of men who attempted in vain to "say the unsayable" in pictures or verbose constructions of pseudo-logical form. Philosophy is logical analysis of all forms of human thought: what it has to say can be stated in comprehensible terms, and there is nothing "unsayable" to which it has to capitulate. Philosophy is scientific in its method; it gathers results accessible to demonstration and assented to by those who are sufficiently trained in logic and science' (p. 308).

Reichenbach contrasts the precision of such meanings abstracted from observation with what he calls the persuasive solutions of 'picture-language'—systems of thought which appeal, not to the intellect, but to 'aesthetic desires'. I will first examine the scientist's conception of this other mode of expression, which for Reichenbach covers not only art, but also ethics and presumably theology[1], and then give my own alternative conception of the language of art.

It is not until very late in his book that Professor Reichenbach gives us a definition of art, and I must ask you to examine it with me because I believe it illustrates an extraordinary misconception of the nature of this human activity, a misconception not confined to scientists. 'Art,' Professor Reichenbach declares without any qualification, 'is emotive expression,' and so that we may be in no doubt as to what he means he expands this dogmatic statement in the following way:

'Aesthetic objects serve as symbols expressing emotional states. The artist, as well as the person who looks at, or listens to, the works of art inserts emotive meanings into physical objects consisting in paint spread on canvas or sounds produced by musical instruments. The symbolic expression of emotive meanings is a natural goal, that is, it represents a value which we aspire to enjoy. Valuation is a general characteristic of human goal-activities, and it is advisable to study its logical nature in full generality, not restricting the analysis to art' (p. 313).

Valuation, in the scientist's view, is not a scientific activity: not a logical act: it is merely an affirmation of desires, and if Professor Reichenbach were right in assuming that the artistic activity is nothing but 'the insertion of emotive meanings into physical

[1] As far as theology is concerned, the limitations of a scientific philosophy have often been demonstrated, but nowhere so ably as by Mascall, E. L., *Words and Images*, London, Longmans, 1957. What Dr Mascall has to say about the nature of sense-experience (for example, the non-sensory or the intellectual element in perception does not consist simply of inference, but of apprehension) is very relevant to the present argument. When he insists (p. 112) 'that images, like language, have an epistemological character and function which is not exhausted in terms of coding and decoding; the image or the image-complex, like the word or the word-complex, is an *objectum-quo*, by the entertainment and contemplation of which the mind is able to enter into intimate cognitive union with the reality of which it is a manifestation', he is virtually anticipating my whole contention.

objects' he might then be right to dismiss it as of no philosophical significance. But Professor Reichenbach's definition is only one of many possible definitions of art, and one that is now old-fashioned and discredited. In aesthetics we should call it the expressionist theory, and it has had more vogue in Germanic than in Latin countries. Benedetto Croce gave it an idealistic formulation which made it completely unreal, and since Croce's time no one has seriously entertained it in the literal sense, unless it be some American behaviourist. That the work of art is in some sense an embodiment of feeling is not to be denied. But what certain philosophers of art now maintain is that the function of the work of art is not to present feelings for enjoyment, but rather to cognition. Paradoxically, the feelings in a work of art are not felt. Art, as Otto Baensch has said, 'like science, is a mental activity whereby we bring certain contents of the world into the realm of objectively valid cognition; . . . it is the particular office of art to do this with the world's emotional content. According to this view, therefore, the function of art is not to give the percipient any kind of pleasure, however noble, but to acquaint him with something which he has not known before.'[1]

Of course, in one general sense art is expression: that is to say, it uses a system of signs to communicate a meaning. So does science and every other human mental activity. But the nature of the activity is determined by its purpose or function, and Reichenbach is wrong in asserting that the function of art is to make a valuation or satisfy a desire. The fundamental purpose of the artist is the same as that of the scientist: to state a fact. And the fundamental purpose of attending to works of art is not to enjoy values, but as in science to establish truths.

I can think of no criteria of truth in science that do not apply with equal force to art. Art has its language of symbols whilst science has a language of signs, but a symbolic language also has its strict system of rules, based on convention. The creative imagination has a logic no less strict than the logic of scientific reasoning, and the same ideal of clarity is held by both activities. Further, there is no sense in which verifiability is a necessary constituent of

[1] Langer, S. K., *Feeling and Form*, London, Routledge, 1953, p. 10. Baensch's original article entitled 'Kunst und Gefühl' appeared in *Logos*, 1923. An English translation is given in *Reflections on Art*, edited by S. K. Langer, Baltimore, The Johns Hopkins Press and London, Oxford University Press, 1959, pp. 10–36.

scientific method in which it is not also a necessary constituent of artistic creation. Great works of art do not survive through the centuries as expressions of desire or as valuations of behaviour. They state such universal truths as the artist is capable of creating; they search for no certainty and express no ideal. They are constructions, concretely physical. Emotions may be inserted into them: they may be clothed in appearances of good and evil, of tragedy and joy; but these expressive functions are not the verifiable content of the work of art. What is verifiable is a perceptible form which communicates a notion of being, a man-made piece of reality.

A scientific philosopher such as Reichenbach regards empirical science as the ideal form of knowledge and insists that sense observation is the only source of knowledge; that it is self-deception to believe the human mind to have a direct access to any kind of truth other than that of empty logical relations. This is virtually a denial that there are any absolute or universal values that can have meaning. We can make emotive noises and call them poetry; we can write a metaphorical language and call it ethics; we can create beautiful objects and get a sensational shock from them; but all these activities, according to the scientific philosopher, have no meaning because they do not lead to verifiable statements.

What, then, is verifiable meaning: what is a scientific fact? The modern scientist has good grounds for his universal scepticism, for in the past seventy years the former ground of all his certainties has crumbled. The process began with the Michelson-Morley experiment, which showed for the first time that our terrestrial standards of measurement are not universal; and it ends, for the present, with a tangle of relativity and indeterminacy. Einstein's theory of relativity has been modified considerably since he first enunciated it, but as Sir James Jeans once said (with reference to Weyl's criticisms of Einstein's theory), it is 'highly probable that all forces reduce to nothing more than our subjective interpretations of special properties of the continuum in which we live'.[1] In short, what the scientist has been driven to recognize more and more is that his observations are not separable from the observer, that subject and object are one. We cannot eliminate ourselves from our observations, and even a scientific method depends on conscious-

[1] *Enc. Brit.*, 13th ed., Supp. Vol. III, p. 330.

ness, which is an unstable element developed by man in the course of his physical evolution, 'an organ still infantile', as Nietzsche called it. Language itself and the symbolic signs by means of which any logical analysis must proceed, are instruments developed by this organ for the control of man's environment; instruments conditioned by his environment, and still in a state of evolution. Sign systems are incomplete because our consciousness is incomplete; and the means by which man is continually extending the area of his consciousness, and concurrently his various means of communication, are not scientific but artistic.

Before I point to the consequences of this misconception for education, which is the main purpose of this chapter, I should like to refer in more detail to that famous observation of Kant's which attributes to man an overall intuition by virtue of which scientific progress becomes possible—the notion that reason must formulate its own *a priori* laws, which are then tested by experiment. It is a notion decisively rejected by the modern scientific philosopher, but not by every modern scientist. Referring to the early experimental scientists, Galileo and Torricelli, Kant observed that they had learned 'that reason only perceives that which it produces after its own design; that it must not be content to follow, as it were, in the leading strings of nature, but must proceed in advance with principles of judgment according to unvarying laws, and compel nature to reply to its questions. For accidental observations, made according to no preconceived plan, cannot be united under a necessary law. . . . Reason must approach nature with the view, indeed, of receiving information from it, not, however, in the character of a pupil, who listens to all that his master chooses to tell him, but in that of a judge, who compels the witnesses to reply to those questions which he himself thinks fit to propose.' This *a priori* rationality, a principle that sustained science so long as the corresponding principle of causality was accepted as universal, has now been overthrown, and in its place we find only statistical averages, or 'posits of probability'. But Kant's categories serve to show that the human mind is capable of a certain independent activity. It is not necessarily conditioned by its environment: it can ask questions—it can formulate ideals, it can, in one word, imagine. It can reach beyond itself, towards values which are not actual, but which become actual in the course of evolution. Such independent mental constructions the scientist calls 'goal activities', and he is rather contemptuous of them. 'The choice of a goal,' says Reichenbach, 'is not a logical act. It is the spontaneous affirmation of desires, or volitions, which come upon us with the compulsion of inescapable urges, or the animation of prospective satisfaction, or the smooth naturalness of unquestioned habits'; and he concludes peremptorily: 'There is no point in asking the philosopher to justify valuations.' To which we might reply with Nietzsche that this is the only activity worthy of a philosopher, for 'the criterion of truth lies in the enhancement of the feeling of power';[1] or, since Nietzsche's use of the word 'power' has led to such a complete misunderstanding of his philosophy, let us say in the simple words of another scientist (Victor von Weizâcker) that 'in order to explore life, one has to take part in life'. Truth is not a verifiable abstraction: and to equate such a necessary word with 'empty logical relations' is to reduce philosophy to a parlour game. Philosophy, to be worthy of the name, is not a game of any kind: it is a mode of action, a free choice of facts in a world of facts. But the philosopher does not necessarily choose his facts in the scientist's laboratory: instead, he may create poetic symbols, which are facts of another kind. He invents a myth, like the *Republic* of Plato, or Augustine's *City of God*, or Nietzsche's *Zarathustra*. Fundamentally, as Sartre says, man is the *desire to be*, and the existence of this desire is not to be established by an empirical induction, but by self-realization. 'There is not first a single desire of being, then a thousand particular feelings, but the desire to be exists and manifests itself only in and through jealousy, greed, love of art, cowardice, courage, and a thousand contingent, empirical expressions which always cause human reality to appear to us as *manifested by a particular man*, by a specific person.'[2] Philosophy is a human activity, not a disembodied energy.

It has always seemed to me that the reduction of science to indeterminacy, and philosophy to a game with counters, far from discrediting idealism, has made it all the more necessary. If, as Reichenbach says, 'the happenings of nature are like rolling dice rather than like revolving stars; they are controlled by probability laws, not by causality'; if the scientist 'resembles a gambler rather

[1] Quoted by Lea, F. A., *The Tragic Philosopher*, London, Methuen, 1957, p. 278.

[2] Sartre, J. P., *Being and Nothingness*, trans. H. E. Barnes, London, Methuen, 1957, p. 565.

than a prophet'—and I accept the modern scientist's own description of himself—then the prophet or some person other than the scientist, perhaps the artist, becomes all the more necessary. Someone must make a choice; someone must say that in this world of rolling dice, 'I will act as croupier and impose my system. The system will not be real: it will bear no relation to the laws of probability. But it will work, and I shall believe in it. More than that; it will enable me to believe that life has some purpose. I have made a choice, whether moral or aesthetic, and if the scientist still persists in saying that it bears no relation to truth, that my choice is merely a "spontaneous affirmation of desires", I can say, with more conviction than the scientist can muster, that the desire I affirm is the desire to live more abundantly, that I live abundantly in my acts of creation, and that this is the only philosophical activity that has any positive meaning for mankind.'

Scientific philosophers like Reichenbach always assume that our desires are selfish, or hedonistic—psychological urges for food, sex, or rest. Reichenbach writes of 'the creative impulse driving a man to write a book or to make his own fence for his garden'—individualistic activities, of no consequence to his fellow-men. In fact the creative impulse finds an outlet not only in the context of a physical world, but also in the context of other human beings. Every choice, moral or aesthetic, is, as Sartre has so well demonstrated, an act which involves the whole human race. Man finds himself in a specific situation—the social situation of his time—and must every day exercise his responsibility. He marries or does not marry; has children or does not have children; whatever he does, it is impossible to evade the problem of responsibility, which is also the problem of creative action. Man does not necessarily act according to the established moral codes. Sartre suggests that we should compare his moral decision to the creation of a work of art. The artist does not act according to established rules; no one tells him what kind of picture to paint. There are no *a priori* aesthetic values which the artist strives to incorporate in his pictures; the values declare themselves, in the coherence of the picture when it is completed, in the relations established between the desire to create and the result attained. The result is not arbitrary—it is successful or it is a failure, and one can only judge it when it is finished. It then takes its place among the rest of the artist's works: then we discover that it has form, style, beauty—values which are not arbitrary but constructive.[1] It is the same with man's moral decisions: they, too, do not follow a pre-established code, but they are not arbitrary. They are what Keats called 'a straining at particles of light in the midst of a great darkness' (letter of 14th February 1819), and are admirable to the degree that they express not abstractions like goodness, truth or beauty, but a particular man's sensuous apprehension of life itself, in its concreteness, its bloom, in its scintillation.

Non-propositional apprehensions—let us now take this dictionary phrase and give it our own further definition. A dictionary elaborates its definitions in conceptual terms—although one famous lexicographer took occasion to kick against a stone and define reality in that non-propositional way. 'Perception, memory, introspection, etc.'—meaning is always conceived as a mental process, communicable and communicated in words. But I am going to suggest that neither the logical idea nor the mental image is the datum in non-propositional apprehension; what is present in consciousness is the created object. Presumably the scientist will say that what is present to consciousness in his empirical observation is also not a logical idea or mental image, but an empirical fact, an object observed in all its concreteness. But I called my object a 'created' object, whereas the object in scientific observation is 'given'—scientific method is an immense effort to preserve its givenness, and to exclude any element of subjective interpretation. But the artist too will pride himself on his objectivity—the object he creates, he will say, is the objective correlative of an emotion, a mood, an idea, or an intuition; in brief, the realization of a state of consciousness. His art, his discipline and craft, are concentrated on the purification of his meaning, on the presentation of an exact symbol.

Consciousness, as William James long ago pointed out, does not exist apart from the object we are conscious of; but we can induce consciousness by seeking a correlative for feeling (emotion, mood, idea, intuition). That is essentially what the artistic process amounts to: it is the presentation to consciousness of an exact correlative for feeling, but the correlative presented to consciousness is always a concrete object, a plastic configuration, sounds, colours, shapes, masses accessible to sensation. The object the artist creates, therefore, corresponds to his state of consciousness:

[1] Cf. Sartre, J. P., *L'existentialisme est un humanisme*, Paris, Nagel, 1946, pp. 74–79. English translation by Philip Mairet, London, Methuen, 1948.

it is his consciousness of that object; it was not first present *in* consciousness, and then expelled like an egg: it grew into consciousness as it germinated, as it was plastically formed. It was matured by an awareness of a context, of a situation, of a matrix; but it came into existence as a created thing, as a creation. Reality, in my sense of the term, is what is in this way created: the objects that grow into consciousness, and remain there in all their concreteness. By comparison the facts *discovered* by the scientist are unreal—where did they come from? who put them there? Nothing to the mind of an artist could be more sophisticated than mathematical formalism, or a belief in the exclusive reliability of sense observation.

'Truth is a predicate of statements,' says the scientific philosopher. But he reduces all verbal statements to error or emptiness, and calls the desert a philosophy. The modern artist, who is always consciously or unconsciously an existentialist philosopher, says that truth is a predicate of the creation of specific symbolic objects. It has nothing to do with a linguistic reaction between the sense organs of the human being and an encompassing universe, as the scientist assumes. The artist knows that his sense organs are quite incapable of encompassing empirically any external reality; but he knows that he is a part of the universal process, a biological entity engaged in the adventure of existence; and by knowing this, by becoming aware of the growing-point that he is in this universal process, he is able to manufacture some grains of the real—just as the photogenic cells of a plant manufacture certain real substances from the air or the ether or the cosmic rays. The two processes are analogous rather than identical, but the work of art is real in the sense that an atom of nitrogen is real.

Works of art are discrete entities, but nevertheless they can combine into discourse, into symbolic coherence. This is best illustrated in the art of music, where each harmonic relation of tones is already a truth created; but such themes can be developed—created facts added to created facts in a created order—until a whole symbolic discourse of sound, a symphony, is present as a reality. The process in the plastic arts is similar, for the painter proceeds from one established tonal relation of colour to the next, modifying each as the creative process proceeds, until a self-contained unity is achieved—what is thus achieved may be a portrait or a landscape or an abstract object that has no reference to the world the scientist observes; but to make it 'real' the artist does not have to take a pump and inflate it with emotion—insert an emotive meaning into the physical object, as Reichenbach suggests: the object has whatever meaning the spectator may read into it, but as an object its reality resides in its harmonies and proportions, which are as verifiable as the logical formulas of the scientific philosopher. What constitutes the *value* of a work of art is not its expression or affirmation of desires or the choice of goals, but the fact that there exists a real object, something snatched from the flux of feeling and *made* to exist, objectively. Its existence, its persistence, is its reality.

In this way the history of art must be conceived, as Max Scheler says, 'as a series of expeditions against the intuitable world, within and without, to subdue it for our comprehension: and that for a kind of comprehension which no science could ever provide'. The mission of all true art is 'not to reproduce what is already given (which would be superfluous), nor to create something in the pure play of subjective fancy (which can be only transitory and must necessarily be a matter of complete indifference to other people), but to press forward into the whole of the external world *and* the soul, to see and communicate those objective realities within it which rule and convention have hitherto concealed'.[1] I would amend these words of Scheler's only in one detail, for the objective realities of art are not seen by the artist and then communicated: seeing is creating, and creation is communication: the objective realities come into existence in the act of creation.

I am proposing to you a philosophy which, though it has its exponents like Cassirer and Langer, Heidegger and Sartre, is totally distinct from the scientific philosophy of Reichenbach and indeed the philosophy prevailing in practically all the academic institutions in this country. I suppose it might be called the existentialist philosophy and I find much support for it among contemporary existentialist philosophers. But I hesitate to call it existentialist philosophy because I did not derive it from the existentialists, but from long meditation on the facts of art—the historical facts and the psychological facts. I prefer therefore to call it aesthetic philosophy, and I claim that it is based on data that are just as objective as the empirical facts of science. A

[1] Scheler, M., *The Nature of Sympathy*, trans. P. Heath, London, Routledge, 1954, p. 253.

Romano–Egyptian portrait on a mummy case is a fact as real as the contemporary propositions of Euclid; Vesalius in the first half of the sixteenth century founded the science of human anatomy, but a century earlier Jan van Eyck had anatomized the soul of man in his portraits, and who shall say which is the most real fact—a dissected corpse in the hospital St Jean at Bruges or the portrait of Margaret van Eyck in the Musée Communal of that same city? The scientist will claim that the circulation of the blood is a verifiable fact, but what then is the van Eyck portrait—a pseudo-statement as the scientific philosopher would say, 'a symbol expressing an emotional state'? Why, then, do we call Van Eyck 'the most exhaustive and the most tantalizing interpreter of human nature' that ever lived (Panofsky)? The widest claim that can be made for science is that it is the history of nature. The widest claim that can be made for art is that it is the creation of nature—that it brings into existence an entirely autonomous world.[1] This is the extreme point of view of André Malraux; for my part I am content to claim that it extends the existing world, enlarges it with new facts, with elements that give continuity to the human experience.

I hope these remarks will not be taken as an attack on science—I am attacking only the pretensions of science: its pretension to be the only sufficient basis of philosophy, or to be identical with Reason itself. For the will to truth which has animated, and continues to inspire, the activities of the scientists of the last few centuries we can have nothing but admiration; and though modern science has to some extent substituted a will to power for the will to truth, that is a social or ethical problem which I am not discussing. I am only asserting, with Karl Jaspers, for example, that 'dissatisfaction with science is the expression of the will to truth that reaches out beyond the fulfilment that science can provide'.[2] Even the choice of subjects for scientific research cannot, as Jaspers points out, be derived from science itself: 'Science is not self-supporting. Where it tries to be, it falls into an infinite abyss of platitudes.' Jaspers says that fundamentally we want more than science can give, and the danger is, of course, that we fall back on what Reichenbach calls 'the picture-language of speculative

[1] Malraux, A., *Les Voix du Silence*, Paris, Gallimard, 1952, p. 614.

[2] Jaspers, K., *Reason and Anti-Reason in our Time*, trans. S. Goodman, London, S.C.M. Press, 1952, p. 33.

systems'. Jaspers himself has, from the scientist's point of view, succumbed to this danger. But I am not offering you a speculative system: I am merely pointing to the concrete existence of those real and obdurate phenomena that we call works of art, and no philosophy is complete that does not incorporate their evidence.

Equally no education is complete that does not incorporate the evidence of art. I have spent the best part of a life-time protesting that an education that ignores the mental processes which lead to the creation of the most permanent achievements of mankind can be no true education. Our whole conception of education has become functional—conceived as serving the provisional interests of a social economy and not as a conquest of reality. Our education is not even scientific in the strict sense, for it is not disinterested. Not only are most scientists victims of what Reichenbach calls 'the fallacy of vocational preoccupation, which makes a man blind to the exigencies of research outside his own narrow field' (p. 192); their fields of research are chosen from extra-scientific motives—the development of atomic power, for example, or an ideal of mechanical perfection. The scientific conception of education is completely subordinate to valuations, desires, goals—what Reichenbach, in characterizing the unscientific nature of rational philosophy, calls 'the compulsion of unescapable urges, or the animation of prospective satisfaction, or the smooth naturalness of unquestioned habits' (p. 314). Education today is a system exactly corresponding to the technological organization of our society, and instead of realizing and regretting the enormous limitation that such a system imposes on the development of the human personality, we take pride in the inhuman efficiency of such a machine.

The scientific philosopher dismisses the imagination as picture-language, or as a pre-scientific form of thought no longer of relevance in this scientific age. ' "Truth is beauty and beauty is truth" [*sic*]—that is a beautiful statement,' says Reichenbach misquoting Keats, 'but not a true one.' On what grounds does he deny the truth of Keats's statement? Because, he says, the question how to classify art is a logical question—a question of the logical nature of valuation, a question to be studied by the psychologist. But I fail to see in what sense a work of art possessing beauty (and Keats had in mind the mathematical proportions of a Greek vase) differs in logical status from the empirical facts revealed to a biologist through his microscope. Both are material organizations, 'silent forms' that can be classified. Both exhibit an order that is fundamentally identical; and if the scientist asserts that the order he discovers in nature is not *meant* to give pleasure, whereas the potter who created the vase had the intention to give pleasure—then I would reply in the first place that the scientist by his own confession does not know whether an intention is present in the order of the universe; and that the intention of the potter was not to give pleasure, but to make a vase that corresponded to his instinct for order. Fundamentally—and I apologize for insisting on what may seem to be a subtle point but which is really the essence of the whole question—fundamentally there is no possibility of making a distinction between science and art in terms of valuation. The work of art is just as much or just as little an empirical fact as the structure of a molecule of carbon; the empirical facts of science are just as much a question of choice, or of chance, or of inspiration, as a work of art. I refuse absolutely to surrender the empirical status of the work of art.

But the empirical status of the work of art has been ignored by our technological age, by our rulers and educators. It is possible that many of us have been educated, and called to the vocation of teacher, and yet have been deprived of the knowledge of one-half of reality: we have been deprived of the beauty that is truth, of the truth that is beauty. It is a mistake, of course, to use these emotive words. What they mean in epistemological terms is that we have been deprived of a mode of communication, 'a mental activity whereby we bring certain contents of the world into objectively valid cognition,' to use Otto Baensch's words again. We have been denied an aesthetic method of apprehension whose functions are complementary to the logical method of definition and verification. We can get away with this half-experience, this half-knowledge, in a technological civilization. But what are the values of a technological civilization? What wisdom has it to offer us? It has a philosophy which is called scientific to correspond with a social organization that is functional, but does this philosophy answer those questions that have puzzled humanity throughout the ages, and that still puzzle any thoughtful man or woman today—the questions asked by the earliest Greek philosophers, by Pythagoras and Heraclitus, Zeno and Parmenides, Thales and Empedocles: the only questions worthy of the strife of thought:

Why does anything exist? Why does not nothing exist? What elements in existence justify the absurdity of continuing to live? To which I have added this final question: Is it possible that life acquires meaning only to the extent that man is creative?

CHAPTER 2

Art as a Symbolic Language

Art may be defined as symbolic language
CASSIRER

A renewed interest in symbolism is one of the characteristics of our time. It is due partly to those social sciences, like anthropology, which have emphasized the great and necessary rôle of symbolism in the life of primitive communities; and partly to the science of psychology which has shown the great and necessary (but often unacknowledged) rôle of symbolism in the mental life of civilized communities. Stemming from these studies there have been more specialized investigations into linguistics and aesthetics which have again assigned a predominant rôle to symbolism. The rationalists of the eighteenth century, or the historical materialists of the nineteenth century, were of the opinion that mankind in its intellectual development had transcended the symbol; today we not only admit the continuing force of symbolic modes of thought, but are even compelled to make a plea for their revival and extension.

'Man is primarily a communicating animal'—such is the opinion of Professor J. Z. Young, an English biologist who has made a special study of the human brain and nervous system.[1] Human beings communicate with one another by means of a great variety of signs, the most obvious being the signs systematized in language, spoken or written. But they also communicate by gesture (in which we may include the subtle but expressive movements of the face

[1] *Doubt and Certainty in Science.* A Biologist's Reflections on the Brain. Oxford, Clarendon Press, 1951, p. 58.

and eyes), by sounds that are not linguistic (music, for example), and by visual images.

A science which goes back to ancient Greek medicine and philosophy has been devoted to the study of these various sign-processes—it is known as *semiotic*. The ancient Stoics, we are told, made semiotic 'a basic division of knowledge co-ordinate with physics and ethics, and included within it logic and the theory of knowledge'.[1]

A related science, which has been given the name of *semantics*, is concerned more specifically with a study of the meaning of signs. In modern times these two overlapping sciences, semiotic and semantics, have become highly organized disciplines, with their own technical terminology, and are associated with some of the greatest names in modern philosophy: Charles Peirce and Mead, Dewey and Russell, Cassirer and Carnap. More specialized studies are due to Ogden and Richards, to Susanne Langer and Charles Morris, and to many others whose names would only be familiar to a specialist in the subject.

It is far from my intention, or capacity, to contribute to this discussion on a technical level. I shall rely on these sciences for a few definitions, but in the main I shall be concerned with the fact that there exist two competing systems of communication, one based on *sound*, the other on *sight*. I shall argue that the system based on sight has been underrated and sadly neglected by modern society, and that any satisfactory social integration or personal intelligence requires the full development of both systems of communication.

In general, semioticians have confined themselves to the study of the various types of discourse which make use of language. Charles Morris has classified discourse, firstly according to use as *informative*, *valuative*, *incitive*, and *systemic*; and secondly according to mode as *designative*, *appraisive*, *prescriptive* and *formative*. The various combinations of these modes and uses give sixteen major types of discourse—scientific, fictive, legal, mythical, poetic, moral, critical, religious, and so on, and a good deal can be said about the characteristics of each type of discourse. Scientific discourse, for example, illustrates (according to Charles Morris) 'the most specialized form of designative-informative

[1] Charles Morris, *Signs, Language and Behavior*, New York, Prentice-Hall, 1946. In an Appendix Dr Morris gives a history of the development of semiotic.

discourse. In it the designative mode of signifying is freed to the maximum degree from the other modes and developed in ways which most adequately perform the task of conveying true information about what has been, does, or will exist. In this respect, it merely elaborates and refines such statements as occur in common speech. As science advances, its statements become more purely designative, more general, better confirmed, and better systematized . . . Science is especially concerned with the search for reliable signs'.[1] Poetic discourse, on the other hand, is primarily appraisive-valuative. According to Morris, it 'signifies by signs which are appraisive in mode and its primary aim is to cause the interpreter to accord to what is signified the preferential place in his behaviour signified by the appraisors'—surely the most unpoetic description of poetry ever tapped out on a typewriter. But Dr Morris makes his meaning clearer when he states that 'the great significance of poetic discourse lies in the vivid and direct way that it records and sustains achieved valuations, and explores and strengthens novel valuations'.[2] To contrast extreme types of discourse such as these is to emphasize the general distinction, first established by Ogden and Richards in *The Meaning of Meaning*, between referential and emotive types of discourse, and our whole discussion might have centred on this conflict which is inherent in language itself, did not a more fundamental conflict—that between linguistic and non-linguistic modes of communication—call for more urgent consideration.

I ought to confess, before proceeding any further, that the title of this essay does not indicate accurately the subject with which I am concerned. At any rate, I ought to begin with a distinction, the one that Susanne Langer makes between the symbol 'which lets us *conceive* its object', and the sign, 'which causes us to *deal with* what it means'. Strictly speaking, as Charles Morris has argued, all symbols are signs, and the true contrast to the symbol is not the sign, but the *signal.* I do not think I need introduce such a refinement, because I am about to substitute another distinction which is more relevant to the discussion. But briefly it is now 'scientific' to use the word 'sign' for any vehicle of meaning, anything that directs behaviour and is not at the moment a physical stimulus; signs can then be divided into 'signals' and 'symbols'

[1] Op. cit., p. 126.

[2] *Philosophy in a New Key*, Harvard University Press, 1951, p. 223.

according to whether they are direct responses of the organism to its environment, or substitutes for such direct responses. To quote an illustration from Morris: 'A person may interpret his pulse as a sign of his heart condition or certain sensations as a sign that he needs food; such signs are simply signals; his resulting words—when substituted for such signals—would however be symbols.'[1] A neater definition is C. F. von Weizsäcker's: 'A sign which cannot be made superfluous simply by pointing to the object simplified, we shall call a symbol.'[2]

It is the contention of a semiotician like Charles Morris that our understanding of symbols is now always dependent in some degree on language, and symbols are distinguished as pre-language, language, and post-language. But a whole group of non-vocal signs—'signs other than those produced by the vocal cords and heard by the ear,' is recognized. Spoken-heard language, Dr Morris admits, 'has never supplanted its great rival—visual signs.' And he goes on to say:

'An age in which printing, photography, painting, film and television have an important place will call for a semiotic which has not neglected the visual sign; music lovers will rightly ask the sign status of musical sounds; and students of human nature will seek insight into the rôle of those signs which play such a prominent place [*sic*] in "thinking" and yet which are not spoken or heard.'

That is precisely the problem I am concerned with now. But it is not merely a problem of whether the science of semiotic or semantics can afford to neglect non-vocal signs; the question is whether in any sphere of human activity, and more especially in the sphere of education and social discourse, we can afford to neglect those systems of non-vocal signs, known more familiarly as the plastic arts, which constitute modes of communication as essential as the modes of communication embodied in vocal (spoken-heard) language.

Let us first note that there is a good deal of ground common to the vocal and non-vocal languages. A painting may convey information, or evaluate a situation, with the same accuracy as a spoken description of that situation. Morris admits that 'a portrait of a person, together with the name of the person, is, as Peirce

[1] Morris, op. cit., p. 26.

[2] *The World View of Physics*, London, Routledge & Kegan Paul, 1952, p. 140.

held, no less a statement than the verbal description of a person'.[1] Music can convey information about a situation or a mood. Morris further admits that:

'Such arts as music and painting may then signify in any of the modes of signifying. And since they can be put to various uses, they can illustrate in various degrees all the types of discourse which have been distinguished. Painting or music, for example, can be designatively informative, appraisively valuative, and so on. Hence a painting or a piece of music can in principle be scientific, poetic, mythological, religious, and the like, terms which we do in fact frequently (and correctly) employ in this way.'

The most that a scientist like Charles Morris will admit—and among scientists I think he would classify himself as a behaviourist—is that non-vocal signs, organized as arts, are 'indispensable for appraisive-valuative discourse, since they can embody vividly and concretely in their icons the very characteristics of the objects which in their appraisive capacity they signify as valuata'. This seems to be an admission, jargon apart, that works of art can have an effect on human behaviour without necessarily being translated into linguistic signs. They can act as substitutes for speech. There is nowhere an admission, as far as I can gather, that works of art have a special rôle in social discourse—that they can express, and communicate, knowledge or values altogether beyond the scope of language.

For an assertion of this truth we must go to the philosophers and to the poets. I think almost all the great poets have been aware that they were in some sense the possessors of what Leone Vivante has described as 'a principle of inward light—an original, self-active principle, which characterizes life and spontaneity as contrasted with mechanism'.[2] What we have to assert, and attempt to prove, is that art is a cognitive activity—that it is not merely an embellishment or intensification of linguistic types of discourse: it is not even a substitute for those types of discourse: it is a unique mode of discourse, giving access to areas of knowledge that are closed to other types of discourse.

This truth, although always evident to philosopher-poets like Goethe and Shelley, was first given full philosophical status by Cassirer in his *Philosophy of Symbolic Forms*, the first volume of

[1] Morris, op. cit., p. 194.
[2] *English Poetry*, London, Faber, 1950, p. 1.

which was published in 1923. It is true that fifty years earlier the symbolic nature of the plastic arts had been clearly recognized by another German philosopher, Conrad Fiedler, but his fragmentary writings have been neglected and even Cassirer seems to have been unaware of them. But Cassirer's recognition, not in the *Philosophy of Symbolic Forms* but in the shorter and later *Essay on Man*,[1] that art 'is not the mere reproduction of a ready-made, given reality . . . not an imitation but a discovery of reality' is identical with Fiedler's recognition of the same truth, and when Cassirer goes on to affirm that 'art may be defined in symbolic language', he is using phraseology identical with Fiedler's.

It would simplify our discussion at this stage if we were to follow Fiedler's example and confine ourselves to the visual arts. The very fact that poetry makes use of words, the material also of rational discourse, complicates any discussion of its non-rational uses; though I believe that the kind of illumination that comes to the consciousness of the poet, and is expressed in words, is not essentially different from the kind of illumination that comes to the painter or sculptor and is expressed in visual images; nor is it essentially different from the kind of illumination that comes to the musician and is expressed in tonal images.[2]

A poem, like a picture or a musical composition, has its unique form, which is a complex of images and cadences, and this form is an embodiment of the artist's feelings and conveys a meaning which is not necessarily co-extensive with the discursive or rational meaning of the words employed. A poem not only *is* different, but *means* more, than its prose paraphrase. It has a physical shape (the black words as they lie on the white page); it has a musical configuration that in itself, as sound, is expressive. At the simplest such a musical configuration is a meaningless

[1] Yale University Press, 1944.

[2] The particular way in which a poem functions symbolically is well described in Rosemund Tuve's book, *A Reading of George Herbert*, London, Faber, 1952, p. 93: 'The meanings of a poem carried to its author often lie too deep for formulation without the aid of metaphor; that is why they must be symbolized. . . . A work of art is a highly conscious achievement; perhaps the human consciousness is seen functioning at its highest when it tries thus to give form to the formless. The welter has its interests, too, but the excitement of literature is that a mind has shaped into loveliness that which otherwise would lie unshaped and dumb. The business of criticism is likewise not with the word unspoken, not with the thing unheard, unshaped, unknown, unmeant, but with the beauty and the power which is taken on by that to which a maker gives form.'

refrain, a 'hey nonny no', or a 'fara diddle dyno'. But every line and verse has this sound-pattern that can be abstracted from the literal content of the statement made in the poem, and when abstracted this sound-pattern would have an expressive function, just as the visual composition of a painting has an expressive function when abstracted from its figurative content. The whole purpose of art, of course, is to make these two functions reinforce one another, so that form comes in aid of feeling—the sound is *responsive* to an unconscious need for expressiveness, for emphasis. A poet can establish, for a particular poem, a pattern of musical expression, and then subtly vary it. Poe's lines 'To Helen' owe part of their mysterious beauty to this principle of variation. A regular pattern is established in the first verse—a steady iambic beat corresponding to the sweep of oars over 'a perfumed sea'. Then the quickened rhythm of the second verse, describing how Helen has brought the poet home over 'desperate seas'

To the glory that was Greece
And the grandeur that was Rome

and finally an invocation in slow rhythm and a last line which ends two voiceless but evocative syllables short of the established pattern:

Ah, Psyche, from the regions which
Are Holy Land!

This is a simple example of symbolic form in poetry, of sound-pattern established almost visually, like musical notation, but at any rate as an aural composition, for the ear, superimposed, as it were, on the literal meaning, an accompaniment in another medium.

The form of the poem, that is to say, is a non-vocal sign, even when it is a shape of words which express meaning in the ordinary semantic sense by their syntax. But let us avoid the formal ambiguities of linguistic art and confine ourselves to the visual arts. We can then more confidently affirm, with Conrad Fiedler, that 'artistic activity is an entirely original and absolutely independent mental activity'.[1]

Fiedler was the first philosopher to suggest that the knowledge

[1] *On Judging Works of Visual Art,* trans. by Henry Schaefer-Simmern and Fulmer Mood, University of California Press, 1949, p. 61.

of reality given by the visual arts is *sui generis* and in no necessary degree coincident with the knowledge of reality which we owe to science or philosophical speculation. Works of art embody an independent and free development of perceptual experience. 'It is the rare privilege of highly organized, sensitive persons,' says Fiedler, 'that they can achieve immediate contact with nature. Their relation to an object does not arise from single effects; on the contrary, they grasp its very existence, and they feel the object as a whole before they break up this general feeling into many separate sensations.'[1]

The artist, Fiedler goes on to say, 'becomes an artist by virtue of his ability to rise above his sensations.' Fiedler contrasts 'the conceptual mastery of the world', which is given in abstract cognition, with the perceptual mastery of the world given in artistic creation. He points out that the scientist, and we might add the educationist, habitually considers a perceptual activity inferior if it does not lead to clear concepts dominating perception. But the scientist and educationist are wrong in believing that 'through abstract thinking alone all the intellectual capacities of human nature have been recognized and fulfilled. To remain at the stage of perception rather than to pass onward to the stage of abstraction does not mean remaining on a level which does not lead to cognition; on the contrary, *it means to keep open other roads that also arrive at cognition*. But if cognition attained by perceptual experience is different from cognition reached by abstract thinking, it can nevertheless be a true and final cognition'.[2]

Fiedler's description of the artistic process as 'a holding on to perceptual experiences in spite of both sensation and abstraction' has been corroborated by the statements of many artists, notably,

[1] Op. cit., p. 28. It is not entirely a question of sensation—although sensation cannot be experienced without perception, nevertheless, Fiedler points out, 'sensation does not stimulate and further, but rather hinders, the growth of our visual conceptions. Our feeling is something else than our visual conceiving, and if the former dominates, then the latter must step back. For example, in sensing the beauty of a particular object, we may occupy ourselves with this sensation entirely, without proceeding a single step towards the *perceptual mastering of the object*. However, at that moment when interest based on visual conception takes hold of us again, we must be able to forget every sensation in order to further our perceptual grasp of the object for its own sake. Because many persons are all too quick to transform perceptual experience into feeling, their perceptual abilities remain on a low level of development.' Op. cit., pp. 29–30. (My italics.)

[2] Op. cit., pp. 34–35.

since Fiedler's time, by Cézanne. Here, for example, is a quotation from a letter of Cézanne's to Emile Bernard (12th May 1904):

'I am progressing very slowly, for nature reveals herself to me in very complex forms; and the progress needed is incessant. One must see one's model correctly and experience it in the right way; and furthermore express oneself forcibly and distinctly.

'The artist must scorn all judgment that is not based on an intelligent observation of character. He must beware of the literary spirit which so often causes painting to deviate from its true path—the concrete study of nature—to lose itself all too long in intangible speculations.'

Or again (26th May 1904):

'Literature expresses itself by abstractions, whereas painting, by means of drawing and colour, gives concrete shape to sensations and perceptions. One is neither too scrupulous nor too sincere nor too submissive to nature; but one is more or less master of one's model, and, above all, of the means of expression. Get to the heart of what is before you and continue to express yourself as logically as possible.'[1]

Cézanne also said, in a phrase which summarizes much that Fiedler had to say: 'All things, particularly in art, are theory developed and applied in contact with nature.' In other words, there can be no divorce between the artist's modes of thought and his perceptual experience. Though he had no command of philosophical discourse, Cézanne was always trying to state that the practice of art, making an object to embody and at the same time define a feeling, is in itself a mode of cognition distinct from scientific or philosophical cognition, and sufficient unto the artist as a principle of reality.

I could quote many other statements made by artists themselves which show that they are always aware, if they reflect on their creative experience, that they are using a language which has nothing to do with literary language, the language of concepts, but which, in its own way, can express the profoundest truths about reality, truths that are not readily expressed in concepts. If we ask what the artist is trying to do we can reply with Fiedler that he is trying to achieve clarity of consciousness. 'Artistic activity begins when man finds himself face to face with the visible world as with

[1] Paul Cézanne, *Letters*, edited by John Rewald, London, Cassirer, 1941, pp. 235–6, 237.

something immensely enigmatical; when, driven by an inner necessity and applying the powers of his mind, he grapples with the twisted mass of the visible which presses in upon him and gives it creative form. In the creation of a work of art, man engages in a struggle with nature not for his physical but for his mental existence . . . the beginning and the end of artistic activity reside in the creation of forms which only thereby attain existence. What art creates is no second world alongside the other world which has an existence without art; what art creates is the world, made by and for the artistic consciousness . . . Art creates the form for that which does not yet exist for the human mind and for which it contrives to create forms on behalf of the human mind. Art does not start from abstract thought in order to arrive at forms; rather, it climbs up from the formless to the formed, and in the process is found its entire mental meaning.

'In the artist's mind a peculiar consciousness of the world is in process of development.'[1]

I am making too generous a use of one author, but no one who has ever written on art has made these points so clearly as Fiedler. Indeed, it is not until comparatively recently that these truths have been rediscovered or re-expressed. A modern philosopher like Susanne Langer, without reference to Fiedler, can suggest that 'the limits of language are not the last limits of experience, and things inaccessible to language may have their own forms of conception, that is to say, their own symbolic devices';[2] and this same philosopher elsewhere admits that artistic expression is 'the verbally ineffable, yet not inexpressible law of vital experience, the pattern of affective and sentient being'.[3] I find the same admission in a recent work by Karl Jaspers, all the more significant in that it comes from such a typically conceptual thinker. 'The fine arts,' says Jaspers, 'make our visible work speak to us. We see things as art teaches us to see them. We experience space through the form that the architect has imposed upon it; we experience a landscape as it has been epitomized in its religious architecture, shaped by human labour, and made a part of life by constant use. We experience nature and man only as they are reduced to their essence in sculpture, drawing and painting. In a sense, it is when this is done,

[1] Op. cit., pp. 48–49.
[2] *Philosophy in a New Key*, p. 265.
[3] Op. cit., p. 257.

and only when this is done, that things assume their characteristic form and reveal their visible quality and soul which had previously seemed hidden.'[1]

Jaspers would make a distinction, as we must do too, between 'art as a code of symbols for metaphysical reality', and 'art in the sense of technical cleverness with no relation to philosophy'. It is the distinction we usually make between art and entertainment, and the failure to maintain this distinction will inevitably lead to a misunderstanding of the symbolic function of art. All 'great art', Jaspers says, is metaphysical art—that is to say, 'an art whose visible creations reveal the underlying reality'. The word 'great' begs the question: let us rather say that art is either *metaphysical*, an activity aiming at the comprehension of reality; or it is *divertive*, an activity that aims at escaping from reality. But we must then make it very clear that metaphysical art is in no sense a philosophical activity: it is as Fiedler says; 'an entirely original and absolutely independent mental activity.'[2]

I hope that I have now made clear this absolute distinction between two activities, one working through non-vocal or iconic signs, the other working through intellectual concepts or logic, but both having as their aim the development of consciousness of reality. Let us now ask what relative attention is paid, by society, to these distinct modes of communication.

The answer is, on the one hand *everything*; on the other hand *nothing*. Everything is done to develop and perfect linguistic modes of communication; to encourage the formation of logical signs and to erect the products of the various types of discourse into systems of knowledge. Our whole civilization is based on the assumption that scientific, legal, technological, political, moral, religious and all the other modes of discourse are not merely adequate, but exclusively adequate, for the acquisition of knowledge and the discovery of truth. On the other hand, so little in general are we aware of non-vocal modes of experience and comprehension that we now conceive them as the special function of an artistic minority, of little relevance to mankind in general. Education is regarded almost exclusively as a system for developing a capacity for forming concepts, and any idea that education should devote

[1] *Tragedy is not Enough*, trans. by Harold Reiche, Harry T. Moore, and Karl W. Deutsch. Boston, Beacon Press, 1952.

[2] Op. cit., p. 61.

at least as much attention to developing a capacity for concrete perceiving has hardly ever occurred to those who formulate and direct our educational ideals.

Over the whole course of human development in historic times there has no doubt been a bias in favour of conceptual thought, and the higher reaches of human thought would never have been possible wtihout the power of conceiving abstract, universal and problematic objects. But the superiority of conceptualization as a mental process can be exaggerated. As William James pointed out:

'Our meanings are of singulars, particulars, indefinites, problematics, and universals, mixed together in every way. A singular individual is as much *conceived* when he is isolated and identified away from the rest of the world in my mind, as is the most rarified and universally applicable quality he may possess—*being*, for example, when treated in the same way. From every point of view, the overwhelming and portentous character ascribed to universal conceptions is surprising. Why, from Socrates downwards, philosophers should have vied with each other in scorn of the knowledge of the particular, and of adoration of that of the general, is hard to understand, seeing that the more adorable knowledge ought to be that of the more adorable things, and that the *things* of worth are all concretes and singulars. The only value of universal characters is that they help us, by reasoning, to know new truths about individual things. The restriction of one's meaning, moreover, to an individual thing, probably requires even more complicated brain-processes than its extension to all the instances of a kind; and the mere mystery, as such, of the knowledge, is equally great, whether generals or singulars be the things known. In sum, therefore, the traditional Universal-worship can only be called a bit of perverse sentimentalism, a philosophic "idol of the cave".'[1]

James thus supports my whole argument, if we add to his observations the fact that by the conception of concretes and singulars we imply the process of the perceptual or visual comprehension of the world. The apprehension of singulars, in any complete sense, is the artistic process itself. It is the comprehending of the things of worth, of adorable concretes and singulars, but it is a process that has been wholly neglected not only by philosophy, but also by all the systems of education ever established by human societies.

[1] *Psychology* (Briefer Course), London, Macmillan, 1892, pp. 242–3.

Such an unbalanced development was made possible by the invention of sign-systems, usually linguistic. There is no reason to assume, as some behaviourist psychologists do, that thought has always been linguistic; there is plenty of evidence to prove that, in the earliest stages of writing, meaning was expressed by visual signs that did not correspond to linguistic signs.[1] In its early stages, writing only loosely expressed the spoken language. 'At the basis of all writing lies the picture,' says Professor Gelb, the latest and perhaps the foremost authority on the subject. 'Just as speech developed out of imitation of sound, so writing developed out of imitation of the forms of real objects or beings.' The evolution of writing from primitive drawings by way of descriptive-representational and identifying-mnemonic devices to word-syllabic systems, and so on to alphabetic systems, has been studied in great detail by modern philologists, who have shown how writing only gradually lost its visual or representational quality, and even its sub-vocal or speech forms, to become a system of signs for the transmission of abstract concepts.

A developed system of writing of any kind did not appear before 3,000 B.C. Writing, therefore, and the whole conceptual mode of reasoning which depends upon it, is of very recent origin compared with man's use of visual symbols—the earliest cave-drawings are perhaps 40,000 years old. I do not make this comparison with any disparaging intention: I merely want to show how basic is the attempt to comprehend the world visually. Now if, on the invention of alphabetic writing, man had dispensed with the representation of visual perceptions altogether, and had discarded art as a useless method of comprehension, then the bias in favour of conceptual thought would be understandable. But on the contrary, driven by the necessities of comprehension and expression, man went on refining his visual consciousness and art became, in every great civilization, the embodiment of his finest feelings and deepest intuitions. By unreflecting consent all men would accord equal honour to Plato and the architect of the Parthenon; to St Thomas Aquinas and the architect of Chartres; to Bacon and Michelangelo; to Spinoza and Rembrandt; to Bergson and Cézanne—not that philosophers and artists should be paired off as contemporaries in this way. We honour our great artists, and count them as among

[1] Cf. I. J. Gelb, *A Study of Writing*, London, Routledge & Kegan Paul, 1952, p. 10 and *passim*.

the most enlightening spirits of history. But we deny the faculties by virtue of which they become great artists—we deny, in our education and in our social estimation of capabilities, any recognition of the fruits of perceptual experience in ordinary people.

So long as civilization was based on handcrafts, there always existed, in the actual mode of living, some counterpoise to abstract conceptual thought. But during the course of the last two centuries millions of people have become divorced from all perceptual effort. Of course, people still have to use their eyes (automatically, with the same kind of reactions that we might expect from a calculating machine, but with less reliability); but there is little need for any positive co-ordination of hand and eye, for any visual exploration of the world, for any constructive use of perceptual experience. A whole method of communication, the language of non-vocal signs, has been thoughtlessly jettisoned by modern society.[1]

But not without protest, of course. Some of the shrillness of modern art is due to its sense of dereliction. It no longer belongs to the people: it is no longer an acceptable mode of communication. The artist has to adopt shock-tactics, in an attempt to reawaken the visual responses of an apathetic public. He is trying to communicate by visual signs with people who are blind. In such a situation it is not the art that should be reformed, but the people that should be given eyes to see. And if they are given eyes to see, they in their turn will wish to express themselves in this distinct and necessary fashion. In learning to use visual signs, to conceive the world symbolically and to create artistic form, they will correct the bias of an exclusively linguistic mode of thought, and, what is equally important, correct the bias of a mechanized mode of life.

[1] To be salvaged, of course, by the publicity men, the practitioners in advertising, who are well aware of the 'subliminal' appeal of visual signs.

PART II

CHAPTER 3

The Creative Process

Any discussion of the psychology of art must begin with an affirmation that is not always acceptable to the psychologist; or, if acceptable, is often conveniently forgotten. This is the fact that the work of art exists as such, not in virtue of any 'meaning' it expresses, but only in virtue of a particular organization of its constituent material elements. We say that this organization is *formal*, but we are soon aware that any metrical analysis of form, any morphology of art, does not yield up art's secret. Form refers back to measures of area, volume, time-intervals, tones; the appeal of these measures, which is called aesthetic because it operates through perception and sensation, is accepted pragmatically, as an evident fact. There have been various attempts to explain this appeal, beginning with the early Greek philosophers, and they have generally been attempts to relate the measurements of art to the measurements of nature, and to see in the proportions of the crystal, of vegetation, of man himself, the prototypes of the proportions discovered in the work of art. I say *discovered* in the work of art because though the Greek architects and sculptors, like Le Corbusier and others today, began to make conscious use of natural proportions, the significant fact is that these proportions appear without conscious intervention in all those works of art that can be characterized as 'beautiful'. This, perhaps, is no more than an hypothesis which has yet to be proved, and certainly a few traditional concepts of natural proportion, such as the Golden Section, do not suffice to explain all the phenomena of art. Form, that is to say, is not necessarily so obvious that it can be expressed in a single formula such as the Golden Section; and we must beware of limiting our notions of form to the canons of a particular tradition or culture. Many of my readers will remember a book that was published in Berlin in the 1920s—Professor Karl Blossfeldt's *Urformen der Kunst.*[1] It was a book that at the time was a revelation of the beauty inherent in plant forms, but Professor Blossfeldt had looked on nature with classical eyes, and found everywhere the motifs of Greek or Gothic architecture and decorative art. About the same time the surréalistes in Paris, inspired by Rimbaud, Lautréamont and Freud, began to find beauty in phenomena of a different kind which, in spite of their strangeness, are equally natural—it might be an octopus, a fungus or the proliferations of disease or decay. Basically no doubt all these forms are the same, or relate to one universal system of formal articulation. What is significant is the selection and combination of forms made by the artist. The forms selected by Karl Blossfeldt tell us something about Karl Blossfeldt, just as the forms selected by a surrealist painter like Max Ernst tell us something about Max Ernst.[2] There is 'no hierarchy in the cycle of natural forms', remarks, very truly, another painter of this school, André Masson: 'The royal structure of the human body is no more *beautiful* than the radiolaria, an oceanic star with solid rays.'[3] The artist, we might say, expresses himself with 'forms already plastic', forms discovered in nature, the signs which, according to Novalis, occur everywhere, and which, in the activity of art, we merely disinter, isolate and recombine.

With what purpose? As we have seen in the last chapter, the purpose of a work of art is not necessarily definable in the terms of rational discourse. Art is a form of symbolic discourse, and its elements are not linguistic but, as Conrad Fiedler recognized seventy years ago, perceptual. We are not in a realm of abstract thought at all, but in one of 'visual cognition'. The work of art remains in what André Masson has called 'the secret world of analogy'. Masson draws attention to some remarks made by Goethe in a conversation reported by J. Daniel Falk which go immediately to the heart of our problem:

'We talk too much, we should talk less and draw more. As for me, I should like to renounce the word and, like plastic nature,

[1] Verlag Ernst Wasmuth, 2nd edition, 1929.

[2] Cf. Max Ernst, *Histoire Naturelle,* Paris, Jeanne Bucher, 1926.

[3] André Masson, *Anatomy of My Universe,* New York, Curt Valentin, 1943.

speak only in drawings. This fig-tree, this little serpent, this cocoon lying there under the window and quietly awaiting its future, all these are profound seals; and he who can decipher their true sense, can in the future do without spoken or written language! . . . Look, he added, pointing to a multitude of plants and fantastic figures which he had just traced on the paper while talking—here are really bizarre images, really mad, yet they could be twenty times more mad and fantastic and still there the question would arise—if their type did not exist somewhere in nature. In drawing, the soul recounts a part of its essential being and it is precisely the deepest secrets of creation, those which rest basically on drawing and sculpture, that the soul reveals in this way.'[1]

One might find expressions of the same idea in Goethe's writings and he indeed was the first to realize that there are two distinct and uninterchangeable non-linguistic modes of communication, one elaborated by man and of limited scope, the other elaborated by nature, of unlimited scope, both of which man may use in that expressive process which we call art.

Nature, we might say, is a world of plastic forms, evolved or in the process of evolution, and man perceives these forms or carries in his memory images of these forms. Images, totally distinct from words or any signs used in discursive reasoning, assume an autonomous activity, combine by way of analogy or metaphor, and produce an effect in us which may be merely personal or sensational and which, when pleasurable, is called beautiful; or may be supra-personal and will then convey what Goethe calls 'the deepest secrets of creation'; or what Dr Erich Neumann has called 'die Gefühlsqualität des Numinosen'.[2] I favour this emphasis on the quality of feeling, for it must never be forgotten that in art the way from the personal to the supra-personal lies along the path of sensation. There are no mental aids in art; without sensibility there is no revelation.

Obviously there is, as Dr Jung has recognized, a creative process at work here which involves the artist as a medium, or as a field of operations. The artist is responsible only as the possessor and activator of a releasing mechanism. It therefore becomes very difficult to apply to this process the ordinary laws of causality.

[1] Goethes Gespräche, J. D. Falk, 14 Juni 1809.

[2] 'Kunst und Zeit', *Eranos Jahrbuch 1951*. Band XX. 'Mensch und Zeit', Zürich, 1952.

I am not referring to the biological difficulty of explaining the sudden emergence of a genius like Michelangelo or Mozart: the science of genetics can juggle with its genes and chromosomes to some purpose in that direction. But given the genius, how explain the Sistine Chapel or *The Marriage of Figaro*? It is not the fact but the quality of genius that calls for explanation, and of this quality genius itself, in its operations, may be in some sense unaware.

Dr Jung has expressed such a view:

'Personal causality has as much and as little to do with the work of art, as the soil with the plant that springs from it. Doubtless we may learn to understand some peculiarities of the plant by becoming familiar with the character of its habitat. And for the botanist this is, of course, an important component of his knowledge. But nobody will maintain that he has thereby recognized all the essentials relating to the plant itself. The personal orientation that is demanded by the problem of personal causality is out of place in the presence of the work of art, just because the work of art is not a human being, but supra-personal. It is a thing and not a personality; hence the personal is no criterion for it.'[1]

Dr Jung has also said, at the beginning of this same essay on 'Poetic Art', that that which constitutes the essential nature of art must always lie outside the province of psychology—'the problem what is art in itself, can never be the object of a psychological, but only of an aesthetic-artistic method of approach'. I am myself an aesthetician, and with this warning in mind I shall disclaim any intention of providing a psychological explanation for phenomena which have been so magisterially excluded from the province of psychology. At the same time it must be observed that it is very difficult to talk about the creative process in art without at the same time giving some information about the thing created, and Jung himself was the first to break his rule—he has made some very important observations about the specific qualities of works of art. He has said, as we have just seen, that art is supra-personal. He goes on to make a distinction between works of art that are deliberate, created by the artist's conscious will and judgment; and works of art that are spontaneous, fully formed before delivered, for which the artist merely acts as a channel. He says of such a

[1] 'On the Relation of Analytical Psychology to Poetic Art', *Contributions to Analytical Psychology*, 1922, London, 1928, pp. 233–34.

work of art that it is 'a force of nature that effects its purpose, either with tyrannical might, or with that subtle cunning which nature brings to the achievement of her end, quite regardless of the weal or woe of the man who is the vehicle of the creative force'. He distinguishes between symbolic works of art which rarely permit of aesthetic enjoyment and non-symbolic works of art which invite such enjoyment and offer us 'an harmonious vision of fulfilment'. And finally, and this is the point of departure for our present deliberations, he suggests that the creative process is an autonomous complex, a living independent organism implanted, as it were, in the souls of man—'a detached portion of the psyche that leads an independent psychic life withdrawn from the hierarchy of consciousness, and in proportion to its energic value or force, may appear as a mere disturbance of the voluntarily directed process of consciousness, or as a superordinated authority which may take the ego bodily into its service.'[1]

The notion of a detached portion of the psyche, capable of independent activity, is difficult to accept, since we are so prejudiced in favour of the unity or integrity of the personality. And yet such an autonomous force is one of the oldest and most persistent ideas in human history. It is the Ancient Greek notion of a *daemon*, which goes back at least as far as Heraclitus; and which was used by Plato specifically to explain the phenomenon of poetic inspiration. Daemons were not always good: they shared, and might even be responsible for, the perversity of mankind. In the Middle Ages they were divided into guardian angels and devils, and the autonomous complexes of modern psychology are equally ambiguous. They may even remain ambiguous, from an ethical point of view, when they emerge into consciousness as works of art. But ethical ambiguity does not affect aesthetic harmony, and it is the source and significance of that harmony which is our present concern.

At the source of all autonomous psychic activities Jung finds a phenomenon which has enjoyed several names and undergone certain transformations as the evidence accumulated. The name which Jung has given to this phenomenon is the *archetype*, a somewhat theological term which may hide, from the uncautious, the essentially materialistic basis of the whole conception, as it took shape in Jung's mind. I think I am right in saying that the term

[1] Op. cit., p. 238.

'archetype' was preceded by the equivalent term 'primordial image', which was more concrete and more directly related to the current terminology of psychology. Indeed, while for the historical description of the archetypes we may have to range over wide fields of myth and fable, as phenomena they are nevertheless firmly rooted in the physiological structure of the brain. Their functions cannot be revealed by anatomical dissection, any more than the 'engrams' and other hypothetical entities of the modern physiologist. But the brain has evolved—has grown in size and complexity through vast stretches of time—and its structure is related to the experiences of countless generations of the human species. It is Jung's reasonable assumption that the profoundest social experiences of mankind must have left some physiological trace in the structure of the brain; and in particular that some of the earliest experiences of the species, long forgotten in the comparative security of historical times, left the deepest traces.

Archetypes, therefore, must be conceived, as the engrams of the physiologist are conceived, as 'inherited with the structure of the brain'; indeed, they *are* engrams, the lowest layer of these physical impresses, and because they are so primordial, Jung described them as 'the chthonic portion of the mind . . . that portion through which the mind is linked to nature, or in which, at least, its relatedness to the earth and the universe seems most comprehensible'. Jung says specifically, and it is a saying to which I shall return, that the primordial images which proceed from this chthonic level of the brain show most clearly 'the influence of the earth and its laws upon the mind'.[1]

The archetypes, therefore, are a function of the brain, but we are not normally aware of their existence. They are not so much unconscious as *unactivated*, dynamos that do not go into action until charged with some psychic current. When they do go into action, they act in a predetermined way—in the way predetermined by their physical constitution and mechanism. They connect up with mnemonic images, deeply buried memories of racial experience, and as these images emerge into individual consciousness, perhaps transformed on the way, they inevitably revive and represent 'countless typical experiences of our ancestors'.[2]

But there is nothing inevitably aesthetic about such revived

[1] *Contributions to Analytical Psychology*, London, Kegan Paul, 1928, pp. 118ff.
[2] Ibid., p. 246.

images, even if we regard them, not so much as concrete symbols, but rather, as Jung himself has suggested, as 'typical forms of apprehension', as 'regularly recurring ways of apprehension'.[1] Ways and forms of apprehension imply a structural organization of the symbolic content, and what is structural *may* be aesthetic. 'A factor determining the uniformity and regularity of our apprehension'—that is another of Jung's definitions of the archetypes, and it comes very near to the Gestalt definition of the aesthetic factor in perception as 'a disposition to feel the completeness of an experienced event as being right and fit'.[2] The farther modern psychology has probed into the distinctive quality of the work of art, the more it has tended to recognize the presence of autonomous processes of organization within the nervous system, and to attribute to these processes the formal characteristics that constitute the aesthetic appeal of the work of art. I refer in particular to the approach of a Gestalt psychologist like K. Koffka to the problems of art.[3]

There is an inherent biological necessity in such aesthetic organization of the data of perception. As Susanne Langer has said 'our merest sense-experience is a process of *formulation.* The world that actually meets our senses is not a world of "things", about which we are invited to discover facts as soon as we have codified the necessary logical language to do so: the world of pure sensation is so complex, so fluid and full, that sheer sensitivity to stimuli would only encounter what William James has called (in a characteristic phrase) "a blooming, buzzing, confusion". Out of this bedlam our sense organs must select certain predominant forms, if they are to make report of *things* and not of mere dissolving sensa. The eye and the ear must have their logic . . . An object is not a datum, but a form construed by the sensitive and intelligent organ, a form which is at once an experimental individual thing and a symbol for the concept of it, for *this sort of thing*'.[4]

I must quote further from Mrs Langer's book, because apparently without any awareness of Jung's psychology, approaching our problem as a logician and philosopher, she arrives at identical conclusions:

[1] Ibid., p. 281.

[2] R. M. Ogden, *Psychology and Education*, New York, 1926, p. 133.

[3] Cf. 'Problems in the psychology of Art', *Art: a Bryn Mawr Symposium*, Bryn Mawr, 1940.

[4] *Philosophy in a New Key*, Harvard University Press, 1942, p. 89.

'A tendency to organize the sensory field into groups and patterns of sense data, to perceive forms rather than a flux of light-impressions, seems to be inherent in our receptor apparatus just as much as in the higher nervous centres with which we do arithmetic and logic. But this unconscious appreciation of forms is the primitive root of all abstraction, which in turn is the keynote of rationality; so it appears that the conditions for rationality lie deep in our pure animal experience—in our power of perceiving, in the elementary functions of our eyes and ears and fingers. Mental life begins with our mere physiological constitution. A little reflection shows us that, since no experience occurs more than once, so-called "repeated" experiences are really *analogous* occurrences, all fitting a form that was abstracted on the first occasion. *Familiarity* is nothing but the quality of fitting very neatly into a form of previous experience . . .

'No matter what heights the human mind may attain, it can work only with the organs it has and the functions peculiar to them. Eyes that did not see forms could never furnish it with *images*; ears that did not hear articulated sounds could never open it to *words*. Sense data, in brief, would be useless to a mind whose activity is "through and through a symbolic process", were they not *par excellence* receptacles of meaning. But meaning . . . accrues essentially to forms. Unless the *Gestalt*-psychologists are right in their belief that *Gestaltung* is of the very nature of perception, I do not know how the hiatus between perception and conception, sense-organ and mind-organ, chaotic stimulus and logical response, is ever to be closed and welded. A mind that works primarily with meanings must have organs that supply it primarily with forms'.[1]

That is the point: form exists and then a meaning 'creeps into it'.[2] But where do these forms come from—what forms the forms? A form, Susanne Langer says, was abstracted on the first occasion; a separate pattern was segregated from the sensory field, and once imprinted on the cortex, was gradually 'developed' by analogous or identical experiences until it acquired what we call meaning. The form became detachable, as a sign or symbol. According to Jung, as we have seen, by reason of their intensity or their frequent recurrence, certain experiences have left formal imprints on the

[1] *Philosophy in a New Key*, pp. 89–90.

[2] Cf. Wolfgang Köhler, *Gestalt Psychology*, 1929, p. 208.

cellular structure of the brain: they are engrams, and as such heritable.

From the aesthetic point of view there are two possibilities here: (1) that a pattern or form can be organized from sense data in virtue of an inner coherence—that we only see a pattern because it has certain physical characteristics, such as symmetry, balance and rhythm; or (2) that among the forms segregated by this organization of the sensory world, some are merely utilitarian, others aesthetic—a view which implies ideal categories of beauty independent of experience. Personally I do not see how the conception of such ideal categories could arise except on the basis of experience—they are meanings read into forms which have been determined by the physical necessities of animal evolution. What is certain is that the forms into which sensory experience is organized were gradually differentiated into two distinct types: signs or symbols whose meaning remained magical, sensory, unexplained; and signs or symbols whose meaning became conventional, conceptual and discursive. We now reserve the word 'signs', or better still, 'signals',[1] for the latter type of communication, and the whole structure of discursive reasoning and non-aesthetic communication is based on such signals, most generally and effectively in the form of word-syllabic systems.

We are to be concerned only with the first method of communication: non-discursive symbols; and only with symbols in so far as they exhibit those characteristics, or convey those sensations, which we call aesthetic. We must first ask why some such symbols have aesthetic characteristics, others not.

It would seem that those non-discursive symbols which are devoid of aesthetic appeal must have lost such appeal, for as we have seen, they only became differentiated from the buzzing confusion of sense impressions in virtue of their attractive form, the 'goodness' of their *Gestalt*.

Jung's theory, if I understand it rightly, is that the symbol loses its original force (and I think the implication is that this original force is aesthetic—a point I shall discuss presently) when it becomes too explicit—when the libido, instead of being retained in the image, is squandered in sexuality or any other physical dispersion of the retained energy. In discussing the relativity of the

[1] Cf. Charles Morris, *Signs, Language and Behaviour*, New York, Prentice-Hall, 1946, pp. 23–27 and page 35 above.

symbol with special reference to *The Shepherd* of Hermas, and also with reference to the symbolism of the Grail, he makes it 'abundantly clear' that it is the repressed libido which evokes a powerful transformation in the unconscious, and endows the symbol with its mysterious efficacy. He even suggests,[1] that an aesthetic form is an essential component of the symbol's efficacy.

I think the necessity for an aesthetic factor is explained by the psychological facts already considered: the symbol only becomes perceptually definite and sensationally effective if it has a good form. Its potency will depend on the relative degree of goodness in the form: the degree of aesthetic appeal depends on the organization of parts into a whole, and on the direct, undifferentiated appeal of the unity achieved by aesthetic organization. In short, we return to the problem of form.

This is not, of course, a problem peculiar to aesthetics. It has been more and more the tendency, during recent years, to reduce science in general to a problem of form, and the contributions to this problem, particularly from physicists and biologists, are of the greatest significance for our study of the aesthetic aspects of symbolic form.[2] Mr Lancelot Law Whyte has dealt with some of the general problems of form,[3] and I have no intention of going over once again the ground he has so adequately surveyed. Admittedly, as we have already noted, there are many analogies between natural forms and aesthetic forms, and perhaps there are no forms conceivable that are not echoes or correspondences of one another. But it would be a poor end to our speculations if all we could prove is that the aesthetic significance of symbolic form lies in its more or less conscious reduplication of natural forms! I am not forgetting that a distinction must be made between natural forms in the widest cosmical sense, and organic forms in the limited biological sense. We know that there have been whole epochs in the history of art that have renounced organic forms, that have taken refuge in geometrical abstractions; there is even a tendency to such abstraction in our own epoch! But it would seem that the more the human psyche tries to escape from organic forms,

[1] Cf. *Psychological Types*, London, Kegan Paul, 1938, p. 291.

[2] For a general discussion of the subject see the symposium edited by L. L. Whyte, *Aspects of Form*, London, 1951.

[3] *Eranos Jahrbuch 1951*, Band XXI, 'Mensch und Zeit', pp. 253–70: 'Time and the Mind-Body Problem. A changed scientific Conception of Process.'

the more it finds itself involved in the universal matrix from which these forms emerge.

At this point we might consider a little more closely the distinction between organic forms, such as we find in a shell, a leaf, a flower, or the human body itself; and those proportions, inherent in these forms, but typical also of a range of phenomena far wider than the phenomena of organic life. Not only is form typical of inorganic as well as organic phenomena, as in the geometrical proportions of a crystal, but proportions can be discerned in the operations of the universe itself, the so-called 'harmony of the spheres'; and there is a similar order discernible in the microscopic world of atoms and molecules. The whole universe is 'patterned', and there can be little wonder, therefore, in the fact that the psychic element in life *conforms* to the all-environing physical mould. Dr Jung has compared the archetype to the ancient bed of a river to which the stream of life may return after some indefinitely long period. As an image it is perhaps too irregular: the stream often flows in channels that are of regular proportions, into basins and cascades of an order that we agree to call beautiful. The freedom, which we inevitably associate with the creative activity, can perhaps be explained as an apparently infinite series of variations on a relatively few fixed forms. There is no need to shrink from such an explanation as from an intolerable restriction of the possibilities of art, for what has the art of music, to a naïve apprehension the freest of all forms of art, ever been but such a play with a determinate number of fixed forms?

A philosopher might complain at this point that we are making metaphysical assumptions. How do we 'cognize' form: by what faculty of the mind do we determine its regularity? Are we not involved in a Kantian system of categories? Perhaps: but personally I believe that our argument can proceed on a purely pragmatic level. The forms of beauty relate to the forms of life, to biological forms; and these are determined by the organic process itself—by efficiency, by natural selection, by environment. Form is determined by physical causes, and 'forms mathematically akin may belong to organisms biologically remote'.[1] But forms, in the sense of regular figures, have a limited range of variation—Plato, in the *Timaeus*, argued that in three-dimensional space there are only five absolutely regular solids. 'These solids inter-penetrate; according

[1] D'Arcy W. Thompson, *On Growth and Form*, 1942, pp. 693–94.

to Plato, they intersect in such a way that out of their perfect harmonies in themselves, they produce all the various discords and resolutions which we find in space within the universe.'[1] The main purport of D'Arcy Thompson's great book *On Growth and Form* is to show how the varieties of form in nature can be explained by a few physical causes.

In the same way a limited number of mathematical figures account for the symbolic significance of the forms of art. A modern physicist has recently remarked that 'Numbers and figures, as the emptiest and most primary forms of thought, are the simplest and perhaps the purest vessel into which inexpressible experiences can still be poured. To be sure, mathematical symbols are not the truth, but they exhibit as much of it as can be exhibited and hide the rest. The formal laws of art are the residues of this experience (which are) still present in the consciousness of the present age. All laws of artistic form have a core of the simplest mathematics. Let us but recall the ratios of musical harmony, the meaning of symmetry and regular sequence in all the arts, the pictorial beauty of mathematically simple figures. And it is the very secret of art that the strictest law of form which has apparently nothing to do with content permits it to express things which escape unrestricted speech'.[2]

The causes that determine the varieties of form in art are likewise few—indeed, in so far as we are concerned with composition, i.e. the disposition of forms within three-dimensional space, the physical limitations are the same in art and nature: a fact which was probably known to Greek artists of the classical period, and certainly to Renaissance artists like Leonardo and Piero della Francesca. We are reduced to the conclusion, therefore, that the forms of art, in so far as they are symmetrical, rhythmical and proportionate, have no psychological significance at all—at least, they are not determined psychically, and any psychological or symbolical or analogical significance they have for human consciousness arises in the act of choice and combination. We may, to adopt the terminology of Wölfflin, choose an open rather than a closed form; we may stand a pyramid on its base or on its apex;

[1] Wind, Edgar, 'Mathematics and Sensibility', *The Listener*, XLVII, 1952, p. 705. Cf. the 'Notice' by Albert Rivaud to his translation of the Timaeus, Budé edition, Paris 1925; also F. M. Cornford, *Plato's Cosmology: The Timaeus of Plato*, London, 1937.

[2] von Weizsäcker, C. F., *The World View of Physics*, trans. Marjorie Grene, London, Routledge and Kegan Paul, 1952, p. 151.

but always we find ourselves manipulating a few simple forms, which are the predetermined forms of visual order, of visual significance. The psychic content of art has to fit into these predetermined forms, like jelly into a mould. What remains of psychological significance, therefore, is the manipulation and variation of typical forms, and the energy displayed in their manipulation, together with such subjective attributes as colour, texture, and that visual mark of nervous sensibility known as 'facture' or 'handwriting'. All these secondary features in the work of art are in themselves also formal and can be referred to the artist's physical constitution or disposition, and though such features may indicate the psychological type to which the artist belongs, they are of no wider significance. Collectively they constitute the talents of the artist: they do not explain genius.

The nearer we get to that central mystery of art the more obvious it becomes, as Jung has often remarked, that there is nothing personal about it. The artist is merely a medium, a channel, for forces that are impersonal, and though there can be no great art without enabling instruments of sensibility and talent, it is the power and purpose with which those instruments are used that make the difference between the major work of art and those trivial but charming expressions of sentiment which are not merely minor in degree, but also essentially different in kind. The fact that the very gifts that enable major works of art to be created are often used by the same artist for minor effects, or as aesthetic exercises, should not blind us to the radical difference which nevertheless exists between the songs and lyrics of Shakespeare or Goethe, and works like *Lear* and *Faust*. The same difference may exist between a painter's sketches and his finished compositions—between a melody and a symphony. What intervenes, to convert the personal into the supra-personal, to give unity to a diversity of effects, is always in the nature of a myth; and because the word myth has associations which are historical or literary we must speak in our present context of the archetype. The archetype is thus clearly differentiated as the principle that gives significant unity to a diversity of aesthetic perceptions. In itself, as Dr Neumann has said, it may be 'bildnislos, namenlos, gestaltlos', but it takes our images and forms, the fine phenomena of our aesthetic perception, and organizes them to some unconscious purpose, gives them a supra-personal significance.

Myth and archetype must therefore be conceived as unifying forces in art, and not as projections from the artist's own unconscious—much less as constructions of his intellect. One can conceive them as magnetic forces that, to use Dr Neumann's metaphor,[1] induce a pattern into a field of scattered perceptions, impressions, intuitions, feelings: and in my opinion we must assume that the force is induced, or brought into play, by a certain ripeness or maturity in the artist. Only artists with a richness of perception and a readiness of expression realize the formal significance of a particular 'constellation' of events in the phenomenal field. The great intuitions come to minds rendered abnormally alert by constant exercise of their talents—a fact which perhaps explains the psychological similarities that exist between artists and mystics.

In comparing form to a mould into which the artist pours a certain content I have ignored the important fact that it is the artist who discovers the form—that is to say, the artist's peculiarity is that he possesses what Schiller called the *formative instinct* (*Formtrieb*), and there is an intimate relationship between the pregnancy of the artist's inspiration and the ability to give that inspiration its appropriate form. The form is found by instinct, ready at hand like a glove already shaped by personal use—or, as Goethe expressed it, the form evolves organically—

geprägte Form, die lebend sich entwickelt.

A failure to realize that fact has been responsible for all the lifeless academicism of the schools. Focillon, in *The Life of Forms in Art*, has expressed the same truth with admirable clarity: '. . . the idea of the artist is form. His emotional life turns likewise to form: tenderness, nostalgia, desire, anger are in him, and so are many other impulses, more fluid, more secret, oftentimes more rich, colourful, and subtle than those of other men, but not necessarily so. He is immersed in the whole of life; he steeps himself in it. He is human, he is not a machine. Because he is a man, I grant him everything. But his special privilege is to imagine, to recollect, to think, and to feel in *forms*. This conception must be extended to its uttermost limit, and it must be extended in two directions. I do not say that form is the allegory or symbol of feeling, but, rather, its innermost activity. Form activates feeling.

[1] *Eranos Jahrbuch*, XXII, 1953.

Let us say, if you like, that art not only clothes sensibility with a form, but that art also awakens form in sensibility. And yet no matter what position we take, it is eventually to form that we must always come. If I were to undertake . . . the establishment of a psychology for the artist, I should have to analyse formal imagination and memory, formal sensibility and intellect; I should have to define all the processes whereby the life of forms in the mind propagates a prodigious animism that, taking natural objects as the point of departure, makes them matters of imagination and memory, of sensibility and intellect—and it would then be seen that these processes are touches, accents, tones, and values . . . Between nature and man form intervenes. The man in question, the artist, that is, forms this nature; before taking possession of it, he thinks it, sees it, and feels it as form.'[1]

What Focillon means by nature is the life-process itself, the underlying dynamics of existence. The whole of our theory of art may therefore be conceived as one that allows for the spontaneous emergence of a psychic energy which, passing through the brain, gives unity to a variety of forms, which forms are in no sense nondescript or arbitrary, but are the typal forms of reality, the forms in which the universe exists and becomes discretely comprehensible to mind. Art might therefore be described as a crystallization of instincts—as the unifying of all feelings and desires; as a marriage of Heaven and Hell, which was Blake's profound intuition of the process. That psychic Energy which is given form by the archetype, Blake defined as Eternal Delight.

It is a process of crystallization which takes place through the senses; we never celebrate the marriage of Heaven and Hell unless we celebrate it in the flesh, in 'Schaudern', in ecstasy, in a piercing vibration of the nerves, in the 'felix transitus' of consummation. In the next essay, I shall try to come a little nearer to the reality of the process in the analysis of certain specific works of art.

[1] Focillon, Henri, *The Life of Forms in Art*, trans. by Hogan and Kubler, New York, Wittenborn, Schultz, 2nd edition, 1948, p. 47.

CHAPTER 4

The Created Form

We must now try to demonstrate our theory in the evolution of art itself, more particularly in the development of typical artists. I shall confine myself mainly to contemporary art, not only because it is the phase of art best known to me, but also because it offers some opportunity of confirming our theories by the cross-examination of the artists themselves.

But there is another and more important reason for confining ourselves to modern art. Excluding the past fifty years, there has prevailed for centuries a conception of art which identified *reality* with *appearance*, and the whole energy of the artist was devoted to the task of giving the reality of his feelings the illusory mask of appearances. This disparity was already obvious to Schiller, and *Letters on Aesthetic Education* are devoted to an examination of the paradox. Schiller pointed out that although a devotion to semblance (Schein) is required of man for the purposes of social intercourse and the mastery of the objective world, when this need is stilled, an inner freedom develops its limitless possibilities, and we become aware of an energy which is independent of outer things. Then we see that a distinction exists between the reality of things and the semblance of things, and that the latter is the work of man. Feeling, Schiller then notes, that feeds on appearances, no longer takes delight in what it experiences, but on what it does; it evades reality and plays with form, with independent energy and freedom of heart. In Schiller's view the separation of form from essence, of reality from appearance, was wholly to the good because it left reality at the mercy of the understanding; it left art in ideal free-

1. Pablo Picasso: Two Studies for 'Guernica',
2nd May 1937. Pencil on gesso
(*The Museum of Modern Art, New York*)

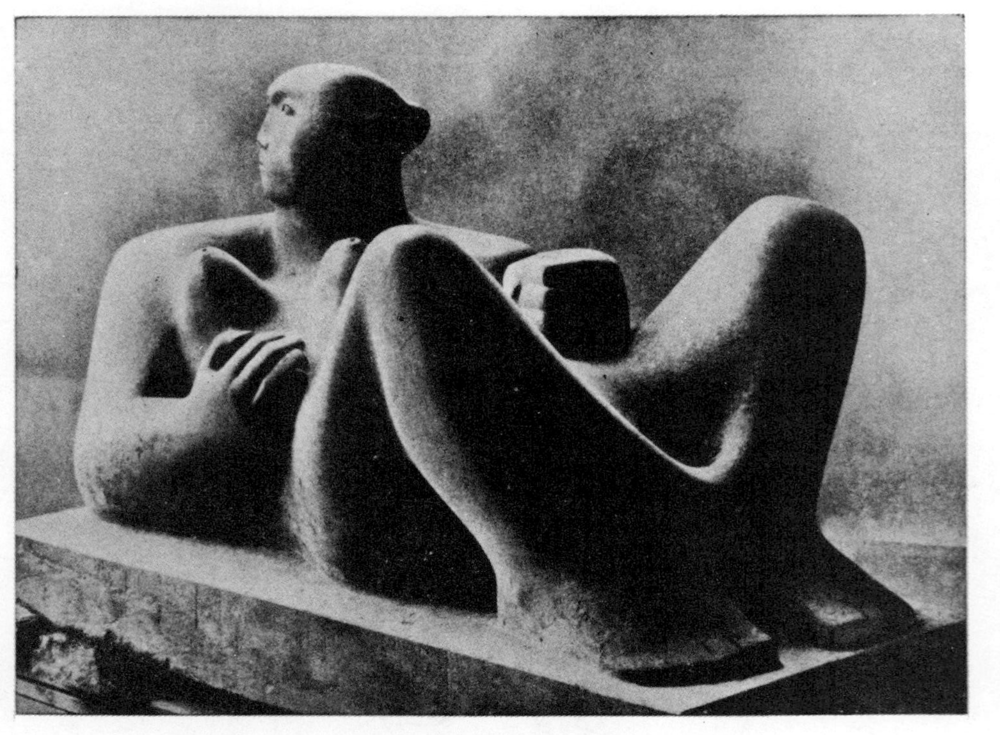

2. HENRY MOORE: Reclining woman, 1930
Green Hornton stone
(*National Gallery of Canada, Ottawa*)

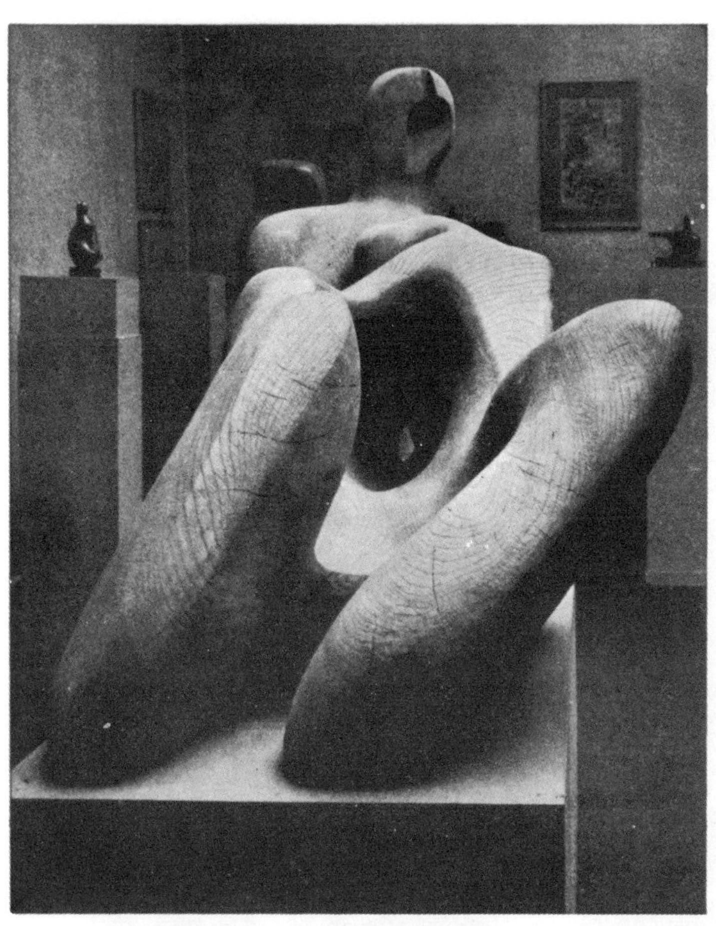

3. HENRY MOORE: Reclining figure, 1937
Elm wood
(*Mr Gordon Onslow-Ford, California*)

4. HENRY MOORE: Four piece composition: reclining figure, 1934
Cumberland alabaster
(*Miss Martha Jackson, New York*)

dom, and gave to man the possibility of enjoying pure beauty. The modern artist cannot accept this divorce from reality; rather, he insists on leaving appearance to the philosopher, or the psychologist, or the photographer, and on being himself the exponent of the inner reality. He has forever finished with an idealism that is based on illusion, and would now master the essence of reality. This means, in our terminology, that he has taken on the job of mastering the unconscious—or, if that seems too ambitious a project, at any rate he will attempt to find some degree of correspondence between the concrete symbols of his art and the subjective reality of his imagination.

I will not stop to discuss whether modern art is unique in this respect—I suspect not, but an investigation of the subject would require a discussion of the precise relation between symbol and sign at different stages of human evolution—for example, for prehistoric man was the bison a symbolic image, as Dr Neumann assumes (he called it 'ein geistig-psychisches Symbolbild'), or was it an eidetic image, a *Scheinbild*, with purely utilitarian connotations?—an open question. But when a modern artist like Picasso paints a bull, there is no longer any question: he is using this animal as a symbol, and as a symbol whose significance can be determined.

Whatever the theoretical justification for the use of such symbols, their predominance in the history of art is inescapable, and Picasso is merely reverting, in this respect, to a predilection which was evident enough in Mycenaean and Minoan art, and is recurrent in the plastic arts, in myth and poetry, throughout the history of western civilization. The bull as a symbol, and the equally archaic symbol of the horse, were embodied in the ritual of the *tauromachia* or bull-fight, a pagan ritual that has maintained, in the hearts of the Spanish people, a hold as strong as the Christian ritual. The art of Picasso, in the course of his development, builds up to the most complete revelation of the unconscious sources and symbolic significance of this same rite. I am referring to his painting called 'Guernica', regarded by some critics of art as Picasso's greatest achievement: it is certainly, in scale and execution, his most monumental work.

Let me recall the origins of this painting. On 28th April 1937 the world was shocked to hear that the Basque town of Guernica had been destroyed by bombs dropped by German aeroplanes in the service of General Franco. Picasso began to paint his picture two days later, on 1st May, and worked on it with maniacal intensity until it was finished some weeks later. During the course of the work he declared: 'In the panel on which I am working which I shall call Guernica, and in all my recent works of art, I clearly express my abhorrence of the military caste which has sunk Spain in an ocean of pain and death.'

The motive of the painting is therefore not in doubt. How is that abhorrence expressed?

By symbols—by the traditional symbols of the bull and the horse, with a number of minor symbols in association with them. Before commenting on the use of these symbols in *Guernica*, let us note that two years before the town of Guernica was bombed, before there was any question of expressing abhorrence for a particular deed, Picasso had used virtually all the same symbols in a large etching which he called 'Minotauromachy'. (*Frontispiece*.)

There is a significant omission in the later picture—the figure of the bearded man who, in 'Minotauromachy', is climbing up a ladder on the left edge of the picture, as if to escape from the scene. It is the archetypal image of the wise man—'the saviour or redeemer' who, as Jung says, 'lies buried and dormant in man's unconscious since the dawn of culture', and who is 'awakened whenever the times are out of joint and a human society committed to a serious error'.[1]

The scene that the Wise Man abandons shows the Minotaur advancing with uplifted arms towards a child who, with a light uplifted in one hand and a bunch of flowers in the other, surveys a horse uprearing, under the threat of the Minotaur, with a woman, apparently dead, stretched on its back. From an opening in the tower-like building in the background, which may be intended as the labyrinth of the Minotaur, two figures in loving embrace, and associated with doves, look down on the scene.

It is a picture so rich in symbolic significance, that one is almost persuaded that Picasso has at some time made a study of Jung and Kerenyi! In addition to the figure of the Wise Man, already mentioned, we have the Minotaur, representing the dark powers of the labyrinthine unconscious; the sacrificial horse, bearing on its back the overpowered libido; and confronting them the divine child, the culture bearer, the bringer of light, the child-hero who

[1] *Modern Man in Search of a Soul*, London, Kegan Paul, 1936, p. 197.

fearlessly confronts the powers of darkness, the bearer of higher consciousness.[1] How easily a Jungian interpretation can be given to this picture may be judged from the following passage from Jung's contribution to an *Introduction to a Science of Mythology*:

'It is a striking paradox in all child-myths that the "child" is on the one hand delivered helpless into the power of terrible enemies and in continual danger of extinction, while on the other he possesses powers far exceeding those of ordinary humanity. This is closely related to the psychological fact that though the child may be "insignificant", unknown, "a mere child", he is also divine. From the point of view of the conscious mind we seem to be dealing with an insignificant content that is gifted with no liberating let alone redeeming character. The conscious mind is caught in its conflict-situation, and the combatant forces seem so overwhelming that the "child", emerging in isolation, appears not to be proportionate to the conscious factors. It is therefore easily overlooked and falls back into the unconscious. At least, this is what we should have to fear if things turned out according to our conscious expectations. Myth, however, emphasizes that it is not so, but that the "child" is endowed with exceeding powers, and despite all dangers, will unexpectedly pull through. The "child" is born out of the womb of the unconscious, begotten out of the depths of human nature, or rather out of living Nature herself. It is a personification of vital forces quite outside the limited range of our conscious mind; of possible ways and means of which our one-sided conscious mind knows nothing; a wholeness which embraces the very depths of Nature. It represents the strongest, the most ineluctable urge in every being, namely the urge to realize itself.'[2]

The 'Minotauromachy' may therefore be regarded as Picasso's affirmation of the grandeur and invincibility of the 'child', a child holding the light of revelation and not at all terrified by the powers of darkness confronting it. An obvious allegory, it might be said, of no great interest because it 'nowhere oversteps the bounds of conscious comprehension';[3] but then this dominant theme by no means exhausts the symbolical significance of the picture. If the

[1] These are Jung's epithets for the divine child. Cf. *Introduction to a Science of Mythology*, C. G. Jung and C. Kerenyi, London, Routledge and Kegan Paul, 1951, p. 122.

[2] Op. cit., pp. 123–24.

[3] Op. cit., p. 127.

dead or unconscious woman represents the libido, why does she carry a sword in her right hand? And what is the significance of the maidens and doves who lovingly look down on the strange scene? All these symbols, no doubt, would yield to rationalistic explanation, but I must be forgiven if I do not dwell on them because what matters, in my present context, is not the interpretation of meaning, but the fact that the artist has employed universal symbols of this kind.[1] Before making any general comment on this process of symbolization I would like to return to 'Guernica'.

We are lucky to possess photographs which show the evolution of this painting in Picasso's studio[2]—not only the various stages in the composition of the canvas itself, but also a considerable number of preliminary sketches of details. (Plate 1.) This preliminary material shows that the constituent symbols of the painting—the bull, the horse, the woman with a dead child, the light-bearer, the figure representing the sacrificed republic—were present in Picasso's mind from the beginning as discrete phenomena. He began with these symbols—the bull, the horse and the woman bearing a light. In some of the composition studies, pencil sketches on gesso made on 1st and 2nd May 1937, a Pegasus is introduced, at first perching on the bull's back, but next day emerging from a wound in the horse's flank. But this symbol was quickly discarded, and others were introduced, notably the one of the victim, at first the traditional republican figure with helm and spear. These traditional accessories are gradually discarded, and in general there is a tendency to get away from literary or historical associations and to let the symbols tell by their inner expressive power. The artist is seen, in these preliminary sketches, exploring the expressive tensions of distortion and exaggeration, until he has substituted his own symbols of power, sacrifice, terror, death and resurrection.

As in the 'Minotauromachy', the horse is the sacrificial animal of the Upanishads, where it signifies a renunciation of the universe. 'When the horse is sacrificed,' comments Jung, 'then the world is sacrificed and destroyed, as it were . . . The horse signifies the

[1] In a drawing made two years later, entitled 'The End of a Monster', Picasso shows a sea goddess emerging from the sea to hold up a mirror to the Minotaur, who lies on the beach transfixed by an arrow.

[2] They are reproduced in *Guernica*, a volume of illustrations accompanied by a text by Juan Larrea, published by Curt Valentin, New York, 1947.

libido, which has passed into the world. We previously saw that the "mother libido" must be sacrificed in order to produce the world; here the world is destroyed by the repeated sacrifice of the same libido, which once belonged to the mother. The horse can, therefore, be substituted as a symbol for this libido, because, as we saw, it had manifold connections with the mother. The sacrifice of the horse can only produce another state of introversion, which is similar to that before the creation of the world.'[1]

This is only a casual comparison, but Picasso's use of these symbols is unerringly orthodox, and the question is whether he is orthodox because he is learned in the history of symbolism, or because he allows his symbols to emerge freely from his unconscious. They not only emerge as orthodox symbols, but in significant association: the sacrificial horse with the figure representing the sacrificed republic, the bull with the horse, the light-bearer with the bull, minor symbols like the flower that grows by the side of the broken sword, and the dove of peace that flies above the carnage.

The question could only be settled by a direct approach to the artist, and this I feel too diffident to make—it would be to invite a confession that in the estimation of psychologists would be damaging to the dynamic force of the work of art. It is generally known, however, that Picasso is not a naïve artist: he is a man of culture, who reads voraciously. It is not inconceivable, therefore, that the traditional symbols he uses are used with deliberate intention. Such symbols are activated by surface emotions, and not by the unconscious. But as Jung has said,[2] 'a symbol loses its magical power . . . as soon as its dissolubility is recognized. An effective symbol, therefore, must have a nature that is unimpeachable . . . its form must be sufficiently remote from comprehension as to frustrate every attempt of the critical intellect to give any satisfactory account of it; and, finally, its aesthetic appearance must have such a convincing appeal that no sort of argument can be raised against it on that score.'

In the past I have praised 'Guernica' as a work of art, and even now I am not going to suggest that it can be dismissed as a work of art merely because its symbols are traditional—that criterion would exclude the best part of all the visual arts ever created by

[1] *Psych. of the Unconscious*, pp. 466–67.

[2] *Psychological Types*, p. 291.

man. But I would maintain that there is a stage in the evolution of symbolism at which the symbols become clichés, and clichés can never be used in a work of art. A dead or exhausted symbol is just as much a cliché as a stale epithet or a hackneyed metaphor. The situation obviously is not improved by beginning with the clichés and then deliberately disguising them. Artistic creation, to the same degree and in the same manner as effective symbolism, implies spontaneity: the artistically valid symbols are those which rise, fully armed by the libido, from the depths of the unconscious.

What redeems this picture, to a degree I would not now venture to determine, is what saves any painting of the past that makes a conscious use of traditional symbolism—any painting making use of the symbols of the Christian faith, or a painting by Poussin making use of the symbols of classical mythology: I mean the fact that every line, every form, every colour, is dominated by the aesthetic sensibility of the artist. What the symbols import into this aesthetic organization is a certain element of collective or traditional significance. A painting of the Madonna may be merely the direct portrait, full of sensuous charm, of a contemporary woman; aesthetically it is never anything else, but the fact that the woman represents the Mother of God imparts into the aesthetic experience a feeling of devotion which is actually a trance-like opening-up of the way to the unconscious, and the woman the artist painted then becomes, not only immediately the Mother of God, but more remotely the representative of still deeper complexes. One way of putting it (it is Jung's way) is that 'humanity came to its gods through accepting the reality of the symbol'; but equally one might say that it was only possible to accept the reality of the symbol because the artist had succeeded in giving it *living form.*

The complex but deliberate symbolism of works like 'Minotauromachy' and 'Guernica' has simplified our task, which is to show the interrelations between the forms of art and the energies of the psyche. I have admitted that to the extent the symbols used by Picasso in these two pictures are deliberate and allegorical, to that extent we may suspect that they have been fished from waters that are relatively shallow; but 'Minotauromachy' and 'Guernica' occupy a small place in the copious repertory of images created by Picasso throughout his career, most of which resist any attempt at rationalistic explanation. Other images are vital, and their vitality comes, not from any identity with the outward world of visual appearances, but from a fidelity to an inner world where vision is archetypal.

I would like now to turn to the work of another contemporary artist, and one well known to me personally for many years, the sculptor Henry Moore. By comparison with Picasso his work presents a certain unity and consistency of development, together with a drastic limitation of theme. Apart from a few abstract works, in themselves nearly always suggested by natural forms, the work of this sculptor consists almost entirely of representations of the female figure, representations that depart considerably from the phenomenal appearances of that object.

A preference for the human form as a motif for sculpture is characteristic of the art from its prehistoric origins, and although there have been periods, in Greece in the fifth century and in Renaissance Italy, when an integrated humanism found expressions indifferently in the form of either sex, in general the male sculptor has devoted his talent to the female form. We do not know whether the first prehistoric carvings of female figures, evidently fertility charms, were the work of men or women; but it is not important, for surely it does not need any profound theory to account for a male preoccupation with the female form. Apart from normal sexuality, it is quite usual for a man to have a mother-fixation, and there is evidence to suggest that an unusual proportion of artists, poets as well as plastic artists, have this psychic bias. But such psychological tendencies merely explain a preference for a particular subject-matter: the aesthetic interest only begins with the transformation which the mother-symbol undergoes in the process of artistic creation.

In the case of Henry Moore, we can simplify our analysis by confining ourselves to a single pose—the reclining figure (Plate 2). His treatment of this theme begins about 1930 in a traditional manner, though it is the tradition of Mayan (Mexican) sculpture rather than of classical Renaissance sculpture. Moore then felt the need to expel all traditional concepts from his psyche, and to proceed to a complete disintegration of the human form (43*a*: 1934)[1] (Plate 4) and then to an abstract reconstruction (51: 1937)

[1] I give references to the illustrations in *Henry Moore: Sculptures and Drawings*, London, Lund Humphries, 2nd edition, 1949. The reader should also refer to Erich Neumann's recent work, *The Archetypal World of Henry Moore*,

(Plate 3). From this geometrical basis, he reanimates the form, gives it recognizably organic shape; and then follows a whole series, continuing to the present day, in which the basic elements of the female figure are the theme for an almost countless series of variations, in various materials. These variations can be studied in greater detail in the numerous sketches in which the sculptor makes a preliminary exploration of his form (139, *a*, *b*; 150*a*; 237).

It would be possible to interpret this development in a purely formal sense. Here is a mass of stone or wood, isolated in space, in dialectical opposition to the space which is its environment, forms weaving and undulating with a life of their own. The aesthetic experience begins with an empathetic response to such a closed world of form—we enter it and fill it and are moved round within it, with sensational reactions which we do not stop to analyse, but which are harmonic and pleasant. But the sculptor himself has told us that 'the humanist organic element will always be for me of fundamental importance in sculpture, giving sculpture its vitality. Each particular carving I make takes on in my mind a human, or occasionally animal, character and personality, and this personality controls its design and formal qualities, and makes me satisfied or dissatisfied with the work as it develops'.[1]

His design, Moore tells us in this passage, is not an intellectual invention: it is not even a direct intuition of form—it is dictated by an inner life, a personality, a daemon, which has entered the block of stone or wood, and imperiously demands a living form.

Moore is here confessing that the creation of a work of art is a genuine, primordial experience—that it is 'the expression of something existent in its own right, but imperfectly known', to repeat Jung's phrase.[2] Moore does not claim to have invented the life of his artistic forms—on the contrary, he asserts that the work of art takes on its own personality, and that this personality controls the design and formal qualities. In other words, Moore confirms Jung's view that 'personal causality has as much and as little to do with the work of art, as the soil with the plant that springs from it . . . The personal orientation that is demanded by the problem of personal causality is out of place in the presence of the work of

New York and London, 1959, where the concepts of analytical psychology are applied to Moore's work in a very comprehensive and illuminating manner.

[1] Op cit., xl, ii.

[2] *Modern Man*, pp. 186–87.

art, just because the work of art is not a human being, but essentially supra-personal'.[1]

Jung's further perception, in this essay on 'Poetic Art', that 'the work of art is not merely transmitted or derived—it is a creative reorganization of those very determinants to which a causalistic psychology must always reduce it'; that it is like a plant which is 'not a mere product of the soil; but a living creative process centred in itself, the essence of which has nothing to do with the character of the soil'; that, in short, the work of art 'must be regarded a creative formation, freely making use of every precondition'[2]—all this is fully and precisely illustrated in Moore's sculpture, and confirmed in his personal statements. The work 'has a power over him that he is quite unable to command',[3] and to watch Moore work is to confirm Jung's description of the poet as one 'who is not identical with the process of creative formation'; who is 'himself conscious of the fact that he stands as it were underneath his work, or at all events beside it, as though he were another person who had fallen within the magic circle of an alien will'.[4]

That being so, it is still permissible to speculate on the significance of the forms proliferated by this dynamic force, using the artist as its channel. In Picasso's two pictures the symbolic figures stand outside the labyrinth itself; and this labyrinth is the archetypal womb, the hollow earth from which all life has emerged.

I might mention, in passing, and without attaching any particular significance to the fact, that Moore's early childhood was dominated by an actual labyrinth, that of the coal-mine. Moore's father was a miner, descending daily into the earth to bring to the surface the substance of fire, which was also the substance of the family's livelihood. It was an enterprise involving danger, and anxiety in the mind of the beloved mother. There are possibilities here of an unconscious association of the labyrinth and the womb.[5] During the war Moore himself descended into the labyrinth, the 'Underground' of the Tube stations, used as bomb shelters, and

[1] *Contributions to Analytical Psychology*, p. 233.

[2] Ibid., p. 234.

[3] Ibid., p. 235.

[4] Ibid., p. 236.

[5] Neumann (op. cit., p. 65) suggests that in these drawings 'the decisive phenomenon is that, in spite of the mining world of the father in which he grew up, the archetypal cave world of the mother nevertheless managed to assert itself to such effect'. I do not agree that Moore's mining pictures are 'weak', but it is perhaps significant that he himself does not like them.

made a series of drawings which, apart from their immediate interest as records of war, re-emphasize his obsession with the labyrinth. In some of his drawings the figures are seen standing outside a cave or labyrinth, and in many others the figures seem to be embedded in rock.

Moore's reclining figures are not substantial solids, as are the sculptures of the classical tradition, but arched and winding caverns. The female body, its superficial protuberances reduced to insignificance, becomes an exposed womb, an excavated mine, and where one might expect emptiness, there is life—the life of shapes and forms which by their convolutions and transformation of masses and volumes, have created an artistic form. We might say that there is a foetus in this womb, but it is the space of the womb itself, the form defined by its rhythmic outlines. In some of his later figures Moore has actually filled these caverns with separate, foetus-like forms, but they were not necessary to express the significance of his symbols.

The Mayan reclining figure which was the point of departure for Moore's series of reclining figures was a god of fertility, Chac Mool, whose particular function was to ensure an adequate rainfall. Round the head are bands of threaded grain, and across the breast an ornament in the form of a butterfly, emblem of regeneration. The hands meet above the womb or belly, and form a hollow depression, basin-like, destined to contain the human hearts demanded as a sacrifice by this cruel deity.

Such symbolism, elaborated no doubt by priests, in the service of a cult, is precise and interpretable. Moore's symbolism is completely unconscious, and is not dictated by any priesthood, or dedicated to any ritual. Nevertheless, it is not entirely unconnected with the same archetypal pattern as the Chac Mool of Mayan religion. Moore assures me that when he first became familiar with the Mexican reclining figure, he had no knowledge of its ritualistic or archetypal significance—to him it was just a piece of sculpture which attracted him by its formal qualities as a work of art. If we interpret Moore's figures as archetypal images of creation, we are then free to relate them to the same archetypal pattern that prevailed in Yucatan more than 3,000 years ago, not as conscious formal imitations, but as identical expressions of the same archetype. The Mayan sculptor proceeded from image to form—his symbols were pre-determined by his cult. The modern sculptor proceeds from form to image—he discovers (or we discover for him) the significance of his forms *after* he has created them. What we must admire, in the modern artist, is the confidence with which he accepts as a gift from the unconscious, forms of whose significance he is not, at the creative moment, precisely aware.

He has that confidence—and this is really the main consideration—because he knows instinctively that there is an intimate connection between the vitality of art and the deeper significance of form. Form is not merely a play with abstractions, a communication of pleasure by the skilful manipulation of proportions and intervals and other geometrical elements. In that way our nerves, our sensibility, may be stimulated—the tone of our physical existence may be enhanced. But it has always been obvious that there was more in artistic creation than could be accounted for by such a direct chain of causality. The forms of art must refer to something hidden, to something not contained in the circuit of nervous reflexes. The aestheticians of former ages—with a few exceptions like Schiller and Fiedler—have been satisfied with an idealistic explanation: art was significant, not in itself, but because it embodied transcendental *ideas*. That fallacy, which even on a basis of the art of the past, should never have been entertained, has forever been exploded by the creative achievements of modern art, achievements which are neither conceptual nor—in the metaphysical sense—transcendental, but which are nevertheless superreal. Modern art—art such as Picasso's and Moore's—is significant but not significant of any expressible ideas. It gives concrete existence to what is numinous, what is beyond the limits of rational discourse: it brings the dynamics of subjective experience to a point of rest in the concrete object. But it only does this in virtue of a certain imaginative play—*eine psychische Spielerei*. The forms of art are only significant in so far as they are archetypal, and in that sense predetermined; and only vital in so far as they are *trans*formed by the sensibility of the artist and in that sense free. The artist releases these dynamic energies within his own psyche, and his peculiarity, his *virtue*, is that he can direct such forces into matter: can 'realize' them as forms of stone or metal, dimensions of space, measured intervals of time. In this sense the artist has become the alchemist, transmuting the *materia prima* of the unconscious into those 'wondrous stones', the crystal forms of art.

CHAPTER 5

Psycho-analysis and the Problem of Aesthetic Value[1]

Thirty-five years ago, with more enthusiasm than discretion, I published an essay on 'Psycho-analysis and Criticism'.[2] I find that I already made there the distinction which is to be the starting-point of this chapter—it will perhaps save time if I repeat my own words. After some remarks on the scope of literary criticism, which I claimed as a separate science, I referred to another consideration which, I said, might put the whole utility of the discussion in doubt, 'the very obvious difference in the subject matter of our two sciences: psychology is concerned with the *processes* of mental activity, literary criticism with the *product*. The psychologist analyses the product only to arrive at the process: art is, from this point of view, as significant as any other expression of mentality. But of no more significance: its significance does not correspond to its value as literature. The psychologist is indifferent to literary values (too often, alas, even in his own work), and may even definitely deplore them, especially when they represent the trimming of subjective phantasies under the influence of some objective standard or tradition. But in any case the psychologist has found and will always find a large body of material in the imaginative literature of all epochs. . . . But whether in the nature of things it is possible for such psychology

[1] The 'Ernest Jones' lecture, read before the British Psycho-Analytical Society, November 15, 1950. First printed in *The International Journal of Psycho-analysis*, Vol. XXXII, Pt. 2, 1951.

[2] *The Criterion*, Vol. III, No. 10, January 1925. Reprinted in *Collected Essays in Literary Criticism*, London, Faber & Faber, 1938.

to add anything positive to the principles of literary criticism is more in doubt. Analysis involves the reduction of the symbol to its origins, and once the symbol is in this way dissolved, it is of no aesthetic significance: art is art as symbol, not as sign'.[1]

It is to that dogmatic statement I now return. I made no attempt at the time to justify this definition of art as symbol, nor to define what in this context I meant by the word 'symbol'. Indeed, I now realize that my statement was in the nature of a lucky guess, which at the time I should have been at a loss to substantiate. Since that time the whole question of symbolic modes of expression has been raised, and symbolism, in a sense to be defined, has become the central principle of aesthetics. That, at first, might seem satisfactory from the psycho-analyst's point of view, but he is doomed to be disappointed. In the last chapter we discovered that certain works of art could have symbolic significance for the psycho-analyst. In the present chapter I am concerned to show that there is a vital difference between the psychic symbol and the aesthetic symbol. Let us first look at the word itself.

The root of the word is in the Greek βολή, βόλος, meaning a throw, and the original sense was that of throwing normally separate things together. Its first use in English seems to have been theological, in the sense of a summary statement of articles of faith, a credo; and from that use it gradually acquired the sense of a visible object standing for something sacred and invisible—for example, wine for the blood of Christ. But in the sixteenth century the word could still be used in its original meaning—for example, the Elizabethan poet, Barnabe Barnes, asks what is life? and one of his replies runs:

A watery bubble symbolized with air.'

We would now say 'inflated', but Barnes's use of the word has a poetic precision—two distinct elements, air and water, seen as thrown together.

I shall not describe all the meanings that have been attached to the word symbol in the past three or four hundred years. The American logician, Charles Peirce, came to the alarming conclusion that there are 59,049 types of 'symbol-situation', and it would need long research to separate those classes that might be defined as aesthetic. But there is a very general distinction to be made

[1] *The Criterion*, loc. cit., pp. 215–6.

between those uses of the word which on the one hand retain the sense of a throwing together of tangible, visible objects, with each other or with some immaterial or abstract notion, and those uses which on the other hand imply no such initial separation, but rather treat the symbol as an integral or original form of expression. A word itself may be a symbol in this sense, and language a system of symbolism. The science of algebra is a still more extreme example of such a system. We might say with Whitehead that 'language and algebra seem to exemplify more fundamental types of symbolism than do the Cathedrals of Medieval Europe'.[1] That is to put art in its place, well below algebra; but Whitehead goes on to distinguish a still more fundamental type of symbolism, and it is symbolism in this sense which concerns us now.

I have borrowed Whitehead's illustration on a previous occasion, but I must use it again. It comes from his book on Symbolism. 'We look up and see a coloured shape in front of us, and we say—there is a chair. But what we have seen is the mere coloured shape. Perhaps an artist might not have jumped to the notion of a chair. He might have stopped at the mere contemplation of a beautiful colour and a beautiful shape. But those of us who are not artists are very prone, especially if we are tired, to pass straight from the perception of the coloured shape to the enjoyment of the chair, in some way of use, or of emotion, or of thought. We can easily explain this passage by reference to a train of difficult logical inference, whereby, having regard to our previous experiences of various shapes and various colours, we draw the probable conclusion that we are in the presence of a chair. I am very sceptical (says Whitehead) as to the high-grade character of the mentality required to get from the coloured shape to the chair. One reason for this scepticism is that my friend the artist, who kept himself to the contemplation of colour, shape and position, was a very highly trained man, and had acquired this facility of ignoring the chair at the cost of great labour. We do not require elaborate training merely in order to refrain from embarking upon intricate trains of inference. Such abstinence is only too easy. Another reason for scepticism is that if we had been accompanied by a puppy dog, in addition to the artist, the dog would have acted immediately on the hypothesis of a chair and would have jumped on to it by way of using it as such. Again, if the dog had refrained

[1] *Symbolism*, Cambridge, 1928, p. 2.

from such action, it would have been because it was a well-trained dog. Therefore the transition from a coloured shape to the notion of an object which can be used for all sorts of purposes which have nothing to do with colour, seems to be a very natural one; and we—men and puppy dogs—require careful training if we are to refrain from acting upon it.'[1]

Let me try to summarize these three degrees of symbolization. There is first of all the *word* 'chair', a monosyllabic sound standing for, and conjuring up, the image of an object made of wood or some other material. What kind of shape or colour of chair we imagine depends on our experience of chairs—the member of a club in Pall Mall will have one image, and the condemned murderer in an American prison quite another; or it may be that in certain contexts we do not need to visualize the chair at all—that will depend on our psychological disposition. In reading the passage from Whitehead I personally visualize Van Gogh's yellow chair; but another person with a more conceptual mode of thought may not visualize any chair at all. He holds the word in mental suspense, as it were, and will only visualize in case of necessity.

Now suppose that the person who cannot visualize the chair is a professor of psychology; he will then tell you that he holds the chair of psychology in a certain University. His use of the word 'chair', not to mention the notion of *holding* that chair, is symbolic. Actually the word 'chair', used in this sense, takes us back to the medieval Cathedral—that compendium of symbolism of all kinds. The very word cathedral is derived from the Latin *cathedra*, and originally referred to the chair of a bishop in his church—chair and cathedral come from the same Greek root καθέδρα. The chair in this sense, therefore, is a symbol of the abstract notion of authority.

Then, thirdly, there is the chair itself: a coloured shape provoking in the artist, not abstract notions, not associations of any kind, but an object with colour and shape, which colour and shape provoke certain sensations which may be pleasant or unpleasant. The chair, as object, becomes the symbol for certain feelings, a *pattern of sentience*, as it has been called.[2]

The basic symbolism involved in aesthetic experience is of this

[1] Ibid., pp. 3–4.

[2] By Susanne K. Langer, *Philosophy in a New Key*, Harvard University Press, 1942.

latter kind. It follows that any conception of art which concentrates on one of the other types of symbolism, to the exclusion of presentational immediacy or sense-perception, is completely off the track. We must decide whether this criticism applies to the psycho-analytical approach to art.

I ought perhaps to add that the phrase 'presentational immediacy', which I take from Whitehead, has not quite the same significance as 'sense-perception' as commonly used. It is a perceptive mode that excludes all details of accident and environment not intrinsic to the thing perceived. The qualities belonging to the thing perceived are abstracted from their involvement in 'the complex organisms forming the community of the contemporary world'. In this sense Peter Bell was a better poet than Wordsworth imagined, for—

A primrose by a river's brim
A yellow primrose was to him,
And it was nothing more.

Further, for Whitehead 'presentational immediacy is an important factor in the experience of only a few high-grade organisms and . . . for others it is embryonic or entirely negligible'. I am not quite sure whether Whitehead is here making a distinction between different types of human beings, or between human beings and animals.[1]

I shall return to the problem of aesthetic symbolism, because I am not entirely satisfied with the theories I have so far discussed; but first I would like to examine the approach that psycho-analysis has in fact made to the definition of aesthetic values.

Admittedly, there is no reason why psycho-analysis should concern itself with the problem at all, unless it can be shown that

[1] Dr. W. R. D. Fairbairn is, so far as I know, the only psycho-analyst who has given adequate recognition to the presentational immediacy of the object in aesthetic experience. (In two papers contributed to the *Brit. J. Psychol.*: pp. 288–303; 'The Ultimate Basis of Aesthetic Experience', 'Prolegomena to a Psychology of Art', 28, 1938; 29, Pt. 2, 1938, pp. 167–81.) He has been impressed, quite rightly, by the phenomenon of the 'found object'—the casually discovered object which, while not being the creation of an artist, functions as a work of art in aesthetic experience—a fact which the surrealists exploited with wonderful effect. I shall refer again to Dr Fairbairn's paper, and for the present merely note that he defines aesthetic experience as 'The experience which occurs in the beholder when he discovers an object which functions for him symbolically as a means of satisfying his unconscious emotional needs'. Discovery, or rather, recovery, is the essential feature of the experience.

art has some therapeutic value, or that aesthetic experience is an essential factor in psychic integration. But that can be done only if we have a proper understanding of what is involved in aesthetic experience.

The psycho-analyst from this point of view would be concerned with the *dynamics* only of aesthetic experience, and not with value judgments. The value of a work of art, it might be said, is its value for the particular mental organization of the individual. One set of circumstances (environment and upbringing) will ensure an aesthetic response only from the *Merry Widow*; another set of circumstances will ensure an aesthetic response only from *Fidelio*. More decisively, the aesthetic culture of a Pacific Island will have no significance for the inhabitants of Bournemouth or Edinburgh; and vice versa. The aesthetic experience is genuine and effective in each case, and from the psychologist's point of view no criterion for comparative evaluation of such disparate art products is conceivable.

But from the point of view of the philosopher of art such a criterion is essential, and does exist.

Freud's own approach to the problem of aesthetic values was always very tentative—indeed, disarmingly modest. Nevertheless it is from his indications of a method that the now quite considerable literature of the subject has grown. It began with Otto Rank's essay *Der Künstler*, first published in 1907, and there are indications that Freud was content to leave this aspect of psycho-analysis to his colleague. Rank's application of the Freudian hypothesis was wholly orthodox: art was given a basis in sexuality, and in the manifestations of the psyche the work of art found a place somewhere between pan-sexuality and hysteria. 'Art develops,' he says, 'from the infantile dreams to the neurosis and attains its peak in times of greatest psychic need, when the people are enabled by means of their artists to balance over the abyss of hysteria with the virtuosity of a sleepwalker.'[1] The artist is fundamentally neurotic,

[1] *Der Künstler*, 4th ed., Vienna, 1925, p. 50. It is only fair to add that towards the end of his life Rank moved towards a completely different and more acceptable theory of art. Art, he suggested, is an irrational language for the expression of what cannot be expressed in rational language. 'In their extremely conscious effort to reproduce what they call the "unconscious", modern painters and writers have followed modern psychology in attempting the impossible, namely to rationalize the irrational.' Elsewhere, in *Beyond Psychology*, New York, 1958, he interprets art and culture generally as an expression of man's need for permanency.

and in his art overcomes his neurosis; and other neurotics, who do not happen to be artists, are nevertheless influenced for the good—they get a vicarious uplift from their appreciation of the work of art.

At the beginning of his book, Rank printed in large type on a blank page a quotation from *All's Well That Ends Well*: 'Is it possible, he should know what he is, and be that he is?' The implication, on which the whole of his hypothesis rests, is that artistic creation is an unconscious, even an automatic process, and that if the artist had any inkling of the sexual motivation of his work, the drive would cease, his Pegasus would be hamstrung. It would seem, therefore, that the artist's slogan should be 'My goodness, my neurosis'.

If Freud's own approach to the problem was originally the same as Rank's, he has nevertheless from time to time thrown out suggestions which go beyond the neurotic hypothesis. For example, already in 1908, in his paper on 'The Poet and Day-Dreaming', he admits that the relation of the phantasies of 'a man of literary talent' gives pleasure, whereas the phantasies of the ordinary day-dreamer merely bore us, or even repel us. But how the writer accomplishes his effect of pleasure remains, Freud says, 'his innermost secret; the essential *ars poetica* lies in the technique by which our feeling of repulsion is overcome. . . . We can guess at two methods used in this technique. The writer softens the egotistical character of the day-dream by changes and disguises, and he bribes us by the offer of a purely formal, that is aesthetic pleasure in the presentation of his phantasies.' That is surely a very significant admission—I mean: the admission that *purely formal* values in a work of art give pleasure. But Freud does not stop there: the work of art has other and more important functions. It is merely a bait to catch the poor fish, an 'incitement premium, or technically, fore-pleasure'. 'I am of the opinion,' Freud concludes, 'that *all* the aesthetic pleasure we gain from the works of imaginative writers is of the same type as this "fore-pleasure", and that the true enjoyment of literature proceeds from the release of tensions in our minds.' So we are back to the dynamics of the artistic event, back to a therapeutic theory of art.

In a paper of 1911, 'Formulations regarding the two principles in mental functioning', Freud gave further support to Rank, but in terms of the pleasure- and reality-principles. 'Art brings about a reconciliation of the two principles (pleasure and reality) in a peculiar way. The artist is originally a man who turns from reality because he cannot come to terms with the demand for the renunciation of instinctual satisfaction as it is first made, and who then in phantasy-life allows full play to his erotic and ambitious wishes. But he finds a way of return from this world of phantom, back to reality; *with his special gifts* he moulds his phantasies into *a new kind of reality*, and men concede them a justification as valuable reflections of actual life. Thus by a certain path he actually becomes the hero, king, creator, favourite he desired to be, without pursuing the circuitous path of creating real alterations in the outer world. But this he can only attain because other men feel the same dissatisfaction as he with the renunciation demanded by reality, and because this dissatisfaction, resulting from the displacement of the pleasure-principle by the reality-principle, is itself a part of reality.'[1]

This is virtually the same formulation as Freud made in the *Introductory Lectures* of 1915–17[2]—the passage beginning 'There is, in fact, a path from phantasy back again to reality, and that is—art'—a passage too familiar to be quoted in full. Again, it is mainly a question of the dynamics of the creative process in the artist, and we are given no clue to the problem of aesthetic values. But in drawing a contrast between the artist and 'those who are not artists', Freud suggests that the artist is exceptional in that he knows how to elaborate his day-dreams, 'so that they lose that personal note which grates upon strange ears and become enjoyable to others; he knows too how to modify them sufficiently so that their origin in prohibited sources is not easily detected. Further, he possesses the *mysterious ability* to mould his particular material until it expresses the ideas of his phantasy faithfully; and then he knows how to attach to this reflection of his phantasy-life so strong a stream of pleasure that, for a time at least, the repressions are outbalanced and dispelled by it.' But all this mysterious ability, according to Freud, has only one object—to win honour, power, and the love of women.

This is a very general theory, and before commenting on it I would like to draw attention to one further contribution of Freud's to the subject—his paper on 'The Moses of Michelangelo',

[1] *Collected Papers*, Vol. IV, 1925.
[2] Eng. trans., 1922, pp. 314–5.

originally published in 1914. It is notable in the first place for its disclaimers. 'I may say,' begins Freud, 'that I am no connoisseur in art, but simply a layman. I have often observed that the subject-matter of works of art has a stronger attraction for me than their formal and technical qualities, though to the artist their value lies first and foremost in these latter. I am unable rightly to appreciate many of the methods used and the effects obtained in art.'[1] But in the course of the essay Freud goes on to affirm that the reason why this statue of Michelangelo has attracted him so strongly must lie in the artist's intention. 'In my opinion,' he says, 'it can only be the artist's intention, in so far as he has succeeded in expressing it in his work and in conveying it to us, that grips us so powerfully. I realize that it cannot be merely a matter of intellectual comprehension; what he aims at is *to awaken in us the same emotional attitude, the same mental constellation* as that which in him produced the impetus to create.' 'Emotional attitude,' 'mental constellation'—those are phrases which at first sight might seem to correspond with the phrases I have already used—presentational immediacy, the pattern of sentience. But that is not what Freud means: he refers to 'the apparently paradoxical fact that precisely some of the grandest and most overwhelming creations of art are still unsolved riddles to our understanding', but he adds that it would only be with the greatest reluctance that he could bring himself to believe that the appeal of a work of art is dependent on 'a state of intellectual bewilderment'. A work of art must have a meaning that can be revealed by analysis; we must be able to *interpret* it.

Freud proceeds to interpret the 'Moses' of Michelangelo, and his interpretation is a classical example of the fallacy of identification. That is to say, in order to interpret this particular work, Freud first identifies himself with the sculptor, to discover what his intention might have been, and then assumes that the sculptor, in order to arrive at the form of his work of art, identified himself

[1] Cf. C. G. Jung, 'Picasso' (*Papers* of the Analytical Psychology Club of New York City): 'When I dare to express myself at all on the subject of Picasso, it is with the express reservation that I have nothing to say on the question of his "Art", but only on the psychology of his art. I put aside as well the question of aesthetics, as the problem of those learned in this direction, and limit myself to the psychology underlying the work of art itself.' Nevertheless, the general implication of this essay is that 'the attempts of a schizophrenic to express himself' have nothing in common with 'beauty', and it is clearly implied that Picasso is schizophrenic.

with his subject, Moses. Incidentally, on the basis of this double process of identification, Freud is able to criticize Michelangelo for not being faithful to the text of the Bible, and for falsifying the character of Moses. Michelangelo, he concludes after his analysis, 'has added something new and more than human to the figure of Moses; so that the giant frame with its tremendous physical power becomes only a concrete expression of the highest mental achievement that is possible in man, that of struggling successfully against an inward passion for the sake of a cause to which he has devoted himself.'

Such a subjective interpretation is based, not on the formal qualities of the work of art, but, as I have said, on an identification of the critic with the subject-matter of the work of art; and if we ask why Freud should have felt an impulsive attraction to this particular subject, and should have mistaken this attraction for the aesthetic value of this particular work of art, we find the answer in Freud's last work: *Moses and Monotheism.* 'It was one man,' Freud wrote in that book, 'the man Moses, who created the Jews. To him this people owes its tenacity in supporting life; to him, however, also much of the hostility which it has met and is meeting still.'[1] As a Jew himself, Freud was forcibly aware of the psychological significance of the historical Moses; an artist who ventured to give expression to this significance was touching Freud on the quick. For that psychological reason the Moses of Michelangelo held him in its grip. 'How often,' he says, 'have I mounted the steep steps of the unlovely Corso Cavour to the lonely place where the deserted church stands, and have essayed to support the angry scorn of the hero's glance! Sometimes I have crept cautiously out of the half-gloom of the interior as though I myself belonged to the mob upon whom his eye is turned—the mob which can hold fast no conviction, which has neither faith nor patience and which rejoices when it has regained its illusory idols.' Emotive language, but not the language of art criticism!

We can no longer avoid a direct questioning of the whole process of *identification.* I have no intention of denying that it takes place in aesthetic appreciation; we may have to admit that a species of identification is the necessary preliminary to the aesthetic apprehension of a work of art. But identification is not enough, as a simple example will show. It comes from the latest work to discuss

[1] Eng. trans. by Katherine Jones, London, Hogarth Press, 1939, p. 169.

the relationship between psycho-analysis and art—a book by Daniel E. Schneider.[1] First let me give Dr Schneider's description of the process of identification as it occurs in art:

'Every artist then must accept the challenge of rigorously accurate thinking—the challenge of attracting, immobilizing, forcing identification upon and "sending" his audience through his art form, giving them no alternative but to "act out" implicitly his interpretation as it swings through conflict, crisis, climax and resolution. This is true for all art. The audience must be drawn in and overcome. It buys its ticket for such substitutive pleasure, and, if cheated of that, it will manifest its hostility by attack or indifference—by "staying away in droves". That the pleasure derived from art form is in part very close to sexual pleasure (though more diffuse and not actually participating—except as audience) cannot be denied by anyone, otherwise we should all prefer to listen to spiritual lectures, and Broadway would become a Mecca for other purposes than its present ones. There would be no need for art form and its intricacies. But art is always outlet, always "acting out" of interpretation. That is the way the true becomes the beautiful.'

The audience must be drawn in and overcome . . . that is the way the true becomes the beautiful—not, you will observe, the way the beautiful becomes the true. Having elaborated this hypothesis, Dr Schneider proceeds to the analysis of various works of art, among them Shakespeare's *Macbeth* and Mr Arthur Miller's *Death of a Salesman*. Incidentally it should be observed that the theory of identification is most easily and most frequently illustrated from the drama or from fiction—very rarely from the plastic arts and music. Dr Schneider has no difficulty in showing that both *Macbeth* and *Death of a Salesman* are magnificent works of art, and judging by the relative degree of enthusiasm aroused in him by each of these works, it would seem that *Death of a Salesman* is a somewhat better work of art than *Macbeth*: there is no escape for the transfixed audience—it is 'sended' (? 'sent'—I do not know how to conjugate this use of the verb) as never before in the history of drama.

But is *Death of a Salesman* as great a work of art as Shakespeare's *Macbeth*? It seems to me that Dr. Schneider is bound to answer

[1] Schneider, Daniel E., *The Psychoanalyst and the Artist*, New York, Farrar, Strauss & Co., 1950.

'yes—even greater'. But I for one, and I think the majority of literary critics, can only regard such a judgment as absurd. Using the same criterion we should have to conclude that Conan Doyle was a greater writer than Henry James; and that the latest Peter Cheyney is far ahead of *Paradise Lost*.

It may be a case of false identification. Freud already distinguished three types of identification[1]—'first, identification is the original form of emotional tie with an object; secondly, in a regressive way it becomes a substitute for a libidinal object tie, as it were by means of the introjection of the object into the ego; and thirdly, it may arise with every new perception of a common quality shared with some other person who is not an object of the sexual instinct. The more important this common quality is, the more successful may this partial identification become, and it may thus represent the beginning of a new tie.' Freud goes on to suggest that the mutual tie that binds a group together is an identification of this kind—a common identification with the leader. He also 'suspects'—he goes no further than this—that 'we are faced by the process which psychology calls empathy (*Einfühlung*) and which plays the largest part in our understanding of what is inherently foreign to our ego in other people'. Now empathy is a term that has been much used in aesthetics—it goes back to Volkelt and Robert Vischer, that is to say, to the 1870s—and long before Freud's time was used to describe Freud's second, and possibly third, kind of identification. But in aesthetics the object of identification is not limited, of course, to 'some other person', or even to a representation of some other person, but can be a plastic object, the essential aesthetic feeling being provoked, however, only when the object is a significant symbol.

It seems to me that Dr Schneider has ignored, or drastically simplified, the complexity of the process of identification, and really confuses empathy with Freud's first type of identification—emotional tie with the object typified in the Œdipus situation. It is significant that *Death of a Salesman*, like *Hamlet*, is a play about an Œdipus situation, so no wonder it unconsciously grips a Broadway audience. And no doubt *Hamlet*, as Dr Ernest Jones was the first to show, has gripped successive generations for a similar reason. But what we have to realize is that a good play—a

[1] *Group Psychology and the Analysis of the Ego*, trans. by James Strachey, Ch. VII. London, Hogarth Press, 2nd edition, 1940.

good work of art of any kind—can grip the public, not for the wrong reason, but for a reason that has nothing to do with aesthetics, nothing to do with beauty or art. *Hamlet* has survived, but thousands of plays that gripped their audiences in their day are now forgotten, and I believe that *Death of a Salesman* will one day be forgotten. What is the difference? It is simple. *Hamlet* is poetry; *Death of a Salesman* is probably not even good prose.

Dr Schneider's view of art is not quite so crude as I have so far made it out to be. He uses some curious phrases—in one place he refers to the 'masturbatory haze' of art which recoils from the task of making itself 'a thing of joy to others'. But he does make a distinction between the content and the form of the dream, and by implication (for he follows Rank in identifying the dream and the work of art) between the content and the form of the work of art. 'What makes the form of the dream,' he says, 'and, as we shall see, the form of art itself is, in addition to its identifications, the power of its economy, the power to combine the manifold "associative radiances" of the symbols in such a way as to enable the analyst (and artist) to interpose rational connecting links and so to "translate" to the dreamer (or to an audience), in logical thought, what one has been unconsciously feeling and thinking, and had suppressed so that it appeared in a dream.' In other words, the work of art is a dream condensed into logical or even rational form, and made objective. In the process the dream, of course, is deprived of its basic sexuality, but it 'stimulates and discharges psychic tensions'. In this way the work of art is made to fit into the dynamics of the psyche. It is a buffer between impossible impulses and reality, between primitive instincts and morality. Its 'form' is the most effective organization of this impact.

A theory which shows much more respect for 'the mysterious ability' of the artist (the phrase, it will be remembered, is Freud's) is that put forward recently in two papers contributed to the *British Journal of Medical Psychology* by Dr Anton Ehrenzweig.[1] Dr Ehrenzweig distinguishes between two types of perception—surface perception and depth perception. These two processes are said to occur simultaneously in different layers of our mind. 'Our depth mind, obeying the archaic pan-genital urge, projects a sexual meaning into any form perceived, while our surface mind counter-

[1] 21, pp. 185–214; 22, pp. 88–109. Since expanded in the author's *Psycho-analysis of Artistic Vision and Hearing*, London, 1953.

acts this projection by projecting, in its turn, an aesthetic ("good") Gestalt into the external world.' In this way Dr Ehrenzweig is able most ingeniously, and even convincingly, to combine the Freudian and the Gestalt theories of art. The unconscious sexual symbolism is the basic material of art, but this crude material is elaborated, to the degree of dissimilation, by our conscious feelings of beauty. A similar distinction was made by Dr Fairbairn, in the papers to which I have already referred. He distinguishes between over-symbolization and under-symbolization—between the true work of art and those false works of art which do not function either because (1) 'the censorship of the artist's super-ego is so rigorous, and necessitates such an elaborate disguise of the urges expressed, that the work of art is deprived of almost all symbolic significance for the beholder'; or (2) the opposite case, 'when the artist's super-ego is weak and his repressed urges are really "urgent", these urgent urges express themselves in the work of art with a minimum of disguise'. Then 'the object is not sufficiently symbolic to pass the censorship of the super-ego. It is, so to speak, too like the real thing'.

Dr Fairbairn then puts forward a principle of 'optimal synthesis'. The artistic activity 'performs the double function of providing a means of expression for the repressed urges of the artist and of simultaneously enabling his ego to pay a tribute to the supremacy of his super-ego, the work of art . . . essentially represents a means of restitution, whereby (the artist's) ego makes atonement to his super-ego for the destruction implied in the presence of repressed destructive impulses'. 'The under-symbolized work of art fails to produce the effect of restitution because the impression which it gives is one of more or less unmitigated destruction. . . . On the other hand, restitution is meaningless apart from the presupposition of destruction; and, consequently, over-symbolization precludes the effect of restitution by excluding the impression of destruction too vigorously.' So it is a case of not too much and not too little, and the work of art, like the Hegelian synthesis, becomes 'the highest unity . . . reached through the full development and reconciliation of the deepest and widest antagonism'. In Freudian terms, the aesthetic experience 'depends upon the resolution of an antinomy created by the simultaneous operation of the libido (the life principle) and the destructive urges (the death principle)'. Hence the importance, in any work of art, of producing an impression of 'the integrity of the object', in other words, of beauty; and the validity of all theories, such as Goethe's, which emphasize the 'serenity' of the work of art.

The advantage of these two theories is that they allow for a *scale* of values. As is well known, the Gestalt psychologists arrange the configurations of perception according to their degree of efficiency, and they have demonstrated that skill, and by implication craftsmanship and aesthetic form, in the ability to select those configurations which are relatively the most effective. Hence the 'good' Gestalt. Dr Ehrenzweig is quick to perceive that 'the new aesthetic principle guides perception to the aesthetically "best" Gestalt and teaches us to appreciate "abstract" form for *its own sake*, without regard to its possible rational significance'. This, in the psycho-analytical approach to art, is an immense step forward, for it not only gets rid of the ambiguous symbolism of representational forms, but even admits that abstract form, as elaborated by the artist, has an aesthetic value independent of its sexual motivation. Indeed, the dynamics of elaboration, the energy we put into creating aesthetic values, is determined precisely by the necessity to hide the sexual meaning of the original perception. I think that this theory possibly allows more freedom to the artist than is present in Dr Fairbairn's theory of optimal synthesis. I do not suggest, however, that there is any contradiction between the integrity of the work of art, which according to Dr Fairbairn would be compulsive, and the artist's freedom to elaborate the form of the work of art. The same impression of integrity could be produced by a variety of forms.

I would therefore like to suggest that we accept this correlation of the two forms of perception, and admit Dr Ehrenzweig's further claim that even those so-called external laws of beauty which we find in natural forms—crystals, flowers, trees, etc.—may be included in pan-genital symbolism. After all, these laws are incorporated in the human body, and the sexually most attractive human form is possibly the one that best illustrates these external laws of beauty. It is an unconscious realization of this geometry of love that gives some of the early paintings of Chirico their mysterious attractiveness.

The only point I want to reserve against Dr Ehrenzweig's theory is a question of a difference of degree, which becomes for all practical purposes a difference of kind. Dr Ehrenzweig, in his evolutionary sweep, can imagine a 'pan-genital crisis when the maddened voyeur libido was deprived, through the erect human gait, of the sight of the female genitals and projected a "pan-genital" significance into any object of the external world'. At that stage all forms acquired a sexual significance, and the new aesthetic principle was evolved as a kind of fig-leaf. All works of art are but species of fig-leaves. We must envisage a process that lasted for millions of years, and is not yet complete. My point is, that at some stage in this historical process the art of propagating new varieties of fig-leaf becomes an intensive activity. The French aesthetician, Henri Focillon, invented the concept of 'la vie des formes', the life of forms, and he showed, in many historical examples, how art forms meet and multiply and breed new forms. I think it would be difficult to prove that this propagation of art-species had any direct correspondence to variations in sexual significance. In other words, while we may freely admit the basic 'pan-genital' significance of art considered as a mode of symbolic expression, the values to which we attach most importance as artists and aestheticians are values of formal elaboration, and our excitement is due more immediately to formal variations on a theme, than to the original significance of the theme itself. The psycho-analyst will retort that this only proves the overwhelming need of our sophisticated civilization to get as far away as possible from the archaic pan-genital urge. Possibly; but my point is that when you get far enough away, the fish has become a fowl. It exists in another element.

If the fish swims in the pan-genital ocean, what then is the quality of the air that our bird-artist breathes? No one, I recognize, will be content with any up-to-date version of the play theory of art. The life of forms is no more, and no less, purposeless than life itself. We must in the end assume that form-elaboration has a biological purpose. We can follow Dr. Rickman and see in this play a reflection of the interplay of the creative and destructive forces of nature. 'When we discern the influence of creation predominating we are moved by something we call beauty, when we see destruction we recoil at the ugly. Our need for beauty springs from . . . our wish to find in art evidence of the triumph of life over death.'[1] This corresponds fairly closely to my own theory,

[1] 'On the Nature of Ugliness and the Creative Impulses', *Int. J. Psycho-*

but I do not favour such neat antitheses as beauty and ugliness, life and death. I prefer to keep to the evolutionary myth, and to see in art the test, the *exercise* of an expanding consciousness. Consciousness, particularly self-consciousness, and the ethical sense that comes with it, is an evolutionary acquisition of man. As a phenomenon it has never, as far as I know, been satisfactorily explained in terms of the survival of the fittest, or of the triumph of life over death. An increasing apprehension of the nature of reality, or of being, is about as near as we can get to a definition of its purpose. In the growth of that apprehensive faculty, art has been the essential means, the instrument for refining the apprehending sensibility.[1] Without the creative arts there would have been no advance in myth or ritual, in language or meaning, in morality or metaphysics.

It may seem that I have been a little grudging in my attitude to psycho-analysis. That is not my intention. I am anxious to protect art and the artist from misinterpretations, and there are many such misinterpretations about—not only psychological misinterpretations, but also political, moral and even aesthetic misinterpretations. But in the end I think we must admit that our debt to psycho-analysis is incalculable. I would say that this new science has come to the aid of the philosophy of art in two ways, which are really two stages of application. The first stage was to show that art could have hidden symbolical signification, and that the power of art in a civilization was due to its expression of the deeper levels of the personality. We thus obtained a scientific justification for our belief that art was more than a representation of appearances. But the second stage was more important—psycho-analysis has proved that the significance of the symbol may be, indeed generally is, hidden; and that the symbol as such need not be representational—it can be super-

Anal., 21, 3, p. 20. Cf. Harry B. Lee, 'The Values of Order and Vitality in Art', *Psychoanalysis and the Social Sciences*, II, p. 245.

[1] To interpret art as 'a manifestation of man's cognitive capability' may be another way of expressing the same idea: but what makes the capability? The psycho-physiological school reduce art to a functional activity of the brain cells, but do not explain what induces these cells to behave in such a peculiar way. Cf. F. Reitman, *Psychotic Art*, 1950, p. 167. I have developed my own views in *Icon and Idea: the Function of Art in the Development of Human Consciousness*, Harvard University Press and Faber & Faber, London, 1955.

real, it can be completely geometrical or 'abstract'. This justifies the freedom of the artist. We had, merely as philosophers, come to the conclusion which Susanne Langer has expressed in these words: 'The first task of the artist is always to establish the primary illusion, i.e. to close the total form and set it apart from reality.'[1] For this determination we have been criticized by Marxist politicians and academic reactionaries, but we know instinctively that such 'setting apart' was not dilettantism, escapism, or esotericism. Now psycho-analysis has shown that our instincts were right; that the process of symbolic transformation which is fundamental to the creative process in art is also biologically fundamental: the necessary transformation of the archaic into the civilized, the passage from the id to the super-ego. This means, in historical or evolutionary terms, that art is symbolization from the beginning—in Susanne Langer's words again, 'form is first, and pictorial meaning is read into it'. Imitation is never the main motive. 'The primary interest is always design, and the very measure of an artist is his instinct for transforming his actual perceptions into wholly plastic elements as he works with them.'[2] The philosopher is content to define works of art as symbols for the articulation of feeling, as patterns of sentience. The analyst has more to tell us about those feelings, and about the biological significance of the patterns we articulate. Let us welcome his contribution to our knowledge of the dynamics of the creative activity; and then let us return to the studio where the forms of art await our further elaboration.

[1] *Hudson Review*, 3, 2, p. 230.
[2] Ibid., 2, 4, pp. 528–9.

CHAPTER 6

Art and the Development of the Personality[1]

I must begin by making clear in what limited and special sense I shall use the three ambiguous words which comprise the title of this paper. By the personality I shall not imply more than 'the point of attention', or awareness, that each individual human being carries about with him. I shall take account of the fact that this is a shifting point, and that its shifts are determined, not only by what goes on in the external world, but also by certain influences behind the point which may determine its direction and control its focus. But I do not think that any particular theory of the unconscious will be necessary for my purpose, and I shall try to avoid the patented terminology of any of the various schools of psycho-analysis.

As for the word 'development', it must not be understood as implying any ethical notions of progress. I shall try to use the word in its biological sense, but I do assume that there is implicit in biological evolution a teleological aim. The evolutionary sequence from amoeba to man only makes sense (and we discourse with one another only on the assumption that there is a sense to be made) if the relationship between mind and matter is conceived as one of progressive adaptation. The point of attention is not static: it is striving all the time to take in, and comprehend, more and more of the external world. In this striving it may be motivated by

[1] Paper read at a meeting of the Medical Section of the British Psychological Society on 12th December 1951. First printed in *The British Journal of Medical Psychology*, Vol. XXV, Pts. 2 & 3, 1952, pp. 114–121.

nothing more than the will to survive. Intelligence (which is the coherent picture we make of the universe we live in) is man's particular offensive and defensive organ—his weapon against the teeth and claws and other inclement forces massed against him. It is, in a very real sense of the phrase, of vital importance to him that he should keep this weapon keen.

When we combine these two words, 'development' and 'personality', we get a phrase which has special significance in modern psychology. We may vary the phrase, and speak of 'the integration of the personality', but we generally imply, not only that man has a personality which is in some sense latent, but that it is desirable to bring it up to the surface, give it some kind of balance or equilibrium, and in some way expand it. This procedure is usually regarded as therapeutic and scientific, but actually it is a conditioning of the personality to a preconceived ideal of happiness or comfort which may be ethically desirable, but is in no objective sense scientific. 'It is possible,' as H. H. Watts, an American critic, has observed, 'to suggest that many of the great gifts that humanity now thoughtlessly enjoys come from the sufferings and visions of those who, in their own era, were "maladjusted".' Too much stability in a community may lead to apathy and decline. The well-adjusted personality, the 'good-mixer', is a terrible bore. A society is kept together by its tensions, by currents that alternate, by an over-all vibration of conflicting forces. Let us assume that it is a good thing to be kept alive, but it is not necessary, for the present discussion, to assume more.

We are to be kept alive in more than one sense: first as individuals, then as communities, and finally as a species. To keep ourselves alive as individuals we must practise mutual aid—that is to say, we must form communities. It now begins to look as though, in order to keep alive as communities, we must practise mutual aid at the community level, and eventually as a species. In order to practise mutual aid, we must communicate with one another, and what I have to say in this paper is concerned primarily with the process of communication. I think that modern psychology has perhaps made a mistake in concentrating on adaptation to the neglect of communication, for it has thereby been able to ignore the nature of the instruments by means of which adaptation is effected. Admittedly a great deal of attention has been paid to *words*, and to the *symbols* rendered up in dream analysis. But this attention has been almost exclusively analytical, and the idea that words and symbols could be used positively, as synthetic structures that constitute effective modes of communication, does not seem to have occurred to our leading psychologists. Myth and ritual, poetry and drama, painting and sculpture—they have treated these creative achievements of mankind as so much grist for the analytical mill, but never as conceivably the disciplines by means of which mankind has kept itself mentally alert *and therefore* biologically vital.

These means of communication, which I shall identify quite generally with the arts of mankind, come relatively late in man's social development, posterior to those conditioned reflexes, acquired skills and habits, upon which his physical and economic well-being depends. It is usually assumed that logical thinking is a still later development, and it can be shown, of course, that such thinking depends on the dissociation of the concept from the image. What has not been questioned is the validity of such conceptual thinking when divorced from reality, and by reality I mean the sensational perception of the external world, visual images or memory images. I do not intend to propagate the vulgar error that philosophy is based on science—that it is in some sense a science of sciences. Philosophy, according to Plato, is based on wonder. 'The sense of wonder,' he said, 'is the mark of the philosopher.' 'It is through *wonder*,' explained Aristotle, 'that men now begin and originally began to philosophize; wondering in the first place at obvious perplexities, and then by gradual progression raising questions about the greater matters too, e.g. about the changes of the moon and the sun, about the stars and the origin of the universe.' We are all perhaps ready to admit the historical independence of philosophy, but what we forget is that philosophy must be continually renewed by this sense of wonder, and that wonder itself is what I would call a liminal awareness—that is to say, sensation stretched to its physical limits. The arts are the exercises by means of which we stretch the intelligence to these limits, and at these limits renew the sense of wonder.

If this sense of wonder is not renewed we get a mental cancer which might be called conceptualism or intellectualism. Bradley has that vivid phrase about the bloodless ballet of concepts, but the ballet is at least a form of art, and what philosophy degenerates into is not a form of art but a recognizable kind of disease. It is not sufficiently realized to what an extent metaphysical speculations and scholarship of all kinds are obsessive-compulsive disorders. It is possible even for pyscho-analysis to become a psychoneurosis of this kind. But it is thinking itself that perishes from this lack of reality-intake: we get the phenomenon known to history as Alexandrianism, which is another name for cultural decadence.

The notion of 'reality-intake' has played a considerable part in the development of psycho-analytical theory, and Freud in particular has seen in art 'a path from phantasy back again to reality'. But art is conceived by Freud, and by most psycho-analysts, as the elaboration of day-dreams, that is to say, as a purely mental process. The whole of the procedure known as sublimation is again usually conceived in terms of mental activity, and though I have no desire to deny that a psychical reality exists just as 'real' as any physical reality, the point at issue is one of relationship, and the hypothesis, which goes back to Pierre Janet, is one of necessary equilibrium: a balance of abstract and concrete, of idea and activity, of individuation and association. These are not isolated balances, for even the projection of a personal phantasy into concrete form involves, not merely the existence of that object in a social environment peopled by other individuals, but also an irresistible need for confirmation. That is to say, we do not believe we have succeeded in expressing ourselves unless the sign or symbol that we have created produces a reaction of approval or disapproval in other human beings. The very faculty of expression could only have developed in a social setting. Neurosis, it would seem to follow, is due either to the inhibition of expression, or to the lack of social confirmation of expression—more generally, then, to a lack of skill in expression.

This view was held by Janet. Speaking of the loss of the sense of reality in what he calls the 'psychasthenic' state of mind, he said:

'One sees that such persons lead a quite special existence, perfectly insignificant from any viewpoint—withdrawn from things, withdrawn from everyone. They are not interested in anything practical; sometimes from infancy onwards they have shown a most astonishing clumsiness. The family of such a patient always declares that he has never been practical, that he does not know how to take account of his real situation or how to succeed in anything. When such persons retain any capacity for activity, one observes that it will always be in an area far withdrawn from material reality: sometimes they are psychologists, above all things they love philosophy and become terrible metaphysicians. When one has had much experience with obsessives, one arrives at the point of sadly asking whether philosophical speculation is no more than a malady of the human mind.'[1]

I must not claim Janet for my general hypothesis, but in this same connection he lets fall a thought which does, I think, anticipate all that I want to say. 'Who would not believe,' he asks, 'that syllogistic reasoning does not demand more brain work than the perception of a tree or a flower with full experience of their actuality? Yet I believe that so-called common-sense is badly deceived on this point. The most difficult operation, that which disappears most rapidly and most frequently in all conditions of mental disability or depression, is *the apprehension of reality in all its forms*. Medical investigation has forced upon us the recognition of this important fact.'[2] But what Janet means by the apprehension of reality is not the resolution of a conflict between the conscious and the unconscious, important as this may be, but the effort of attention required to perceive things with the certainty that they actually exist. It may be that he was thinking in the main of experimental activities in the scientific laboratory, but that is not how we perceive a tree or a flower 'with full experience of their actuality'. That experience is given in the fullest degree in the creation of a work of art, which is precisely the apprehension of reality in this sense. I paint, said Cézanne, in order to realize my sensations; and he meant in order to give a concrete equivalent of his sensations. All art is just that: an objective symbol for a feeling or emotion. It is the validation, to the senses, of processes that are otherwise purely conceptual.

Art, in this sense, is merely instrumental. It is a faculty, relatively constant in human development in historical times, by means of which man adjusts himself perceptually to his environment. I believe that as a faculty it has enabled man to develop his special skills—in primitive times such skills as hunting and court-

[1] Janet, P., *Les Névroses*, Paris, 1909. Quoted from the translation by Elton Mayo, *The Psychology of Pierre Janet*, London, Routledge and Kegan Paul, 1951, p. 97.

[2] I take these apt quotations from Elton Mayo (pp. 99–100), but not before referring, at his instigation, to the original text. In this case, *Les Névroses*, pp. 361–2.

ship, in later times his science and philosophy, his intelligence generally.[1] Art is the composition of perceptual experience into meaningful or significant patterns, and all knowledge and intelligence is a reading or interpretation of such patterns. A myth is a reading of ritualistic patterns, and from myth arises all religion and philosophy. Magic is a reading of animistic symbols, and from magic arises all knowledge of the external world, all science. But it is not only a question of origins: my contention is that science, philosophy and religion only serve an ontogenetic or evolutionary purpose in so far as they continue to be nurtured and invigorated by activities that are sensuous and aesthetic.

All this can be, and has been, demonstrated at the linguistic level. There is a close relationship between the vitality of thought and the metaphorical faculty; idea is an offspring of the marriage of hitherto unrelated images. Newton had *to see* the apple fall before he could 'hit upon' (as we say) the theory of gravity. The procedure might thenceforth be purely 'logical', and I have no desire to question the possibility of arriving at useful conclusions by processes that are strictly verbal. But we have to admit that life is larger than logic—that there are areas of experience or consciousness that are not accessible to cognition. But they are not inexpressible. We can invent symbols which are acceptable equivalents for these logically inexpressible areas of experience or consciousness, and that is what the artist is busy doing. He invents such symbols, and he is a successful artist if his community accepts and uses these symbols. And so, parallel to, and distinct from, the discursive logic of language, arises a logic of non-discursive symbols.[2] We express our states of consciousness, our points of awareness, in lines, colours, proportions, visual images, sounds, and all these means of expression are capable of infinite elaboration or articulation. They are just as flexible as language, and they have virtually no limitations. The work of art, as we say, can express 'the unutterable'.

[1] Again I must refer the reader to the fuller development of this theme in *Icon and Idea.*

[2] Cassirer, E., *Die Philosophie der Symbolischen Formen,* (3 vols.). Berlin, Bruno Cassirer, 1923, 1924, 1929. Eng. trans. by Ralph Manheim, Yale University Press, 1953, 1955, 1957.

Cassirer, E., *Language and Myth,* New York, Harper, 1946.

Langer, S. K., *Philosophy in a New Key,* Oxford University Press, 2nd edition, 1951.

What should strike us immediately as odd is that such an essential mode of communication (or modes of communication) should be confined to a skilled *élite* whom we call artists. It is generally supposed that in the earliest days of the development of language, when words were still associated with magic, invocation too was an art confined to an *élite*, the priesthood; and right down to the end of the Middle Ages there was an identity between those skilled in verbal expression, the clerks, and the priesthood or clergy. We have healed that dichotomy to such an extent that a man who cannot express himself in a literate and logical way is now regarded as a delinquent outcast, to be rescued and regenerated by special commissions of U.N.E.S.C.O. But if we go back to those same Middle Ages, and beyond, we find that the man who could not then read or express himself logically was a natural artist. Everything he made had expressive meaning, and the larger articulations or elaborations of his skill, such as the churches he built, had great beauty. It almost looks as though there were some compensatory balance between these two modes of expression, the symbolic making way for the logical, the discursive ousting the non-discursive forms. And then, perhaps, we remember that the greatest minds, not only of the Middle Ages but also of Antiquity, were masters of both modes of communication—Plato, St Augustine, St Thomas Aquinas—to mention only the greatest.

Can we any longer escape this question—or rather, these questions: If, as is historically evident, there are latent in man these two modes of consciousness and communication; and if, as also seems evident, they are interrelated in their scope and development—can we then deny the necessity of bringing them both to their maximal efficiency? In other words, can we conceive the integration of the personality on any basis that does not develop in equal potency the symbolic and the discursive faculties?

Jungian psychologists might claim that this is precisely the way in which they have conceived the integration of the personality. Realization of the self, wholeness of the personality, they say, is attained when the conscious logical mind is brought into conjunction with the symbolizing processes of the unconscious and a reconciliation is effected. Such is the way of individuation, leading to psychic equilibrium, to wholeness of being, perhaps—though Jung himself is chary of using the word—to happiness.

But a price must be paid. According to Jung[1] this 'unconditional affirmation of all that constitutes the individual' brings with it isolation. 'Its first consequence is the conscious and unavoidable exclusion of the individual from the undifferentiatedness and unconsciousness of the herd.' Jung is very positive about this. 'Neither family, nor society, nor position can save [the developed personality] from [isolation], nor the most successful adaptation to actual surroundings, nor yet the most frictionless fitting in with them. The development of the personality is a favour that must be paid for dearly. But people who talk the most about the development of personality are those who least consider the results, which are such as to frighten away all weaker spirits.'

This ideal of spiritual isolation, of being a law (but a *law*) unto oneself, is common to several of the great religions and philosophies—to Greek Stoicism, to Taoism, to Buddhism, even to certain Christian sects. I am not going to condemn it as an ideal—indeed, it is an essential part of that discipline by means of which we reach that degree of mental concentration or attention which permits us, not only to perceive a tree or a flower with full experience of their actuality, and, I would now add, to perceive a work of art with the same full experience of its actuality; it is the state of mind in which we create a work of art—the state of mind in which we conceive a metaphor, or grasp the unity of a group of particular forms or sounds—the state of mind in which what Coleridge called the esemplastic power, the formative imagination, can work. But what I find lacking in Jung's psychology, and indeed in any of the psychological systems of today, is any suggestion that the integrated personality must be an active, creative personality, giving substance to its thoughts, making out of the plastic materials of the external world symbols to communicate its states of consciousness.

I realize the need there is to escape from what Jung has called 'the fateful identity with the group soul'. But isolation is equally fateful. 'We must love one another or die.' We establish love by communication, and over against the unconscious group soul, we must create a conscious group soul, a community of integrated and interrelated personalities. The means towards this end are always *active*. It may be a prejudice of mine, and admittedly I have no therapeutic experience to support my hypothesis, but I

[1] Jung, C. G., *The Integration of the Personality*, London, Kegan Paul, 1940.

do not believe in the possibility, or at any rate the permanency, of any purely mental solutions of neurotic conflicts. In other words, all therapy must in some degree be what psychologists call 'occupational'. What a dreary word that is! And what dreary occupations are devised for the patients in a mental hospital! It does not seem to have occurred to the psychotherapist to investigate the relative value of such occupations. For economic reasons it may be preferable to dig the cabbage-patch rather than to pick oakum, and to serve the purposes of analysis a patient may be encouraged to paint. But never with any sense of aesthetic awareness, of creative achievement! We tend rather to invent a special category, neurotic art, helplessly admitting that art in the normal sense of the word is not in question. In short, in all our therapy there is no qualitative approach to the products of the imagination, no inkling of the possibility that in the progressive achievement of quality lies the way to something more than the isolated integration of the personality—to a way of life that is communal and creative, and communal because creative.

There is one psychologist who has perceived these truths, not in the abstract and theoretical manner in which I am presenting them now, but in the living experience of self-analysis—I refer to Joanna Field, whose book, *On Not Being Able to Paint*[1] has the greatest possible significance for our discussion. It is not a very ambitious book—the author probably felt that she was describing a single experiment, and that verification must come from others working in the same field with the same methods. But, nevertheless, to anyone who has struggled defeatedly with the problems of a sick civilization, this book will have the force of a sudden illumination. Joanna Field began with a personal problem —her inability, in spite of conventional methods of training, to paint, and by discovering *how* to paint, and observing, as a trained analyst, what was happening to her personality in the process, she discovered the necessary interplay, in living and in painting, of the functions of imagination and action, of dream and reality, of incorporated environment and external environment. But this, the psychologist might say, is the very basis of our psychotherapy, and there is nothing new in it. But there is all the difference between an external environment that is passively perceived and accepted, and one that is actively created or manipulated. The practice of

[1] Field, J., *On Not Being Able to Paint*, London, Heinemann, 1950.

art enables us to establish an active and pragmatic relationship between the self and the external world. As Joanna Field says, 'art is not only a created fusion between what is and what might be; it is also a created way of giving the inner subjective reality of feeling an outer form, in order that it may be shared, and so also tested and verified; it is a making of new bottles for the continually distilled new wine of developing experience.'[1] 'In order that it may be shared'—that is an important qualification which I shall come back to; but first let me make clear, by quotation from Joanna Field's book, the exact nature of this process of 'making real':

'My own experience,' she writes, 'not only with the free drawings but in earlier experiments, had certainly shown how essential for anything but blind living was the emotionally coloured image, as well as the intellectual concept. Thus it was not until I had given up looking for direct help, either from intellectual concepts or factual observations of the external world, and concentrated first upon images, that I had begun to live at all, in any real sense. It was by following up all the apparently unconnected, but rich and sensuous and many-coloured images that the mind continually deposits on the shore of consciousness, like a sea upon its beaches; it was by studying "what the eye likes" rather than what the reason affirms and verifies, that I had at last become able to begin to live reflectively rather than blindly. . . . Having reached some idea of what function the arts might be fulfilling, it was now possible to see more what Cézanne might have meant when he said: "Réaliser: tout est là!" Having seen how it could be that the artist, by embodying the experience of illusion, provides the essential basis for realizing, making real, for feeling as well as for knowing, the external world, it was now possible to look further into the artist's rôle to see how it is that he adds to the generally accepted views of external reality; how in fact art creates nature, including human nature. Thus it seemed to follow that the artist is not only one who refuses to deny his inner reality, but also and because of this, is potentially capable of seeing more than other people, or at least, more of the particular bit he is interested in.'[2]

[1] Op. cit., p. 155.

[2] Op. cit., p. 162. Cf. John Macmurray, *Reason and Emotion*, London, 1935: 'Personal spontaneity is always objective, always in terms of the independent reality of an object which absorbs us. There is no other self-expression possible. If we block the avenues of the outpouring of self, if we withdraw from the reality of the world, if we allow our actions to be subjectively determined by

Such were the reasons that persuaded Joanna Field to persist in the practice of a particular art, painting; I must allow myself to steal one more quotation, a passage in which she describes the effects of her experience:

'I had discovered in painting a bit of experience that made all other usual occupations unimportant by comparison. It was the discovery that when painting something from nature there occurred, at least sometimes, a fusion into a never-before-known wholeness; not only were the object and oneself no longer felt to be separate, but neither were thought and sensation and feeling and action. All one's visual perceptions of colour, shape, texture, weight, as well as thought and memory, ideas about the object and action towards it, the movement of one's hand together with the feeling of delight in the "thusness" of the thing, they all seemed fused into a wholeness of being which was different from anything else that had ever happened to me. It was different because thought was not drowned in feeling, they were somehow all there together . . . something quite special happened to one's sense of self."[1]

What happened, of course, was the miracle of integration. We can use the word 'miracle' because it is such a rare, such a hitherto inexplicable event. But it can happen to anyone. That, at least, is my conviction, and I think it is Joanna Field's too. We have only to get rid of the idea that creativeness is 'an omnipotent fiat from above', and to realize that it is, as Joanna Field says, 'something which comes from the free reciprocal interplay of differences that are confronting each other with equal rights to be different, equal rights to their own identity'. And above all, the free reciprocal interplay of different personalities. I thought I had finished quoting from Joanna Field's book, but she ends by speaking of the forces that frustrate such a free interplay of personalities.

'In order to "realize" other people, make them and their uniqueness fully real to oneself, one has in a sense to put oneself into the other, one has temporarily to undo that separation of self

mere instincts and habits, following our inclinations, we do not express ourselves, we frustrate our own self-expression, surrender our freedom and suffocate all creative spontaneity. The artist does not act by impulse, still less by the compulsion of rules, but by the nature of the reality which he apprehends. By doing this he becomes free and his action becomes a self-expression. In no other way can self-expression be achieved.'

[1] Op. cit., p. 165.

and other which one had so laboriously achieved. In one's own imaginative muscles one feels the strain of the model's pose, in one's own imaginative body one feels the identity of one's opponent, who is one's co-creator. But to do this and yet maintain one's integrity, neither to go wholly over to the opponent's side, nor yet retreat into armour-plated assertion of one's view-point, that is the task demanded. To be able to break down the barrier of space between self and other, yet at the same time to be able to maintain it, this seems to be the paradox of creativity.'

This reminds me of the famous passage in Keats's letters, which I have often given as the first axiom of poetic creation—that in which he describes the quality that goes to form a man of achievement in literature as *negative capability*. The poet, said Keats, is continually informing and filling some other Body. It follows that poetic creation is a social activity, and all the arts involve what Joanna Field calls 'contemplative action', action with reference to a social environment. I think it would follow from these considerations that in the very process of achieving the integration of the personality, we should at the same time solve the problem of social integration. A society in which every man would be an artist of some sort would necessarily be a society united in concrete creative enterprises: in a single creative enterprise, because in such a society the arts are unified.

In conclusion I would like to use a metaphor which comes from the so-called Dark Ages: it is an image which Johannes Scotus Erigena took from Dionysius, to illustrate his notion of *adunatio*: the union of the many in the one without ceasing to be many. 'Many people may see one thing, and see it all at once, as when a crowd is watching the golden ball on a spire, and no one says, Take away your glance, so that I may see what you see! for all can see it together. Many lamps in a church give one light. Many sounds make one harmony.'[1] It was an image used for a theological purpose, but it is equally apt for a sociological purpose, for the work of art is precisely that bright external point in the contemplation of which all attentive minds unite.

[1] Cf. Bett, H., *Johannes Scotus Erigena*, Cambridge University Press, 1925, p. 83.

PART III

CHAPTER 7

Poetic Consciousness

Poetry is primordial, but we have no poetic survivals from prehistoric times to compare in evidential value with the plastic arts of the Stone Age. Nevertheless most of the earliest written records of mankind are poetic in structure, and when we repeat 'In the beginning was the Word', we imply that the word was poetic.[1] Language is now an instrument of rational discourse; but that was not its original purpose. It was evolved from obscure and incoherent beginnings, and was certainly at first an attempt to express feelings or to name things, to make a fixed and constant association between a vocal sound and a visual or somatic sensation, and to use these sounds persuasively in conversation with other men. The Evangelist seems to assert that in the beginning was a naming of the gods; and we may generalize that assertion and say, with Hölderlin, that in the beginning there was an establishment of being, of distinct entity, by means of the word. 'Was bleibet aber, stiften die Dichter.' Heidegger has commented on this saying of Hölderlin's, interpreting it as a description of a principle at work in the creation of existential being. 'The poet names the gods and names all things as what they are. The naming does not consist merely in something already known being supplied with a name; it is rather that when the poet speaks the essential word, the

[1] Cf. *The New Science of Giambattista Vico,* trans. by T. G. Bergin and M. H. Fisch, Cornell University Press, 1948. 'The word logic comes from *logos,* whose first and proper meaning was *fabula,* "fable", carried over into Italian as *favella,* "speech". In Greek the fable was also called *mythos,* "myth", whence comes the Latin *mutus,* "mute". For speech was born in mute times as mental (or sign) language, which Strabo in a golden passage says existed before vocal or articulate (language) whence *logos* means both "word" and "idea" ' (§ 401).

existent is by this naming nominated as what it is. So it becomes known as existent. Poetry is the establishment of being by means of the word.'[1]

The poet speaks *the essential word*, says Heidegger. This implies that poetry is not the use of a ready-made language. It is that particular kind of speech, as Heidegger says (still interpreting Hölderlin) which 'for the first time brings into the open all that which we then discuss and deal with in everyday language. Hence poetry never takes language as a raw material ready to hand; rather it is poetry which first makes language possible. Poetry is the primitive language of a historical people'.[2]

Such a theory of the primacy of poetic language had already, before Hölderlin's time, been advanced by an obscure Italian philosopher whose revolutionary ideas have only in our time been given their full effect by the advocacy of Benedetto Croce—I mean, of course, Giambattista Vico. Vico, in his 'New Science', *Scienza Nuova*, boldly asserted, in opposition to the old science, that is, in opposition to the whole intellectual tradition of western philosophy, that 'in the histories of all nations, poetry appears as the first and primary mode of expression, as the vehicle of their first articulate life and expresses, not the peripheral, the pleasurable, or even the commodious dimensions of life, but the most intimate, stern and fundamental necessities of the life of the people, that is, their laws, their wisdom, their religious rites, their sacred formulas of birth, marriage and death, of initiation, of war and peace, and their rude speculations on the cosmos'.[3] Poetry thus becomes, not a

[1] *Existence and Being*, trans. Douglas Scott, London, Vision Press, 1949, p. 304.

[2] Ibid., p. 307.

[3] A. Robert Caponigri's summary of *Il Diritto Universale*, II, 379, and *La Scienza Nuova Seconda*, p. 173 et seq., in *Time and Idea: The Theory of History in Giambattista Vico*, London, 1953, p. 83. Cf. the following passages from *The New Science:* § 456. 'In this way the nations formed the poetic language, composed of divine and heroic characters, later expressed in vulgar speech, and finally written in vulgar characters. It was born entirely of poverty of language and need of expression. This is proved by the first lights of poetic style, which are vivid representations, images, similes, comparisons, metaphors, circumlocutions, phrases explaining things in their natural properties, descriptions gathered from their minuter or their more sensible effects, and, finally, their striking and even their trifling collateral circumstances.' § 460. 'From all this it appears to have been demonstrated that, by a necessity of human nature, poetic style arose before prose style; just as, by the same necessity, the fables or imaginative universals, arose before the rational or philosophic universals which were formed through the medium of prose speech. For after the poets had

faculty developed by already cultured peoples for their delectation, or for the effective expression of ideas already rationally formulated (Horace's 'Aut prodesse aut delectare poetas'), but the primary act of apprehension and formulation, 'the expression of the pre-reflective or spontaneous consciousness of man'.[1] Further, and here Vico anticipates Conrad Fiedler's theory of the plastic arts,[2] there is no real distinction between this primary poetic expression and the first consciousness of some new aspect of reality: 'expression is the state of consciousness in its concrete actuality'.[3]

When this poetic consciousness develops a form, a structure (but still not a reflective form), when it becomes what Hölderlin called 'the most innocent of all occupations' and what Heidegger calls simply 'conversation', then we get, according to Vico, the myth. Poetry is no longer merely linguistic, but has become a myth-making activity, and once the myth is established, the consequent spiritual activities of man may develop: unification, integration, reflection, intellection. But, Vico asserts in one of his basic axioms, 'men at first feel without observing, then they observe with a troubled and agitated spirit. Finally they reflect with a clear mind.' And this axiom, he says, 'is the principle of the poetic sentences, which are formed with senses of passions and affections, in contrast with philosophic sentences, which are formed by reflection and reasoning'.

In the first stages of this development—the development from spontaneous expression to conversation, from the concrete actuality of a moment of consciousness (and of expression) to the formal articulation of a myth or an idea, between mere consciousness and passionate advertence, we have passed from what I will call the *intensive* aspects of poetry to the *extensive* aspects of poetry. We now distinguish these aspects thanks to our powers of reflection, and on the basis of the poetic material that has accumulated in historical times. In other words, the distinction we make is artificial, as is the whole academic science of poetry, poetics in the

formed poetic speech by associating particular ideas, as we have fully shown, the peoples went on to form prose speech by contracting into a single word, as into a genus, the parts which poetic speech had associated.'

[1] I must again refer the reader to the development of this theory in *Icon and Idea*, Harvard University Press and London, Faber and Faber, 1955.

[2] Caponigri, op. cit., p. 167.

[3] *Scienza Nuova Seconda*, §§ 218–19; Caponigri, p. 169.

Aristotelian sense. It is our failure to preserve a sense of poetry as a primordial activity of consciousness, distinct from poetic thinking or myth-making, that has so often led to a misunderstanding of the nature and function of poetry today, especially among psychologists.

The intensive aspects of poetry are due to the particular character of the words used in the spontaneous act of naming or advertence, and to the syntactical structure, or wholeness or unity which these words assume as they are uttered. The extensive aspects are due to the images, fantasies and reflections which these words convey, first to the poet in the act of advertence, then to the poet's audience, at the moment of understanding.

What we still debate, and the only excuse for reopening the subject now, is the degree to which these two aspects of poetry depend upon one another. To what extent is the degree of consciousness achieved in poetic utterance dependent on its verbal structure? Can the awareness conveyed by a poem be conveyed by any other verbal means—that is to say, by prose? Is the distinction between poetry and prose intensive only (that is to say, a question of verbal efficacy); or is it also extensive (that is to say, a distinct mode of discourse)? Poetry, it is easy to agree, is a spontaneous mode of expression: it is also at the moment of utterance a heightened state of consciousness. How shall we define such a state of specifically poetic consciousness; and what reality does such a state of consciousness reveal that is not accessible to mental acts of reflection?

To answer all these questions would require a treatise even more comprehensive than Aristotle's, and my ambition does not extend so far! This chapter cannot attempt much more than a definition of the problem of poetic creation; and if I can ask a clear question, maybe a psychologist will come along and give a clear answer.

Let us first consider the intensive aspects of poetry for these, being objective and measurable, should be relatively easy to account for.

It is agreed, for example, that poetry is distinguished from prose by its metre, but since prose also has its metre, or discernible accent, it is necessary to add that poetic metre has a certain degree of regularity or repetitiveness. But relativity is of the essence of the situation: not only does poetry exhibit a wide range of metres, but poets use them optionally and irregularly, until the dividing line between poetic metre and prose metre becomes very indistinct. The most we can assert, therefore, is that poetic metre tends towards regularity, and may always have a regular pattern as a kind of sounding board; whereas prose metre must, if it is to retain its separate identity, avoid any suggestion of regular or repetitive rhythm. We might express this distinction, therefore, by saying that the rhythms of prose are syntactical, and subordinate to grammatical structure, which is in its turn subordinate to some ideal of clarity or consistency; whereas the rhythms of poetry are sensuous (aesthetic), and determined by internal necessity, by the need to find some vocal correlative for a state of consciousness. What is vocal in such a situation is not necessarily logical or even comprehensible.

I will not pursue this distinction between poetry and prose, since it is of merely academic interest, and clear enough in experience. The *Song of Solomon*, or Whitman's *Song of Myself*, may not conform to a pedantic definition of poetry, but no one but a pedant doubts that these verbal structures are essentially poetic.

However, I will just mention one further and somewhat subtle distinction: prose is reflective, explanatory of a given situation: it may state ideas that are already precise or it may crystallize diffuse ideas or unravel ideas that are too imprecise, too vaguely conceived. Poetry, on the other hand, being exploratory, cannot be used transitively; but it has become a common practice, in historical times, to use its metrical rhythms tentatively, in the hope of precipitating an image or an intuition. Prose is an instrument we use with a practical purpose; poetry is an instrument we can use speculatively, as a means of improvisation. This does not imply that poetry is to be conceived as a pastime. I merely want to emphasize, that in a reflective and sophisticated age, poetic consciousness is not man's natural state. We therefore often practise versification with the hope that we may write poetry. Inspiration remains the only source of poetry; but so rare is the commodity that most modern poets have to induce it artificially.[1]

Apart from its metrical form there are two further characteristics of poetry which we should bear in mind. One of these again it has in common with prose, and indeed with the plastic arts: the visual image. But in poetry and in the uncorrupted plastic

[1] In a less sophisticated age, it is possible to believe that poetry is always spontaneous. Cf. Leopardi, *Epistolario*, Vol. I, p. 496.

arts the image has an essential function. It exists in its own right, in its presentational immediacy, as an indissoluble expressive formula and not as an extension of logical discourse, not as illustration or signification. The poetic image is received and felt, but it is not observed and reflected on; it is a moment of original vision, an intuitive extension of consciousness, an act of apprehension but not yet of comprehension. Cassirer, at the very end of the second volume of his *Philosophy of Symbolic Forms*, expresses this distinction admirably. He has been speaking of the conflict of meaning and image which he regards as one of the essential features of religious thought, and he continues:

'Only when we turn from the mythical image world and the world of religious meaning to the sphere of art and artistic expression does the opposition which dominates the development of religious consciousness appear to be in a sense appeased, if not negated. For it is characteristic of the aesthetic trend that here the image is recognized purely *as such*, that to fulfil its function it need give up nothing of itself and its content. In the image myth sees a fragment of substantial reality, a part of the material world itself, endowed with equal or higher powers than this world. From this first magical view religion strives towards a progressively purer spiritualization. And yet, again and again, it is carried back to a point at which the question of its truth and meaning content shifts into the question of the reality of its objects, at which it faces the problem of "existence" in all its harshness. It is only the aesthetic consciousness that leaves this problem truly behind it. Since from the outset it gives itself to pure "contemplation", developing the form of vision in contrast to all forms of action, the images fashioned in this frame of consciousness gain for the first time a truly immanent significance. They confess themselves to be illusion as opposed to the empirical reality of things; but this illusion has its own truth because it has its own law. In the return to this law there arises a new freedom of consciousness: the image no longer reacts upon the spirit as an independent material thing but becomes for the spirit a pure expression of its own creative power.'[1]

I shall return later to these compact observations: for the moment they serve to emphasize the distinction that exists between

[1] *The Philosophy of Symbolic Forms*, Vol. II: *Mythical Thoughts*, trans. Ralph Manheim, New Haven, 1955, pp. 260–1.

the function of the image in poetry and its function in those modes of thought that are not poetic, but religious (I am of course implying a distinction between myth and religion), or reflective.

The second non-metrical intensive aspect of poetry I have in mind is one of which perhaps we have only become fully aware since the development of a Gestalt psychology. A poem is a *closed* form, originally Vico's 'poetic sentence'. But even the longest poems, epics like the *Iliad* or *Divine Comedy*, have their formal divisions, each in itself a closed form, and these forms combine to make a unity, a consciousness of *wholeness*. Again Cassirer will provide us with the perfect expression of this distinction:

'If we content ourselves with considering the material aspect of the cultural forms, with describing the physical properties of the signs they employ, then their ultimate, basic elements seem to consist in an aggregate of particular sensations, in simple qualities of sight, hearing, or touch. But then a miracle occurs. Through the manner in which it is contemplated, this simple sensory material takes on a new and varied life. When the physical sound, distinguished as such only by pitch and intensity and quality, is formed into a word, it becomes an expression of the finest intellectual and emotional distinctions. What it immediately is, is thrust into the background by what it accomplishes by its mediation, by what it "means". The concrete particular elements in a work of art also disclose this basic relation. No work of art can be understood as the simple *sum* of these elements, for in it a definite law, a specific principle of aesthetic formation, are at work. The synthesis by which the consciousness combines a series of tones into the unity of a melody, would seem to be totally different from the synthesis by which a number of syllables is articulated into the unity of a "sentence". But they have one thing in common, that in both cases the sensory particulars do not stand by themselves; they are articulated into a conscious *whole*, from which they take their qualitative meaning.'[1]

In poetry not only is the 'melody'—the phrasing or cadence of a rhythm—in itself a Gestalt: the poem also is a unity of such rhythmic forms, and these rhythmic forms are sympathetically related to the images they convey—simple images being expressed in simple rhythms, complex images needing and inducing elaborate rhythms. In an elementary sense, each line (especially in

[1] Op. cit., Vol. I: *Language*, New Haven, 1953, pp. 93–94.

fixed metres like the Alexandrine and the heroic couplet) is a Gestalt; but by enjambment and other devices, a series of lines may be united into the regular form of a quatrain or sextet, or into the irregular form of a stanza or free verse phrase. The sonnet, for example, has a distinct Gestalt, easy to recognize; but poems far more irregular in their structure are also formally coherent, and we must assume that this shape or Gestalt is in itself significant. It is even plastically significant: the visual impact of a page of poetry is quite distinct from that of a page of prose. Prose has a functional façade: poetry a symbolic one.

We must therefore conceive the poem as in some sense a recollection or recovery of the original word-gesture from which language itself developed by a process of fragmentation and elaboration.[1] If we listen to a surviving form of relatively primitive poetry, a Spanish *flamenco* for example, we are conscious of a continuous sound-pattern, highly inflected, but not rationally grammatic—a long-drawn-out cry of anguish or joy. The poetry is in this configuration of sound: a *volume* of sound with analogues in the plastic volumes of sculpture. It is this *vocal* symbol that constitutes the felt impact of the poem.

It would be tedious to elaborate these intensive aspects of poetry, which begin with the original magic of the single word-gesture and extend to the formal structure of the epic and of poetic drama, but they are essential to the very nature of poetry, and to neglect them in favour of the extensive aspects of poetry, as many philosophers and psychologists do, is to introduce a fundamental fallacy into our discussions. What I intend to discuss in this chapter is poetry of the originative type, poetry in the sense defined by Vico and Hölderlin. There is much that passes for

[1] Cf. Susanne K. Langer, *Philosophy in a New Key*, 1942, Harvard University Press, pp. 130–3. Mrs Langer quotes an article by J. Donovan on 'The Festal Origin of Human Speech', published in *Mind*, Vol. XVI (O.S.), pp. 498–506, and Vol. XVII, pp. 325–39, suggesting that in the excitement of the ritual dance in primitive societies certain rhythmic groups and syllables 'got intimately associated with the peculiar feelings and perceptions that came most prominently into the minds of the festal players during that excitement'. Mrs Langer comments that the theory is interesting '(1) because it assumes that the original use of language lies in *naming*, *fixating*, *conceiving* objects, so that the communicative use of words is only a secondary one, a practical application of something that has already been developed at a deeper psychological level; and (2) because it suggests the very early, very primitive operation of *metaphor* in the evolution of speech'. Cf. also Otto Jespersen, *Language: Its Nature, Development and Origin*, London, 1922.

poetry that is not poetry in this sense; and in particular there grew up during the Renaissance an *advertive* or, as I would rather say, a *transitive* conception of poetry which we must examine briefly and then dismiss, to leave our minds clear for a consideration of poetry in the stricter sense.

An advertive or transitive use of poetic form becomes possible when a separation occurs between the state of poetic consciousness and the act of expression; when the poet is conscious of form in the act of expression; when expression is no longer spontaneous and immediate; that is to say, when sensibility and thought are dissociated. These are all variations of the same statement—I am describing that dissociation of sensibility, or corruption of consciousness, from which ensued the decline of all the arts except music during the seventeenth and eighteenth centuries.[1]

When poetry began to recover its vitality towards the end of the eighteenth century, it was with a personal and subjective tone distinct from the unselfconscious mythopoetic tone of earlier civilizations. I do not wish to imply that in earlier civilizations every man was a poet—in a certain sense he was, because there was no printing press to manufacture clichés, and every man spoke with his own voice. The distinction is, that in primitive society common speech is a derivation, however remote, from poetic utterance; whereas in the reflective or sophisticated stages

[1] We owe the phrase, 'dissociation of sensibility', to Mr T. S. Eliot, who thus defines it: 'The poets of the seventeenth century, the successors of the dramatists of the sixteenth, possessed a mechanism of sensibility which could devour any kind of experience. They are simple, artificial, difficult, or fantastic, as their predecessors were; no less nor more than Dante, Guido Cavalcanti, Guinicelli, or Cino. In the seventeenth century a dissociation of sensibility set in from which we have never recovered; and this dissociation, as is natural, was aggravated by the influence of the two most powerful poets of the century, Milton and Dryden. Each of these men performed certain poetic functions so magnificently well that the magnitude of the effect concealed the absence of others. The language went on and in some respects improved; the best verse of Collins, Gray, Johnson, and even Goldsmith satisfies some of our fastidious demands better than that of Donne or Marvell or King. But while the language became more refined, the feeling became more crude.' (*Selected Essays*, 1917–32, London, Faber & Faber, 1932, pp. 273–4.)

The parallel notion of a corruption of consciousness in art is developed by R. G. Collingwood, at first tentatively in *Speculum Mentis*, Oxford, 1924. Cf. Chap. III, s. 3, 'The Monadism of Art'; and then more specifically and fully in *The Principles of Art*, Oxford, 1938. Cf. (p. 282): 'A bad work of art is the unsuccessful attempt to become conscious of a given emotion: it is what Spinoza calls an inadequate idea of an affection. Now, a consciousness which thus fails to grasp its own emotions is a corrupt or untruthful consciousness.'

of social development, common speech has become completely divorced from poetry, which is now a separate and exceptional mode of expression, a mandarin dialect.

We are limited to our contemporary experiences of poetry, and these are, as I have said, individual, introverted, little private ecstasies that may none the less be genuinely poetic. Primitive poetry was created in conditions of undifferentiated social consciousness—*Ganzheitserfahrung*, to use Erich Neumann's term—that is to say, conditions in which the consciousness of self was as yet undeveloped, or was not strong enough to withstand the pressure of social consciousness. We, who are aggressively self-conscious, in order to write poetry, or even to appreciate poetry, must retire deep within ourselves and make contact with a suppressed social consciousness, namely, the collective unconscious.[1] Only in this way can we recover the immediacy which was the original characteristic of poetic utterance. For many centuries now man has so effectively separated his self-consciousness from his social consciousness that he has lost all vital contact with poetic modes of expression. For the original poetic activity he has substituted, in so far as he aspires to poetry, either (*a*) an intellectual activity, which consists in giving reflective thought a metrical form; or (*b*) a play activity, which consists in manipulating words and metrical forms for pleasurable effects, for entertainment. Again, it was Vico who exposed the fallacy, for art was in this manner 'dissociated from the highest aspirations and movements of the spirit', which for Vico were 'the attainment of the true and the good', but which we might also describe as the apprehension of truth or reality. Vico's commentator, Robert Caponigri, whom I have already quoted, again gives a clear summary of the consequences as foreseen by Vico:

'From this dissociation of art from the vital interests of spirit

[1] I am referring in this paragraph not only to Jung's well-known hypothesis of a collective unconscious, but also to Trigant Burrow's notion of a social organism with a common consciousness which has been disrupted by the development of self-consciousness. 'The rudiment of consciousness is self-consciousness. In its origin it is self-reflexive, self-relational. That is, consciousness in its inception entails the fallacy of *a self as over against other selves*. It is in this inevitable *faux pas* of man's earliest awareness, of his original self-consciousness (original sin), that consists the error or lapse in the process of his evolution.' *The Social Basis of Consciousness*, Kegan Paul, London, 1927, pp. 119–20. Cf. also *The Biology of Human Conflict*, Macmillan, New York, 1937, and *Science and Man's Behaviour*, Philosophical Library, New York, 1953.

there spring two forms of aestheticism, both of which have found eloquent advocacy in western thought. There is, in the first instance, that aestheticism which would carry this dissociation of art from life to the extreme of a cult, making of art a refuge from life, a realm into which the human spirit may retreat from the task of the discernment of values, of the real from the unreal. There is also that aestheticism (in reality a variant of the first) in which the relationship of art to life is conceived extrinsically; art is made an external appanage of life, with the function of pleasure, of instruction or amusement. By contrast to both, Vico's theory of spirit would integrate art and life, recognizing in art the first movement of the spirit toward the idea and toward the fullness of its own being in total presence.'[1]

Aesthetics is not a word used by Vico, though it was invented in his life-time by Baumgarten, and it is perhaps confusing to use a derivative word, aestheticism, for what is in effect the fundamental intellectualist fallacy, which is to forget the priorities expressed in the Aristotelian phrase that 'there is nothing in the intellect which was not first in the senses'. The denial of the intellectual or cognitive status of the senses as such, which Vico was the first philosopher to protest against, is really the corruption of consciousness in its source: it is to exclude from the process of cognition those modes of apprehension which are concrete and immediate in favour of the remoter artifices of logic and rhetoric.

We might for a moment consider the logic of the dream: We can say that a dream develops logically because we know, on the evidence of dream-analysis, that in its totality it has significance or meaning. But how does it develop from one moment to another? Very much as poetry develops, by the *rapprochement* of images not hitherto associated. And here we begin to touch on the mystery of poetic creation, which is the intrinsicality of its dynamism. Jung has warned us against the fallacy of 'unconscious ideation', which he calls a *contradictio in adjecto*. We must not ascribe the functioning of the dream, nor, I would say, the functioning of poetic imagery, to any 'subject' with a conscious will. The psyche is no doubt a conscious-unconscious whole, but the hyphen in that conglomerate expression is a dividing-line between the personal Ego and the impersonal Self, between the will and certain 'patterns

[1] Op. cit., p. 85. Cf. also B. Croce, *The Philosophy of Giambattista Vico*, Eng. trans. by R. G. Collingwood, London, 1913, pp. 48–49.

of behaviour', which we call instinctive when we observe them objectively in animal life, and archetypal when we discover them in the unconscious of man.[1]

On the evidence of his knowledge of the behaviour of images in the minds of his patients, Jung has been able to discern *formative principles* in the unconscious, and his most fundamental views and ideas, he says, derive from these experiences. They lead him to suppose that unconscious regulators of fantasy work according to a number of basic patterns. And just as the fantasies are guided by these pre-existent patterns of behaviour, 'so it is with the hand that guides the crayon or brush, the foot that executes the dance step, with the eye and the ear, with the word and the thought: a dark impulse is the ultimate arbiter of the pattern, an unconscious *a priori* precipitates itself into plastic form, and one has no inkling that another person's consciousness is being steered by the same principles at the very point where one feels utterly exposed to the boundless subjective vagaries of chance. Over the whole procedure there seems to reign a dim fore-knowledge not only of the pattern, but of its meaning. Image and meaning are identical, and as the first takes shape, so the latter becomes clear.'[2]

The essential truth of the poetic experience is contained in the basic doctrine of Jungian psychology, but we must proceed to make distinctions, for poetry is not identical with dream, nor even with myth. Dreams have a logic of their own because they are a shadow-play reflected from psychotic conflicts, they are motivated by an 'individuation process', and so on. But poetic images have an unmotivated existence, as objects for contemplation; a form of vision, as Cassirer said in the passage I quoted, that contrasts with all forms of action, a world of illusion that has its own truth and its own law, and develops in perfect freedom—freedom from any necessity, whether internal or external, subjective or objective. There is, of course, the necessity of correlation: the poetic image may be identical with or symbolize (the root meaning of the word 'symbol' indicates two or more objects thrown together) a feeling value—the feeling value of the archetype, of the numinous whatever-it-is that demands a naming. But only in freedom, from infinite possibilities, can the poet choose a name.

[1] 'The Spirit of Psychology', in *Spirit and Nature: Papers from the Eranos Year Books*, New York and London, 1954, p. 411.

[2] Op. cit., p. 414.

The name he chooses is magically apt, and in word-magic we must acknowledge the primordial intensive aspect of poetry. Cassirer has pointed out that myth and language are inseparable and mutually condition each other. 'Word and name magic are, like image magic, an integral part of the magical world view.' And in all this, he says, 'the basic pre-supposition is that word and name do not merely have a function of describing or portraying but contain within them the object and its real powers. Word and name do not designate and signify, they are and act. In the mere sensuous matter of language, in the mere sound of the human voice, there resides a peculiar power over things . . . the mythical-magical power of language is truly manifested in articulated sound.'[1]

It would be possible to illustrate this magical quality of the word in primitive poetry, but the attempt would be hazardous because we no longer respond to such poetry with the emotional equipment of primitive man. Nevertheless, we speak without any sense of incongruity of the 'magic' of the poetry we do appreciate, and we have only to take an example of indubitable poetic magic, of poetry that has a universal appeal, to find a quality in it which we cannot account for rationally.

Take Ariel's Song from *The Tempest*:

Full fathom five thy father lies;
Of his bones are coral made:
Those are pearls that were his eyes:
Nothing of him that doth fade,
But doth suffer a sea-change
Into something rich and strange.
Sea-nymphs hourly ring his knell:
Hark! now I hear them,—ding-dong, bell.

It is an incantation, a dirge celebrating death and mortality, comparable to that earliest poetry that has survived from remote antiquity, the Egyptian Book of the Dead. We are in the presence of the fundamental mystery of being, and it is the consciousness of this mystery, and the blind emotion with which the poet confronts this mystery, that creates a desire, not to 'designate and signify', but to affirm the triumph of life in death, the enduringness of a poetic transformation. The very words that celebrate death are magical, 'something rich and strange', vital images with which the

[1] Op. cit., II, p. 40.

poet confronts death and oblivion. 'This awareness of intense individual vitality in the midst of or against an awareness of natural inevitable change, or even destruction,' observes Kathleen Nott, 'enters the reader's mind directly, as a simple unanalysed excitement. I do not say that this acute awareness of standing on the shore of time is the only poetic theme, anyway the only conscious poetic theme. I do say that this awareness is the *sine qua non* of poetic experience in general. It *is* the poetic emotion.'[1]

We cannot explain such magic. We can count syllables, mark rhythm, observe alliteration and paraphrase metaphors, but it is like taking a clock to pieces to discover the nature of time. The magic vanishes, and we neither know what made the separate elements of the poem cohere into this particular word pattern, nor why the sound-value of this pattern should affect us so deeply. We have to conclude, with Jung, that 'a dark impulse is the ultimate arbiter of pattern'. The pattern can take shape from a wide range of sensory images: a chord of music is an image and so is the vocal sound of a word.[2] *Ra*, the name of the Egyptian sun god, is an aural image; so is *Jehovah* and so is *Allah*. Between such primordial nominative poetry and the lyrical poetry of Ariel's Song there is a long process of development. Nominative poetry has become metaphorical poetry: poetry has acquired structure and extensive formulation. It has acquired 'an aesthetically liberated life'. This is Cassirer's expression again, who further observes that 'the lyric is the one [form of poetry] which most clearly mirrors this ideal development. For lyric poetry is not only rooted in mystic motives at its beginning, but keeps its connection with myth even in its highest and purest products. The greatest lyric poets, for instance Hölderlin and Keats, are men on whom the mythic power of insight breaks forth again in its full intensity and objectifying power. But this objectivity has discarded all material constraints. The spirit lives in the word of language and in the mythical image without falling under the control of either . . .

[1] *The Emperor's Clothes*, London, 1953, p. 214.

[2] Cf. T. S. Eliot, *The Use of Poetry and the Use of Criticism*, London, 1933, pp. 118 and 119: 'What I call the "auditory imagination" is the feeling for syllable and rhythm, penetrating far below the conscious levels of thought and feeling, invigorating every word; sinking to the most primitive and forgotten, returning to the origin and bringing something back, seeking the beginning and the end. It works through meanings, certainly, or not without meanings in the ordinary sense, and fuses the old and obliterated and the trite, the current, and the new and surprising, the most ancient and the most civilised mentality.'

Word and mythic image, which once confronted the human mind as hard realistic powers, have now cast off all reality and effectuality; they have become a light, bright ether in which the spirit can move without let or hindrance. The liberation is achieved not because the mind throws aside the sensuous forms of word and image, but in that it uses them both as *organs* of its own, and thereby recognizes them for what they really are: forms of its own self-revelation.'[1]

Such poetry, the poetry of self-revelation, is the specifically modern form of poetry, the poetry created by Shakespeare and Donne, by Goethe and Hölderlin, by Baudelaire and Rimbaud—the poetry described by Keats as 'the true voice of feeling' or by Marianne Moore as 'imaginary gardens with real toads in them'.

It is to poetry as a form of self-revelation that I shall turn in the following chapter. The poet, whenever we can identify ourselves with him, is always a self. We cannot identify ourselves with the primitive poet because there is no revelation of a self. There is no self in Homer; we cannot even tell whether the poet of the *Odyssey* was one self or many selves: whether a blind old man, as tradition says, or a beautiful young woman (Nausicaa) as Samuel Butler ingeniously maintained. The self that names, *der Dichter der stiftet*, was engaged in an objective activity: he was revealing the visible world, exploring the confines of a social consciousness. The modern poet is engaged in a subjective activity, discovering 'something deeply intrinsic in mental activity',[2] also therefore exploring the confines of consciousness, but of self-consciousness. The distinction, of course, is not absolute. There are modern poets for whom, in Gautier's phrase, the visible world is still real; and even the invisible world has to be made visible by sensuous analogies. But the difference of attitude, of orientation, has produced two distinct types of poetry, and one is of the past, and irrecoverable, the other of the future, and in process of formation.

[1] *Language and Myth*, trans. Susanne K. Langer, New York and London, 1946, p. 99.

[2] Leone Vivante, *English Poetry and its Contribution to the knowledge of a Creative Principle*, London, 1950.

CHAPTER 8

The Creative Experience in Poetry

In order to come close to the creative experience in poetry, it is necessary, either to describe an experience of one's own, or to discover some revealing evidence among the manuscripts of an acknowledged poet. There are obvious disadvantages in relying on one's own experience. Time has not tested the products of that experience, and nothing is so deceitful as the poetic afflatus. Even if our poems were acknowledged by our contemporaries, we should still have the uneasy feeling that they might be no more than a manifestation of the Zeitgeist. I shall speak as a poet who is under the illusion that he has had authentic experiences of poetic creation; but I shall take as an example for analysis a poem that in England has had a high reputation for more than one hundred and fifty years, a poem that is complex enough to exhibit all aspects of poetry, whether intensive or extensive, and whose composition is fully documented: Coleridge's ode, which he called *Dejection.* It was first published in the London *Morning Post* on the 4th October 1802 but it had been written exactly six months earlier in a form very different from that given to the public. The full version was first published by Professor Ernest de Selincourt in 1937. It has been republished more recently,[1] but the poem in its completeness cannot be said to be well known. Yet not only is that original version a great and moving poem, but a comparison of the two versions, and a consideration of the reasons which led Coleridge to revise his original version before publication, raise problems of the greatest critical importance.

[1] Selincourt, Ernest de, *Wordsworthian and Other Studies*, Oxford, Clarendon Press, 1947, pp. 57–76.

The original version is a continuous poem of 340 lines. What might be called the standard version, first published by Coleridge in 1817 in a collection of his poems called *Sibylline Leaves*, is merely 139 lines long, and the *Morning Post* version of 1802 is even shorter still. In its ruthlessly lopped state the poem is no longer a continuous train of thought, and is therefore divided into eight numbered and rearranged sections. Apart from these large structural changes, numerous small revisions have been made in the remaining text that completely disguise its origin and alter its tone. The considerations which Coleridge had in mind in making these alterations were partly personal and partly critical. But before we can discuss them we must take into account the circumstances in which the poem was composed.

Coleridge has married in haste and repented at leisure. For our present purposes it is not necessary to take sides in the quarrel, for we are only concerned with Coleridge's feelings in the matter, and of these there is no doubt. He gave full expression to them in a letter written in October of this same year 1802 to his friend and benefactor, Thomas Wedgwood. Here is a passage from this revealing document:

'After my return to Keswick, I was, if possible, more miserable than before. Scarce a day passed without such a scene of discord between me and Mrs Coleridge, as quite incapacitated me from any worthy exertion of my faculties by degrading me in my own estimation. I found my temper injured, and daily more so; the good and pleasurable Thoughts, which had been the support of my moral character, departed from my solitude. I determined to go abroad—but alas! the less I loved my wife, the more dear and necessary did my children seem to me. I found no comfort except in the driest speculations . . . About two months ago after a violent quarrel I was taken suddenly ill with spasms in my stomach—I expected to die—Mrs C. was, of course, shocked and frightened beyond measure—and two days after, I still being very weak and pale as death, she threw herself upon me and made a solemn promise of amendment—and she has kept her promise beyond any hope, I could have flattered myself with . . . If any woman wanted an exact and copious Recipe, "How to make a Husband compleatly miserable", I could furnish her with one—with a Probatum est, tacked to it. Ill-tempered Speeches sent after me when I went out of the House, ill-tempered Speeches on my return, my friends received with freezing looks, the least opposition or contradiction occasioning screams of passion, and the sentiments which I hold most base, ostentatiously avowed—all this added to the utter negation of all, which a Husband expects from a Wife—especially, living in retirement—and the consciousness that I was myself growing a worse man. O dear Sir! no one can tell what I have suffered. I can say with strict truth, that the happiest half-hours, I have had, were when all of a sudden, as I have been sitting alone in my Study, I have burst into Tears.'[1]

Such was Coleridge's state of mind when he wrote *Dejection.* But he did not tell Wedgwood the whole truth—he did not tell him that the passion he had once felt for Sarah Fricker, his wife, he now felt for Sara Hutchinson, the sister of Mary who was to become Wordsworth's wife.

All thoughts, all passions, all delights,
Whatever stirs this mortal frame
All are but ministers of Love,
And feed his sacred flame . . .

The beautiful ballad which opens with these lines had been inspired by this new and deep and hopeless passion and had been written three years before this letter to Wedgwood. That was in December, 1799, and the following summer, in order to be near the object of his new passion Coleridge had moved to the Lake District, and during the next few years they saw much of each other. During all this time Coleridge's health was rapidly deteriorating—apart from the spasms in the stomach mentioned to Wedgwood he suffered from giddiness and rheumatic pains, and it was then that he first had fatal recourse to opium. He was indeed a miserable man, but he was also a deeply religious man, and his convictions forbade any thought of divorce. He had three women to minister to him in his sickness, to sympathize with his misery—Mary and Sara Hutchinson, and Dorothy Wordsworth, who was as hopelessly in love with him as he was with Sara. It was in a mood induced by the tenderness of these ministering angels that he wrote the poem he called *Dejection.*

It is such an intimate poem, so self-revealing and so revealing of a complex passionate situation affecting others, that no other

[1] *Collected Letters of Samuel Taylor Coleridge,* edited by Earl Leslie Griggs, Vol. II (1801–06), Oxford, 1956, pp. 464–5.

excuse would be necessary for the considerable excisions which Coleridge made in the published version. But there was another consideration to which I have already referred of a more theoretical nature. Coleridge held the view that the best poetry is not written out of what we might call private situations. The best poetry is *objective*, as we say—it is *aloof*. In the *Biographia Literaria* he praises Shakespeare for possessing this quality. A sign of his genius, he said, 'is the choice of subjects very remote from the private interest and circumstances of the writer himself. At least,' he adds, 'I have found, that where the subject is taken immediately from the author's personal sensations and experiences, the excellence of a particular poem is but an equivocal mark, and often a fallacious pledge, of genuine poetic power.'

I think there is no doubt that Coleridge had this particular poem of his own in mind when making such a statement. This general principle of objectivity or aloofness in art is not to be confused with the impersonality of primitive poetry: the 'objective correlative' is always correlated to a subjective state of mind. For the moment it is perhaps sufficient to note that objectivity, or 'aesthetic distance' as it is sometimes called, is a principle recognized by aestheticians in all the arts, and it is perhaps a distinguishing mark between certain schools of art—the classical artist, for example, accepting it as a matter of course, but the realist, and more particularly the expressionist artist, going to the opposite extreme to find the basis of his work in the immediacy of his personal emotions.

In the original version of Coleridge's poem there is no attempt to disguise the dramatis personae; Wordsworth appears as William, and Sara, Mary and Dorothy are mentioned by name. In the *Morning Post* versions, William became Edmund; in the final *Sibylline Leaves* version, all names whatsoever are suppressed, and only a vague 'virtuous Lady' is apostrophized—'O Lady! we receive but what we give,' instead of 'O Sara! we receive but what we give'. The process of depersonalization was complete.

Thanks to our knowledge of the circumstances in which it was composed, and to the evidence offered by two distinct versions, one immediate and spontaneous, the other pondered and selective, we are able to distinguish clearly between the intensive and extensive aspects of this particular poem. The two versions must be studied side by side before any conclusion about their respective merits can be reached. My own conclusions, after such a careful study, are not at all ambiguous. The original poem is a human document of great interest, essential to an understanding of the personality of a great poet; but the revised version which Coleridge published is an infinitely better work of art. Indeed, nearly all the specifically poetic lines in the poem are in the final version; the lines that have been sacrificed are almost without exception rhetorical or prosaic. It seems as though the poetic spirit in Coleridge soars aloft whenever he ceases to address Sara in person and descends to become sentimental in her presence. There are exceptions: for example, this description of a happy moment of domestic bliss:

Such joy I had, that I may truly say,
My spirit was awe-stricken with the excess
And trance-like depth of its brief happiness

And there is one longer passage which is very moving and essential to an understanding of the situation out of which the poem arose:

I speak not now of those habitual ills
That wear out life, when two unusual minds
Meet in one house and two discordant wills—
This leaves me, where it finds,
Past cure, and past complaint,—a fate austere
Too fix'd and hopeless to partake of fear!

. . . Methinks to weep with you
Were better far than to rejoice alone—
But that my coarse domestic life has known
No habits of heart-nursing sympathy,
No griefs but such as dull and deaden me,
No mutual mild enjoyments of its own.
No hopes of its own vintage, none O! none—
Whence when I mourn'd for you, my heart might borrow
Fair forms and living motions for its sorrow.

But that is all. The great passages of the poem are in the public version, and are presented as direct utterances of the poet's own spirit, as a 'sudden flash of transcendental feeling'[1]:

[1] An expression I take from a book which, though innocent of modern psychology, showed a deep understanding of the poetic process: *The Myths of Plato*, by J. A. Stewart, London, 1905.

There was a time when tho' my path was rough,
The joy within me dallied with distress;
And all misfortunes were but as the stuff
Whence fancy made me dreams of happiness;
For hope grew round me, like the climbing vine,
And leaves and fruitage, not my own, seem'd mine!
But now ill tidings bow me down to earth,
Nor care I that they rob me of my mirth—
But oh! each visitation
Suspends what nature gave me at my birth.
My shaping spirit of imagination!

My shaping spirit of imagination! It will perhaps now be evident why, of all poems that were possible, I have chosen for analysis this poem of Coleridge's. It contains within its lines an exact description of the problem we are discussing. Let me quote one more passage:

For not to think of what I needs must feel,
But to be still and patient all I can;
And haply by abstruse research to steal
From my own nature, all the natural man—
This was my sole resource, my only plan:
Till that, which suits a part, infects the whole,
And now is almost grown the habit of my soul . . .

O Lady! We receive but what we give,
And in our life alone does Nature live
Ours is her wedding garment, ours her shroud—
And would we aught behold of higher worth
Than that inanimate cold world allow'd
To the poor loveless ever anxious crowd,
Ah! from the soul itself must issue forth
A light, a glory, and a luminous cloud
Enveloping the earth!
And from the soul itself must there be sent
A sweet and potent voice of its own birth,
Of all sweet sounds, the life and element.

Coleridge proceeds to identify that sweet and potent voice, this beautiful and beauty-making power, with joy, with the celebration and utterance of a feeling of spiritual identity with the creative forces of nature.

The poem, we see, proceeds quite directly from a conflict in Coleridge's mind, a moral and emotional embarrassment caused by his loss of love for his wife, and his concurrent passion for a woman not his wife. This personal conflict is seen by Coleridge as parallel to a conflict between metaphysical speculation and poetic expression. The emotional conflict creates a tension which is relieved by the act of poetic utterance; in some way, or to some degree, the poetic quality of the utterance is related to the intensity of the conflict. There supervenes in this emotional conflict an intellectual conflict, a fear that he (Coleridge) may be deprived of the capacity for poetic utterance by an indulgence in 'abstruse research', that spontaneity may be endangered by reflection.

Such is the personal equation implicit in this one poem. But can we generalize from this particular case? Not, of course, with any scientific validity, but whenever we uncover the springs of modern poetry—and it should be remembered that I am now discussing the post-Renaissance subjective type of poetry—there we soon detect a conflict of this nature. *Hamlet* and *King Lear* are, at the beginning of the period, the prototypes of such psychic conflicts, resolved in poetry.

Twenty-five years ago, in 1934, a psychological study of these problems was published by the Oxford University Press—Maud Bodkin's *Archetypal Patterns in Poetry*—a pioneering work which has not had sufficient acknowledgement. The archetypal pattern in poetry, according to Miss Bodkin, is always one of conflict—'The pattern consists of emotional tendencies of opposite character which are liable to be excited by the same object or situation, and, thus conflicting, produce an inner tension that seeks relief in the activity either of fantasy, or of poetic imagination, either originally or receptively creative.' Miss Bodkin does not presume to make any dogmatic assertion about the nature of the opposed tendencies, but she suggests that they arise from an ambivalent attitude towards the self—'a certain organization of the tendencies of self-assertion and submission' such as we find in tragedy. 'The self which is asserted is magnified by that same collective force to which finally submission is made; and from the tension of the two impulses and their reaction upon each other, under the conditions of poetic exaltation, the distinctive tragic attitude and emotion appears to arise.'[1]

This description would apply to Coleridge's poem (and Miss Bodkin does proceed to trace the same archetypal pattern in Coleridge's *The Ancient Mariner*, and in less detail in *Kubla Khan*). The collective force is present in Coleridge's acute sense of social morality, his 'fate austere, Too fix'd and hopeless to partake of fear!' His self is asserted in his defiant love of Sara, friend devoutest of his choice, and there is no possible reconciliation of those two contrary drives—only the relief of poetic utterance, of a projection of the conflict into the objective form of poetry. The relief is all the greater the more objective that projection can be made. We also call the process sublimation. The poet in the end cannot get rid of the perilous conflict unless he forgets himself, and creates a symbolic conflict in which the hidden self, in tragic renunciation, submits to Fate, or Truth, or God—by whatever name we designate the collective wisdom of the race or group.

Such is the mechanism of the creative imagination, of the formative will in the unconscious of the poet. But have we forgotten the fact which I stressed at the beginning of the last chapter—the fact that poetry does not consist wholly in an archetypal pattern of drama or action, that it is not only a form of art, but also a personal style? Whence comes the distinctive verbal magic of poetry, 'the sense of musical delight', as Coleridge called it?

I believe that it comes from the same source—or at least, that only an inner conflict of sufficient intensity can elicit those magical images that contribute the sonorous intensive aspect of poetry. Ariel's Song is a crystal jet from the same imaginative fountain as *Hamlet* or *King Lear*, as *The Tempest* itself, in which the Song has its organic station and function. *The Tempest* is also a great poem about self-assertion and submission, and all its beauties, of expression, unity and intellect, proceed from its unique intensity. Ariel's Song is not an incidental beauty—it too is produced and modified by the predominant passion of the poetic drama. It is, indeed, a crystallization of the theme of the drama—the sea-change that reconciles youth and age, life and death, mortal man and immortal beauty. The words wait in the inchoate recesses of

[1] Op. cit., p. 23.

the poet's mind, ready to spring into active discourse whenever the intensity of the internal conflict calls for them.

Poeta nascitur non fit—that Latin tag has been repeated for two millennia as a confession of the defeat we experience if we try to explain the secret sources of poetry. I do not think that any modern philosopher or psychologist would be so rash as to claim that he had solved the age-long mystery. But I think he would claim that the concept of the unconscious, and more particularly the concept of the archetypes, have thrown much light, if not into the sources of poetry, at least on the mechanism of poetic experience, the formative process in the imagination. The psychologist has penetrated some distance into the recesses of the poet's subjectivity and found there, not darkness, but a clever piece of machinery.

The metaphysicians still maintain, of course, that it is not a piece of machinery at all, but is rather what Jacques Maritain calls a wholly mysterious 'divination of the spiritual in the things of sense'.[1]

Some kind of immateriality is, of course, intrinsic to the poetic process. Poetry is consistent only in its shadowiness, its indeterminacy, its intangibility. In writing poetry we have a sense of the inexhaustible depth of our subjectivity; and out of that depth, flowing as spontaneously as water from a spring, comes this sensuous utterance in rhythmic verse. Of course, it is spiritual or psychic, as water is earthy. Spirituality is generated by it, as 'a sudden flash of transcendental feeling', but not added to it. Poetry creates its own potency, as Coleridge asserts in the poem we have examined:

O pure of heart! thou need'st not ask of me
What this strong music in the soul may be!
What, and wherein it doth exist,
This light, this glory, this fair luminous mist,
This beautiful and beauty-making power.

A light, a glory, a fair luminous mist—we cannot find more precise words to describe the experience of poetry. But what we have to insist on, against the theologians on the one side and the psychologists on the other side, is the originality and integrity of

[1] *Creative Intuition in Art and Poetry*, New York and London, 1953, p. 3 *et passim*. For a more detailed discussion of Professor Maritain's theory of poetry, see the appendix to this chapter (p. 136 below).

the process. There is no discernible reality, spiritual or otherwise, behind the process, no 'definite intellectual actuation' prompting the poetic flow. There is only within the total psyche a state of 'intrinsic indeterminacy'. This is Leone Vivante's phrase, and at this point I seek the support of his deeply sensitive, long considered philosophy. All art has as one of its distinctive features an intrinsic sensuous quality: it is sensuous at the moment of its origination, 'framed with senses of passions and affections', to recall Vico's phrase. It is a sensuous process within the psyche, and any distinctions of spirit or matter are foreign to its innocent nature. To quote Vivante at some length:

'We cannot understand the importance of this factor, nor its full meaning, nor the possibility of its very existence, except through the conception . . . of a positivity implying indeterminacy, co-extensive with subjectivity, and containing—in embryo, *a parte subjecti*—the whole gamut of our psyche. We cannot, except through this conception, understand the union between sense and meaning nor the aptness of sense to express the highest values. Nor can we understand why, when we enter the realm of sensibility, we enter the realm of God—a world more sensible, richer, truer, less one-sided, at one and the same time more impersonal and more intimately personal, far more favoured by taste, and by grace, and wisdom, than the world of voluntary thought, which is that of external construction, and not of intimate growth.

'Philosophers have generally undervalued sensation, and (a most lamentable, in my opinion, and almost incredible error) they have put the principle of the synthesis outside it. They have considered sensation as entirely passive, a reality without problems and without mysteries. Poets have not followed the same way.

'The fact is that the fundamental problems—and the fundamental realities—of psychic activity are met in sensation no less than in sentiment, no less than in will, no less than in the cognitive activity. I mean, for instance, such problems as the unity, or inner transparency, of the psychic present; the problem of a cause not entirely derived; the reality, or else the illusion, of an actual origin of value (or quality); the degree of reality of mental activity.'[1]

We have to admit that the illumination cast by modern psychology on these 'fundamental problems' of creativity is almost nil. Myth and dream, symbol and image—all the paraphernalia of depth-

[1] Vivante, op. cit., p. 324f.

psychology—are conceived as shadow play, and it is their analysable signification, and not their sensuous actuality, that attract the analyst. The depth-psychologist may claim that therapy is his only concern, and that the sensuous quality of works of art would merely distract him. That is to misunderstand the nature of art, and precisely its most intrinsic values. It is to disregard the unity of the psyche, which is not a unity of concepts, of spirit or intellect, or even of images, but of sensation. Thought in its deepest recesses is a sensuous, formative process: spontaneous, not controlled by any extrinsic will or consciousness. Though the psyche may be impelled to thought by conflict; though it may flow into channels that have been prepared by racial experience, as when the poet innocently repeats a fable or a myth that other poets in remote ages had invented—nevertheless, the thought of the poet is originally sensuous because it has its origins in physical perception and flows along the organs of sensation, and even as it flows, forms into determinate patterns of delight.

The sense of delight is, I think, the sense of illumination, of revelation, what Maritain calls specifically 'the poetic sense', 'a meaning which is immanent in that object which is a poem or co-substantial with it'. And it follows, says Maritain, that 'the intelligible sense, through which the poet utters ideas, is entirely subordinate to the poetic sense, through which the poem exists'.[1] This poetic sense, which may be clear or obscure, analysable or unanalysable, is a self-sustaining reality, 'which is without comparison vaster and stronger, of a far greater spiritual breadth, than that of the planning will'.[2] The poem is a sensuous unity, a totality of utterance, and meaningful as unity or totality. To break it down into image and idea is to ignore the fact that there are no internal sutures, no possibility of separating image from image, image from idea, or either from the language in which they are expressed.

Do we then end with a mystery, and a veto on psychological attempts to explain it? Not exactly. We end with the reality of being or existence, and the experience of poetry is a proof of its intrinsic originality, of its ceaseless novelty, of its unpredictable form. There is a chain of cause and effect in our practical life, in our intercourse with the external world; but deep within man's

[1] Maritain, op. cit., pp. 258–9.
[2] Vivante, op. cit., p. 328.

subjectivity there is an effect which has no discernible cause, which is a process of discovery, of self-realization, a rending of the numinous veil of consciousness. The immediate object of the poetic experience refuses to be identified: it is infinite and eternal, formless and uninformed. In so far as this poetic experience can be described, Francis Thompson described it in these paradoxical words:

O world invisible, we view thee,
O world intangible, we touch thee.
O world unknowable, we know thee,
Inapprehensible, we clutch thee!

View, touch, clutch—these are sensible modes of knowledge, and what we know by these means can be described only by the one simple but ambiguous word: Truth.

The experience I have been describing was described more eloquently and more subtly sixteen and a half centuries ago by the great Chinese poet, Lu Chi. In conclusion I will quote the last section of his Essay on Literature, the famous poem *Wen Fu*:

Such moments when Mind and Matter hold perfect communion,
And wide vistas open to regions hitherto entirely barred,
Will come with irresistible force,
And go, their departure none can hinder.
Hiding, they vanish like a flash of light;
Manifest, they are like sounds arising in mid air.

So acute is the mind in such instants of divine comprehension,
What chaos is there that it cannot marshal in miraculous order?
While winged thoughts, like quick breezes, soar from depths of heart,
Eloquent words, like a gushing spring, flow between lips and teeth.
No flower, or plant, or animal is too prodigal of splendour
To be recreated under the writer's pen.
Hence the most wondrous spectacle that ever whelmed the eye,
And notes of the loftiest music that rejoiced the ear!

But there are other moments as though the Six Senses were stranded,
When the heart seems lost, and the spirit stagnant.
One stays motionless like a petrified log,
Dried up like an exhausted river bed.
The soul is indrawn to search the hidden labyrinth;
Within oneself is sought where inner light may be stored.

Behind a trembling veil Truth seems to shimmer, yet ever more evasive,
And thought twists and twirls like silk spun on a clogged wheel.
Therefore, all one's vital force may be dispersed in rueful failure;
Yet again, a free play of impulses may achieve a feat without pitfall.
While the secret may be held within oneself,
It is none the less beyond one's power to sway.
Oft I lay my hand on my empty chest,
Despairing to know how the barrier could be removed.[1]

Appendix

I hesitate to enter into argument with a philosopher so skilled in traditional dialectics as Maritain, and I have the greatest respect for his book, *Creative Intuition in Art and Poetry*. But his brilliant rhetoric is, I believe, used in the service of a theological conception of truth, and profound as is his general philosophy of art, he introduces an intellectual prejudice which confuses the issue we are discussing.

In disagreement with certain earlier French critics, Maritain draws a distinction between poetic experience and mystical experience. They are distinct in nature: 'poetic experience is concerned with the created world and the enigmatic and innumerable relations of beings with each other; mystical experience with the principle of things in its own incomprehensible and supramundane unity'. 'Poetic experience is from the very start oriented towards expression, and terminates in a word uttered, or work produced; while mystical experience tends towards silence, and terminates in an immanent fruition of the absolute.'[2]

This is an acceptable distinction, as is also Professor Maritain's further distinction between poetry and metaphysics. '. . . metaphysics is engaged in abstract knowledge, while poetry quickens art. Metaphysics snatches at the spiritual in an idea, by the most abstract intellection; poetry reaches it in the flesh, by the very point of the flesh sharpened through intelligence.' But Maritain

[1] Trans. by Shih-Hsiang Chen, The Anthoensen Press, Portland, Maine, 1952. A more accessible translation (which, however, has been drastically criticized) accompanied by a full and interesting commentary, is given by E. R. Hughes in *The Art of Letters*, Bollingen Series, New York, 1951.

[2] *Creative Intuition in Art and Poetry*, pp. 234–5.

somewhat dims these neat distinctions by adding, as afterthoughts, that different in nature as poetry and mysticism may be, 'they are born near one another, and near the centre of the soul; in the living springs of the preconceptual or supraconceptual vitality of the spirit'; and that metaphysics gives 'chase to essences and definitions, poetry to any flash of existence glittering by the way, and any reflection of an invisible order'.

To understand what Maritain means by an invisible order, or a preconceptual or supraconceptual vitality of the spirit, we must refer back to a distinction which he has made earlier in his book at the expense of Dr Jung. He is very emphatic at this point, and indeed his whole philosophy, and that of all the obscurantists of this issue, depend upon it. He says that we must not be misled by the word *unconscious*; and he warns us that the word as he uses it does not mean what it says—it 'does not necessarily mean a purely unconscious activity. It means most often an activity which is *principally* unconscious, but the point of which emerges into consciousness'. It means, in fact, what is distinguished by psychologists as the preconscious, but Maritain continues to use the word 'unconscious'.

He then proceeds to his point. 'My contention,' he says, 'is that everything depends . . . on the recognition of the existence of a spiritual unconscious, or rather, preconscious, of which Plato and the ancient wise men were well aware, and the disregard of which in favour of the Freudian unconscious alone is a sign of the dullness of our times. There are two kinds of unconscious, two great domains of psychological activity screened from the grasp of consciousness: the preconscious of the spirit in its living springs, and the unconscious of blood and flesh, instincts, tendencies, complexes, repressed images and desires, traumatic memories, as constituting a closed or autonomous dynamic whole. I would like to designate the first kind of unconscious by the name of spiritual, or, for the sake of Plato, musical unconscious or preconscious; and the second by the name of automatic unconscious or *deaf* unconscious—deaf to the intellect, and structured into a world of its own apart from the intellect; we might also say, in quite a general sense, leaving aside any particular theory, *Freudian unconscious*.'

And then in a footnote Maritain adds that his distinction is altogether different from Jung's distinction between the *personal* and the *collective* unconscious—'both of which are part of the spiritual unconscious inasmuch as they enter the sphere of the preconscious life of the intellect or the will, and are thus spiritualized, and both of which are a part of the automatic unconscious inasmuch as they are shut up in a merely animal world, separate from the life of the intellect and the will.'[1]

It might seem that Professor Maritain is merely describing the super-ego, but he does not mention this term; inasmuch as the Freudian concept of the super-ego implies that it proceeds from the unconscious, by natural steps dictated by the reality-principle, I fear it would not satisfy him. Professor Maritain is a Christian apologist (as also was Coleridge) and he is anxious to retain in the poetic pattern a place for what he calls 'the spirit'—something wholly distinct from what we call 'the psyche'.

I am not concerned with the theological issue: I am only anxious to avoid a confusion between poetics and theology. For Professor Maritain proceeds on the assumption that his definitions are acceptable, and on their basis he maintains that the intellect itself is unconscious, or that there exists an unconscious that is intellectual, that there exists 'at the single root of the soul's powers', 'something which is preconceptual or non-conceptual and nevertheless in a state of definite intellectual actuation'. Obviously, we might suppose, he is referring to the archetypes; but no, for he goes on to say that this 'something' is not 'a mere way to concept', an 'impressed pattern', 'but another kind of germ, which does not tend towards a concept to be found . . . which is already an intellective form or act fully determined though enveloped in the night of the spiritual unconscious'.[2] Maritain is here positing a wholly new faculty of the mind which he proceeds to identify with poetic intuition. Poetry, therefore, is no longer an intrinsically sensuous process, a naming of things present to consciousness but not yet realized. Poetry is rather an intellective act which by its essence is creative, and forms something into being instead of being formed by things: and what (asks Maritain) can such an intellective act possibly express and manifest in producing the work if not the very being and substance of the one who creates? The implication is that this is a state of mystical awareness, 'a kind

[1] Op. cit., pp. 91–92.

[2] Op. cit., pp. 111–12. Cf. (p. 97) the discussion of *species impressa*, impressed pattern, 'a mere way to the concept'.

of experience or knowledge without parallel in logical reason, through which things and the self are obscurely grasped together', 'one of the basic manifestations of man's spiritual nature. . . .' It is really the traditional theory of possession, of inspiration.

It is perhaps only a question of terminology, and it might prove more difficult for Professor Maritain to reconcile his theory of poetry with a belief in divine dispensation than it is for me to translate the same theory into the empirical language of depth psychology. We must both confess that we are in a realm of indeterminacy: out of this realm emerge the patterns of poetry. To ascribe these patterns to 'a kind of inherent knowledge' or to a process of 'intellectual actuation' may not seem to differ much from identifying them with something so indefinite as an archetypal pattern of feeling. But it is more dangerous to be near the truth and yet not truthful, than to be far from the truth, a position obvious to anyone. Plato, as Maritain notices, clearly separates poetic inspiration from reason, from intellectual cognition. He did so because he realized that though inspiration can be called a form of cognition (for it 'cognizes' aspects of reality, just as the intellect does); and though each form of cognition may be said to proceed logically (that is to say, by constructive shapes or configurations); nevertheless the two modes of cognition are totally distinct in their operations.

Poetry is not necessarily visual: it can and does deal with concepts, and Coleridge's poem, which I have quoted, is full of concepts. 'The deeper logic of thought,' writes Leone Vivante, 'is the very life of poetry—and of art. The subtlest, most delicate and most secret, most remote, forgotten kinships of concepts are revealed in poetry.' But how revealed? That is the important question, and the answer is not in doubt. They are revealed by a process that we call realization, or even materialization, a sensational process. They find their objective correlatives, their sensuous images that no longer haunt thought's wildernesses as disembodied abstractions, but are incarnated in things of sense. Maritain seems to recognize this distinction, for example, when he speaks of the essential difference between the poetic sense and the logical sense —when he admits that the words in a poem 'are not only signs of concepts or ideas, but objects also, objects which are endowed with their proper sonorous quality. Their function as signs, in their mutual interrelation, depends at the same time on this physical sonorous quality itself—and on the images they convey—and on the fog or aura of unexpressed associations they carry with them—and on their intelligible or logical meaning (only a part of the whole).[1]

In this complete description of the poetic process, what has become of the spiritual unconscious? 'What matters,' repeats Maritain, 'is only the poetic sense'; and all his statements and illustrations go to show that this sense resides in the words of the poem—the intelligible meaning of the words and the *imaginal* meaning of the words—'and the most mysterious meanings of the musical relations between the words, and between the meaningful contents with which the words are laden.'[2]

[1] *English Poetry*, p. 258.
[2] Op. cit., p. 259.

CHAPTER 9

The Scream of Juno's Peacock

During the past hundred years a revolution in the visual arts has taken place that is without precedent in the history of our western civilization. In its incipient stages, which we call impressionism, expressionism, post-impressionism and cubism, it was still possible to characterize this revolution as a variation of previous modes of visual cognition; but with the invention of *abstraction* it became necessary for the first time to conceive a completely new mode of visual cognition—briefly, a mode of cognition that turned inwards, to render visible whatever images might come into consciousness by recollection or introspection, instead of turning outwards, to render visible whatever images had come into consciousness from the external world by the normal channels of sensory perception. Paul Klee expressed this new aim in a famous aphorism: 'Art does not reflect the visible but makes visible.'

It is my intention in this chapter to examine the nature of this revolution in the arts and to ask whether it signifies a defeat of the human spirit, a descent into nihilism or despair, or on the contrary a spiritual or even a cosmic renewal of any kind.

I shall refer in more detail later (Chapter 14) to Plato's myth of the Age of Kronos, a myth devised to account for those cataclysmic changes in human destiny that puzzled archaic man. In the present chapter I would like to discuss the same myth as it appears in the work of W. B. Yeats, who was the first modern poet, so far as I know, to relate the strange manifestations of contemporary art to some cyclic change of the kind envisaged in Plato's myth. But before I venture into this, to me, unfamiliar territory, let me explain that I do so with the hesitation and modesty, not only of one who is profoundly ignorant of the esoteric tradition of which it is a part, but also as one who is sceptical of all attempts to explain human phenomena by recourse to superhuman agencies. I accept Plato's cosmic ages, as I accept Nietzsche's eternal recurrence and Yeats's cycles or gyres, as convenient myths to explain inconvenient experiences. They indicate that the human imagination is always more resourceful than the human intellect: that art has the capacity, and the audacity, to transcend history. They indicate more than this, for the vital function of the imagination is not to escape from reality, but to make it viable. As Professor Eddington once suggested, in an appropriate metaphor, it is possible that 'reality is a child which cannot survive without its nurse, illusion'.

I would like to recall the context in which Yeats's remarks about non-representative art occur. They are to be found in his discussion of 'The Great Year of the Ancients', which is Book IV of *A Vision*. To the archaic mind, and to the modern poet who is often a poet in virtue of his archaic modes of feeling, there is nothing irrational or unscientific in imagining a 'great' year on the analogy of our short-term terrestrial year, a recurrent event governed by some cosmic revolution of the stars, corresponding to the smaller scale of the revolution of our own planetary system. Yeats quotes Cicero: 'By common consent men measure the year by the return of the sun, or in other words by the revolution of one star. But when the whole of the constellations shall return to the positions from which they once set forth, thus after a long interval re-making the first map of the heavens, that may indeed be called the Great Year wherein I scarce dare say how many are the generations of men.'

Once Yeats has accepted this idea of a Great Year, equal to many thousands of our terrestrial years, then it is not illogical for him to suppose that such a year has its seasons, not necessarily corresponding climatically to our own seasons, which are governed by the heat of a single star, but perhaps subject to cosmic influences such as do undoubtedly exist. The phases and duration of such seasons could possibly be determined by mathematical calculation, and such calculations have been attempted by philosophers and astrologers.

We need not rely on them for our present discussion! But the whole concept might involve archetypal months and seasons, and at the end of the Great Year there would be a period of wintry darkness, from which eventually the Universe would slowly renew itself and put forth the Spring flowers of a new Great Year.

In the midst of his discussion of these concepts and calculations, Yeats suddenly remembers 'that most philosophical of archaeologists Josef Strzygowski'. Strzygowski haunts his imagination, he says. This is because the philosophical archaeologist had situated the source of European civilization in the Near East—not India or China, but Asia Minor, Mesopotamia and Egypt—and had elaborated a kind of geographical symbolism in which the East is the realm of intellectual power or authority (its symbol the sceptre), the South of humanism (its symbol the human figure), the North the realm of abstraction (superhuman form), and the West perhaps a reflection of these other realms, a realm of emotional freedom.

Yeats's cosmography is an elaborate system derived partly from the pre-Socratic philosophers, partly from Jakob Boehme and Swedenborg, and partly from his own visions. From Boehme he took the word 'tincture'. There are two tinctures, the 'primary' and the 'antithetical', and as far as I can understand Yeats's use of the terms they seem to correspond to those states of mind or mental energy which we call extraversive and introversive.

To return to Yeats's geographical symbolism: the South, he says, with its humanistic tendencies, represents the introversive or antithetical tincture; the North the primary or extraversive tincture, to which the Great Year is now due to return. And that is why he was haunted by Strzygowski, for Strzygowski confirmed his vision by finding 'amid the nomad Aryans of northern Europe and Asia the source of all geometrical ornament, of all non-representative art'. And then follows a prophetic passage which is my excuse for introducing these curious speculations:

'It is only when he [Strzygowski] comes to describe such art as a subordination of all detail to the decoration of some given surface, and to associate it with domed and arched buildings where nothing interferes with the effect of the building as a whole, and with a theology which so exalts the Deity that every human trait disappears, that I begin to wonder whether the non-representative art of our own time may not be but a first symptom of our return to the *primary tincture*'—that is to say, to an objective, extraversive phase of existence.'[1]

Yeats traces the evolution of art through the 28 Phases of his cosmographic revolution. I am concerned only with his description of Phase 22, which runs according to his reckoning from 1875 to 1927—Yeats was writing in 1925. This period, he says, 'is like that from 1250 to 1300 (Phase 8) a period of abstraction, and like it also in that it is preceded and followed by abstraction. Phase 8 was preceded by the Schoolmen and followed by legalists and inquisitors, and Phase 22 was preceded by the great popularizers of physical science and economic science, and will be followed by social movements and applied science. Abstraction which began at Phase 19 will end at Phase 25, for these movements and this science will have for their object or result the elimination of intellect. Our generation has witnessed a first weariness, has stood at the climax . . . and when the climax passes will recognize that their common secular thought began to break and disperse.' Then, after a reference to Tolstoy and Flaubert, Yeats suggests that there came into our civilization 'synthesis for its own sake, organization where there is no masterful director, books where the author has disappeared, painting where some accomplished brush paints with an equal pleasure, or with a bored impartiality, the human form or an old bottle, dirty weather and clean sunshine'. In other words, what we might call an ethic of objectivity. Yeats confesses that he is filled with excitement as this new gyre begins to stir, and suggests that even the ignorant must be impressed by the contrast between the concepts of Newton and recent mathematical research, with its objective world intelligible to intellect. He concludes: 'men, for the first time since the seventeenth century, see the world as an object of contemplation, not as something to be remade, and some few . . . even doubt if there is any common experience, doubt the possibility of science.'[2]

There are many profound thoughts in this passage, and some amazingly confident assertions which luckily are not strictly relevant to our purpose. But certain correlations are made and these together constitute 'a period of abstraction'—the physical sciences, economics, literature and painting, all have become objects of contemplation—an objective world intelligible to the

[1] *A Vision*, London, 1937, p. 258.
[2] Op. cit., pp. 299–300.

intellect. In his description of Phase 22 in an earlier part of the book even the world of action is found to exhibit the same features —and to become terrible, 'for men will die and murder for an abstract synthesis, and the more abstract it is the further it carries them from compunction and compromise; and as obstacles to that synthesis increase, the violence of their will increases'. Yeats had the Russian Revolution in mind, and mentions Karl Marx in this same paragraph. He makes the following generalization about the whole of this Phase: 'There is no longer a desired object, as distinct from thought itself, no longer a *Will*, as distinct from the process of nature seen as a fact; and so thought itself, seeing that it can neither begin nor end, is stationary. Intellect knows itself as its own object of desire; and the *Will* knows itself to be the world; there is neither change nor desire of change. For the moment the desire for a form has ceased and an absolute realism becomes possible.'[1]

One wonders exactly what forms of abstract art Yeats had in mind at the time he was writing *A Vision*. Through his friend Ezra Pound he had been in touch with whatever abstraction was practised in England at that time, with the paintings of Wyndham Lewis, for example. We can assume he was familiar with Picasso's work, but there is no evidence that he knew the far more systematically abstract art of Kandinsky and Mondrian. He might have read, at the time of the publication of the first English translation (1914) Kandinsky's book, *Concerning the Spiritual in Art*, in which for the first time the possibility of a modern abstract art was foreseen. He might have discussed the theory of abstract art with T. E. Hulme, but this would have been before 1917, when Hulme was killed. He does not seem to have read Hulme's *Speculations*, which was published in 1924, until 1933.[2] I mention these tedious facts to show that Yeats's knowledge of abstract art, when he wrote *A Vision*, must have been superficial, and that it is very unlikely he had any knowledge at all of the considerable body of theoretical or philosophical exegesis which was being written during his lifetime by the artists themselves, above all, by Kandinsky, Klee and Mondrian. All the more remarkable, therefore, his intuitive realization of the significance of this contemporary movement in art.

Above all Yeats could not have been aware of a fundamental

[1] Op. cit., p. 163.
[2] Cf. *Letters of W. B. Yeats*, London, 1954, p. 810.

division within the abstract movement which nevertheless is an illustration, and an elaboration, of the distinction which he himself had made and which I have just quoted, the distinction between the work of art as thought itself, as absolute realism, a process of nature accepted as a fact, and the work of art as the desired object, a formal expression of the Creative Mind. But this is a distinction now apparent in contemporary art, and of the greatest significance from a philosophical point of view. It is the distinction between a nihilism or apathy that accepts and expresses the 'crepuscular decomposition' which is the historical fact, and a creative positivism that revolts against the tyranny of time and seeks the timeless perfection of an abstract non-figurative art.

It is true that this revolt against the actuality of history, against what is loosely called 'social realism', may also be interpreted as a negation, but it will be one of my purposes in this chapter to maintain that the negation of the historical present is not to be confused with an apathetic nihilism devoid of any positive effort or thought; that on the contrary, this a-historical art whose characteristics I shall define, is the only positive evidence of renewal at present discernible in the visual arts of our time.

I shall now try to trace very briefly the origins and development of these two types of art, both of which are, confusingly, but not unreasonably, called 'abstract'.

From one point of view, that of the classical idealist, any departure from the criteria of representation established during the Renaissance—criteria derived from a nostalgic interpretation of Greek art and its Roman derivatives—is to be regarded as a step towards nihilism—*ein Verlust der Mitte*, as Professor Sedlmayr calls it[1]—a loss of the mean, of balance or equilibrium. From this point of view the rot begins in the eighteenth century; romanticism is one of its manifestations; naturalism in literature and impressionism in painting are advanced stages in the disease. Presumably from such a point of view the corresponding changes in science and social organization, in philosophy and religion, are also part of the same process of decomposition. Their inevitability, even if that is accepted, is not their justification. They are all aspects of the same process of 'Degeneration' or '*Entartung*', and periodically such changes from the conventional standard of realism are denounced by some angry prophet: Max Nordau,

[1] Sedlmayr. Hans, *Art in Crisis: the Lost Centre*, London, 1958.

Tolstoy, Spengler, Goebbels, Berdyaev. As Bernard Shaw said in the pamphlet he wrote in answer to Max Nordau, the same alarm has been raised at the onset of every new wave of energy in art; and these alarms, like prophecies of the end of the world, always have had their public.[1]

Nordau's degenerates were artists like Wagner, Ibsen and Tolstoy; the artists of our own time, say Stravinsky, Eliot and Pasternak, would have seemed to him, as no doubt they seem to Sedlmayr, cases from a more advanced stage of the same process of degeneration; whereas the general body of contemporary art and literature would be but the final melancholy proof of Nordau's thesis. But this thesis, and the thesis of all these prophets of doom, has one aspect of truth. Wagner and Ibsen, the Impressionists and the Post-Impressionists, are intent on destroying, not only what Nordau calls 'civilization', but the rationality that has brought this particular civilization into being. The 'common secular thought', as Yeats calls it, is no longer acceptable, and this common secular thought against which our artists are in revolt includes the most fundamental assumptions of that thought, those of time and space.

The pioneers of the modern movement in art, the poets and painters of the first decade of this century, were consciously metaphysical in their thought—some of them even called themselves 'metaphysical'. The word 'cubism' is a spatial concept; the word 'futurism' is a concept of time; the word 'surrealism' is a concept of space-time. Futurist painting, declared the manifesto of the group published in 1912, contains three new pictorial concepts:

1. The solution of the problem of volumes in the picture, for we oppose the liquefaction of objects which is a fatal consequence of impressionistic vision.
2. The translation of objects according to the *lines of force* which characterize them, by means of which an absolutely new plastic dynamism is achieved.
3. The third, which is a natural consequence of the first two points, is the rendition of the emotional atmosphere of the

[1] *The Sanity of Art: An Exposure of the Current Nonsense about Artists being Degenerate*, London, 1911. Shaw's essay was originally written twelve years earlier for the American anarchist journal *Liberty*, edited by Benjamin Tucker. Max Nordau's book was first published in Germany in 1893.

picture which is a hitherto unknown source of pictorial lyricism.[1]

The Russian Constructivists in 1920 made a similar declaration in their 'Realistic' Manifesto of 1920. Declaring that 'the realization of our perceptions of the world in the forms of space and time is the only aim of our pictorial and plastic art', they laid down 'five fundamental principles':

1. In painting they renounced colour, for colour is an accidental element, exterior and superficial, and has nothing in common 'with the innermost essence of a thing'.
2. They renounced the descriptive line, for description is the accidental trace of man on things—'it is not bound up with the essential life and constant structure of the body'. Line can be affirmed only as a direction of the static forces and their rhythm in objects.
3. They renounced volume as a pictorial and plastic form of space, for space can only be affirmed in depth.
4. They renounced mass as a sculptural element—the force of resistance and the inertia of an object do not depend upon its mass, but upon its extension in depth.
5. They renounced the age-old delusion according to which the basic element in art is the static rhythm. They affirmed that kinetic rhythms are the basic forms of the perception of real time.[2]

Picasso denies the linear or evolutionary conception of time: 'I also often hear the word "evolution". Repeatedly I am asked to explain how my paintings evolved. To me there is no past or future in art. If a work of art cannot live always in the present it must not be considered at all. The art of the Greeks, of the Egyptians, of the great painters who lived in other times, is not an art of the past; perhaps it is more alive today than it ever was. Art does not evolve by itself, the ideas of people change and with them their mode of expression.'[3]

It may be that by 'metaphysical' these artists meant little more

[1] Cf. Umberto Boccioni, 'Opera Completa', Foligno, 1927, pp. 185ff. Trans. R. Goldwater and M. Treves, *Artists on Art*, New York and London, 1947, pp. 436–7.

[2] *Gabo*, London, Lund Humphries, 1957, p. 152.

[3] Statement of 1923, and originally published in *The Arts*, New York, 1923. Quoted from *Picasso: Fifty years of his Art*. By Alfred H. Barr, Jun., New York (Museum of Modern Art), 1946, pp. 270–1.

than 'numinous' or even 'romantic', but when we examine the statements of artists who had an adequate philosophical vocabulary, Kandinsky, Klee and Mondrian, then we can no longer disguise from ourselves the metaphysical nature of the revolution they envisage. These three artists in particular—and they are representative—are consciously and coherently expressing, both in their writings and their paintings, a will to abstraction which is at the same time a rejection of the phase of history into which they had been born.

The will to abstraction is not, of course, a new phenomenon in the history of art: as Yeats, following Strzygowski, points out, it is a characteristic of early Gothic art and of the art of the North generally. But it is not Strzygowski, but Wilhelm Worringer, who has given the most complete account of this historical phenomenon, and Worringer's writings on the subject were certainly familiar to Kandinsky and Klee, and perhaps also to Mondrian. Worringer, developing the theories of Theodor Lipps and Alois Riegl, shows that no explanation of art as 'objectified self-enjoyment' (Lipps's definition) can account for the facts of art history. Many works of art appear, on the contrary, to be a denial of the self and self-enjoyment, a retreat into a realm of inorganic abstraction. This self-denial, according to Worringer, is the outcome of a great inner unrest inspired in man by the confused phenomena of the outside world, spiritual dread of space.[1] The art of the East characterized by Yeats as intellectual is an art dominated, according to Worringer, by an immense need for tranquillity. The happiness these people sought from art 'did not consist in the possibility of projecting themselves into the things of the outer world, of enjoying themselves in them, but in the possibility of taking the individual thing of the external world out of its arbitrariness and seeming fortuitousness, of eternalizing it by approximation to abstract forms and, in this manner, of finding a point of tranquillity and a refuge from appearances.'[2]

I know of no better theoretical explanation of the tendency to abstraction that we find in many historical types of art, notably in Islamic art, but also in the Pre-Renaissance art of the North. But the main stylistic consequence of this tendency to abstraction was the strict suppression of the representation of space, in other

[1] *Abstraction and Empathy*, Eng. trans., 1953, p. 15.

[2] Op. cit., p. 16.

words, a two-dimensional art. We shall see that modern art, on the contrary, is often very much pre-occupied with the representation of spatial values—that is to say, of space itself. Space itself is an absolute (an essence) which the modern artist would like to separate from the individual existence of natural phenomena. Time, too, in the abstract art of music, and even when represented as a rhythmic arrangement of two-dimensional forms, can be similarly isolated.

I do not wish to spend too much time expounding Worringer's well-known thesis, but I must emphasize his general conclusion, which has been supported by much subsequent research and judgment, that 'every stylistic phase represents, for the humanity that created it out of its psychic needs, the goal of its volition and hence the maximum degree of perfection. What seems to us today a strange and extreme distortion is not the fault of insufficient ability, but the consequence of differently directed volition. Its creators could *do* no otherwise because they *willed* no otherwise'. These words were written long before the universal proliferation of an abstract style[1] such as we have witnessed in the past twenty-five years; they were prophetic and they remain true. But we should perhaps pause for a moment to ask what does Worringer, and German art historians in general, mean by a 'directed volition' in art or philosophy? The 'will' as a social force, into which individuals are willy-nilly swept, remains a Germanic concept, and in recent years has, as we all know, been much criticized, and even ridiculed not only by materialistic philosophers, but by empiricist and logical positivists in general. It is the inexcusable excuse for all forms of historicism.

Worringer, to do him justice, is always ready to trace the origins of a style in art to geographical and climatic factors. In his book on Egyptian art he subscribes to the formula of Frobenius: 'The relationship of a culture to the soil is the condition or the explanation of the essence of that culture. Culture is the soil rendered organic by man.' The culture of Egypt can be explained as an oasic culture. But something else has to be taken into consideration—the catastrophic phenomenon of inundation, for example. Up to a point we can explain Egyptian culture as 'the

[1] Originally published in the *Zeitschrift für Aesthetik und allgemeine Kunstwissenschaft* in 1909, but added as an appendix to the third edition of *Abstraktion und Einfühlung* in 1910.

culture of a colony of mixed races, foredoomed by the special conditions of its existence to become stereotyped as a hot-house growth of artificial conventions, a forced product of civilized life maintaining its formative impulse out of the rationality of institutions and not out of the irrationality and individuality of their exponents. It is always said that the Egyptian is in a special degree conditioned by the organizations forced upon him if he is to extract from the special natural circumstances of Egypt a maximum of productiveness. And this maximum is forced upon him because immediately alongside the strips of oasis yawns the desert.[1]

This is materialistic enough to satisfy a Marxist. Where then does the will come in? Worringer's whole point is that in Egyptian art, by exception, it does not come in. There is no spirituality (and no sensuousness) in Egyptian art simply because there is no awareness of space—and an awareness of space is, as it were, the beginning of a will to art—'space is always only a form of the relationship of the ego to the surrounding world.' . . . The organization of space, in the architectonic sense, is the process by means of which 'the subjective feeling for existence' is rendered relative and metaphysical. Space in Egyptian architecture is only a surviving rudiment of a primeval magic of caverns—reminiscences of subterranean earth-workings. The Egyptian was not hostile to space—but neutral and indifferent. 'Rigidity, inhuman, non-human rigidity, is the mark of this culture. How could there be a place in it for the ever-fluid quality of space?'[2]

Space is metaphysical consciousness—such is Worringer's summary of the whole matter, and the will enters into the scheme of things with this awareness. 'Space is becoming, eternal becoming, endless melody of becoming—victory over everything that is bound up with mere being, the opening up of what lies eternally beyond all corporeality.'

There is another and a less mystical explanation of the origins of a will to art which is nevertheless related to a consciousness of space. I refer to the researches of Piaget and his colleagues into the origins of intelligence in the child, for there it is shown that out of the first tentative gropings of the infant into space is born *intention*, the desire to discriminate; and where there is a desire to discriminate there is already an aesthetic volition. But Piaget's

[1] *Egyptian Art*, Eng. trans., 1928, pp. 11–12.
[2] Op. cit., pp. 87–88.

researches do not contradict Worringer's theory: on the contrary, they give it biological support.

To go back to Yeats for a moment. He distinguishes four faculties: Will and Mask, Creative Mind and Body of Fate. Mask is the object of the Will; Body of Fate the object of the Creative Mind, and these pairs of opposites are antithetical. Will and Creative Mind are the primary and antithetical tinctures and seem, as I have already suggested, to be identical with the extraverted and introverted directions of mental activity, perhaps with instinct and rationality, but nothing is very precise in this system. But as a system it has a suggestive application to our present concerns. For example, Yeats says that 'the *Will* looks into a painted picture, the *Creative Mind* looks into a photograph, but both look into something that is the opposite of themselves. The *Creative Mind* contains all the universals in so far as its memory permits their employment, whereas the photograph is heterogeneous. The picture is chosen, the photograph is fated, because by Fate and Necessity—for I need both words—is understood what comes from without, whereas the *Mask* (which is the object of the Will) is predestined, Destiny being that which comes to us from within. We can best explain the heterogeneity of the photograph when we call it the photograph of a crowded street, which the *Creative Mind* when not under the influence of the Mask contemplates coldly; while the picture contains but few objects and the Contemplating Will is impassioned and solitary. When the *Will* predominates the *Mask* or Image is "sensuous"; when the *Creative Mind* predominates it is "abstract", when the *Mask* predominates it is "idealized", when *Body of Fate* predominates it is "concrete".'[1]

We might identify Yeats's *Creative Mind* with the intellectual and pragmatic spirit of Egyptian art, and his *Will* with that metaphysical consciousness of space out of which is born the will to art, that is to say, the will to find an embodiment for feeling in the wrought image, which Yeats calls the *Mask*. Without explaining the very complicated system of phases whose progression constitutes the revolution of the Great Wheel, we may note that in certain of the twenty-eight phases, the fourth and the twenty-seventh, man separates himself from instinct—which I identify with the empathy (*Einfühlung*) of Worringer—and tries to enforce upon himself and others all kinds of abstract or conventional ideas

[1] Op. cit., pp. 86-87.

—ideas which, according to Yeats, 'are for him, being outside his experience, mere make-believe'. Yeats's primary and antithetical tinctures, which he himself can correlate with so many other oppositions—will and mind, physical and spiritual, Nature and God, democratic and aristocratic—are all aspects of change or evolution, the upward and downward directions of the Great Wheel; first youth, then flexible maturity, then rigid age. But each phase, each condition, implies and evokes its counter-force. 'A civilization,' says Yeats, 'is a struggle to keep self-control, and in this it is like some great tragic person, some Niobe who must display an almost superhuman will or the cry will not touch our sympathy. The loss of control over thought comes towards the end; first a sinking in upon the normal being, then the last surrender, the irrational cry, revelation—the scream of Juno's peacock.'[1]

Such loss of control we have seen in our time: the death of God (to use Nietzsche's phrase to summarize a depersonalization of religion, not least striking in those who still believe in God); the surrender of individual conscience to the tyranny of the State; the consequent growth of mass violence and mass destruction; the abdication of philosophy, its retreat into verbal analysis; the inadequacy of scientific rationalism; and finally the dehumanization of art. But each of these processes is internally complicated by reactions and protests, and within its dissolution contains the seeds of renewal. The Great Wheel, we might say, never ceases to turn, and as it reaches its nadir, there is already present the momentum that will carry it past the lowest point and upwards towards a new zenith.

Such an observation is not inspired by optimism. I will take as an example of what I mean certain characteristics of the Dada Movement, which came into being in Zürich during the First World War. The chief protagonists of this movement, Tristan Tzara, Hugo Ball, Hans Arp, Richard Hülsenbeck, had been thrown together fortuitously by the war which they sought to evade in the neutral territory of Switzerland. If they had a common philosophy, it was a political one—a hatred of war and a contempt for *bourgeois* social values. Some of them had been influenced by the Futurism of Marinetti and were to that extent aware of the metaphysical claims of that movement. But as Hülsenbeck admitted in a history of the movement published in 1920,

[1] Op. cit., p. 268.

anything that Dada took over from Futurism was taken over without any suspicion that it had philosophical implications. These artists 'actually had no idea what they wanted', but this state of negativeness was in itself significant. The will to art was dead, and yet they remained artists. Thus arose the concept of 'anti-art'—an art not merely to shock the *bourgeoisie*, but to ridicule the traditional concept of art itself. This movement might have remained insignificant, but for its association with Marcel Duchamp, who had found a refuge in New York, where he was joined by Francis Picabia, who was then to act as a liaison between New York and Zürich. Duchamp had been influenced by the metaphysical concepts of futurism; he sought to represent in his painting abstract qualities like energy and rhythm. This gradually led him, in his own words, to 'break forever the enslaving chains of Naturalism', and he describes his most famous painting, *The Nude descending the Stairs*, as 'an organization of kinetic elements, an expression of time and space through the abstract presentation of motion'.[1] But Duchamp seems to have realized that he could not thus escape from the traditional notion of a painting; *The Nude descending the Stairs* certainly was and remains a work of art, with aesthetic qualities which we might identify with similar qualities in a painting by Cézanne or Leonardo da Vinci. Duchamp gradually abandoned the activity of painting: he was content to present any object, a hatstand or a lavatory bowl, just for the sake of its objectivity, its obstinate and aggressive existence. Only in this way could he escape from aesthetic preoccupations.

The opposite fate is illustrated by the case of Kurt Schwitters. Schwitters adopted the Dada programme with enthusiasm, and proceeded to make his pictures out of rubbish—the contents of waste-paper baskets and ash-cans. But he was not able to escape from his aesthetic preoccupations. His *Merzbilder*, as he called them, fell into patterns of sensuous beauty and are now among the most sought-after bibelots of the *bourgeois* collector. In Schwitters the instinct that always seeks equilibrium or rest triumphed over the mind that would destroy art in order to maintain the momentum of the Wheel; in Duchamp the creative mind has triumphed over the instinct that seeks rest and by abstention allows the Wheel to complete its downward course.

[1] *Collection of the Société Anonyme*, Yale University Art Gallery, 1950, p. 148.

This downward course was completed by two phases of the modern movement which are known as surrealism and informalism, but in the next chapter I shall attempt to show that these labels, hastily improvised by critics, have no precise significance, and that we must distinguish, among the many manifestations subsumed under them, antithetical elements of nihilism and renewal.

But first let us note very briefly the events that have by now led to the completion of the historical cycle, as far as that completion can be revealed in the concrete icons or masks of art.

In the year 1910, in Munich, Kandinsky had discovered the need and the possibility of a new orientation of art towards abstraction. His discovery coincided with the publication and diffusion of Worringer's thesis on *Abstraction and Empathy* and the further development of the artist may have been influenced by the theories of the philosopher. It was a happy conjunction of events, for, as Worringer has said, 'the whole period was disposed for a radical reorientation of its standards of aesthetic value.'[1]

The time was indeed ripe, for it was not merely in Munich that this reorientation began to reveal itself. I shall not trouble the reader with dates and priorities, but within five years the abstract tendency revealed itself in Russia, in France, in Holland—indeed, throughout Europe and even in America. There were degrees of abstraction, degrees of compromise with nature and with aestheticism, but the direction of the tendency was not in doubt. It led to an art of precise formal images completely detached from the sensuous perception of the external world. This detachment was already complete in certain compositions by Mondrian of the year 1917. The Creative Mind had succeeded in detaching itself from the historical present, from the dependence of the Will on its organic environment.

Concurrently a movement with an entirely contrary direction had arisen from the dispersed activities of the Futurists and the Dadaists. It took conscious shape in Paris about 1922, and had an intelligent protagonist and co-ordinator in André Breton, a poet and critic well versed in psycho-analysis. It received its first clear and unequivocal plastic expression in a painting by Picasso, the *Three Dancers* of 1925. Between 1925 and the outbreak of war in

[1] *Abstraction and Empathy.* Foreword to the new impression, 1948. Eng. trans., 1953, p. vii.

1939 the movement spread throughout the world (excluding Russia and China) and although the war destroyed its unity, in so far as this was expressed in organizations and publications, it has survived as one of the characteristic types of contemporary art, and has given birth since the war to a new movement variously known as tachisme, action painting or informal art. In all its manifestations this movement has been an expression of the instinctive Will, and though equally with abstract art it has retreated from the historical present, it has sought refuge in that interior world where images proliferate in apparent independence. These images are multiform rather than informal, and have sensuous substance though no emotional affect. If abstract art is objective or 'concrete', informal art might be contrasted as subjective and diffuse (discrete).

Both types of art are often characterized as 'irrational', but that is a question-begging word, for was art ever rational? All the visual arts are irrational in the sense that they make use of images rather than signs—reason depends on an agreed system of signs, whereas in art every image, until it becomes a cliché and therefore dead, is individual and arbitrary. Or to express the same thought in a different way: art embodies feelings, rational language communicates thoughts or explains actions. If 'irrational' means contrary to reason, then it is inapplicable to art, for one cannot say that feeling is irrational: it is not contrary to reason, but independent of it: a different process of reaction, visceral rather than cerebral, of the heart rather than of the head. Art is a language of images, independent of the language of signs; and this language of images may be used to communicate what we loosely call feelings, but which may be all that is inexpressible in linguistic signs or mathematical symbols—not only feelings, but in general intuitions of the unknown. It is because it has this all-important function that we may suppose that the art of the present day, apparently so informal and irrational, is nevertheless trying to communicate some important information about our existential situation.

CHAPTER 10

The Principle of Speculative Volition

Although most people have now abandoned the extremely sophisticated belief that a work of art (for the moment let us confine our discussion to the plastic arts) should be the representation of a scene or event, the work of art itself is a physical or worldly object. It is a certain organization of forms and colours, or of sounds in music, that embodies, and is capable of communicating to other people a mental experience. It is a raw material shaped until it makes visible to other eyes what otherwise is only visible to the inner eye of the artist. As such it can be defined, as Susanne Langer defines it, as an image of feeling, but feelings, as Sir Russell Brain has pointed out, do not exist in the void, but are evoked by, or directed towards, something. For this reason 'the image of feeling which constitutes a work of art will include also something which the feeling is about. To say even that a work of art is "an image of feeling" is inadequate because it fails to take into account the object or idea to which the feeling is directed. Such an association is *an experience*, and a work of art is an image of an experience in which the representation of feeling plays an essential part. The whole experience is mental, and to try to distinguish in it a physical object and an emotional reaction to it is to dissect a living whole into abstractions'.[1]

This is an acceptable definition of the process that is the work of art, and we must bear in mind the integrity of this experience. But we must then point out that such a definition does not tell us anything about the origins of the experience, beyond suggesting

[1] *The Nature of Experience*, London, Oxford University Press, 1959, p. 52.

that it may be a feeling evoked by an object or by an idea. This would presumably allow for a mental (subjective) beginning to the process, as well as a perceptual (objective) beginning. Still confining ourselves to the visual arts, we might assume that the feeling embodied in the work of art was provoked by some external object, a *motif* such as a landscape or a human face. But equally the feeling might be provoked by a memory or a dream, or might even on occasion be wholly unmotivated, that is to say, gratuitous. There are feelings such as longing or nostalgia, even love, which seek embodiment, and of which we do not become conscious until the work of art brings them into a visible existence. I do not suggest that this invalidates Sir Russell Brain's definition of art, but it should be realized that the experience of art is a circular process which may be set in motion at any point—the possible points being image, feeling, percept, idea, material, or even the handling of tools. The consciousness of the artist is a sensitive surface upon which the impact of any of these phenomena will set up a formative reaction, a crystallization which is the work of art.

What motivates the artist, sets this process in motion, is what Stravinsky has called 'a foretaste of discovery'. 'This foretaste of the creative act accompanies the intuitive grasp of an unknown entity already possessed but not yet intelligible, an entity that will not take definite shape except by the action of a constantly vigilant technique. . . . The very idea of putting my work on paper, of, as we say, kneading the dough, is for me inseparable from the pleasure of creation. So far as I am concerned, I cannot separate the spiritual effort from the psychological and physical effort; they confront me on the same level and do not present a hierarchy.'[1]

Stravinsky provides a phrase which admirably describes the process: *the principle of speculative volition.* He is, of course, discussing music, but what he says is true of all the arts. It is through the unhampered play of its functions, he says, that a work is revealed and justified. 'In the pure state, music is free speculation.'

Though Stravinsky warns us that it is futile to try and observe the inner workings of the creative process from the outside, or even in one's self, nevertheless the whole purpose of this chapter is to make the attempt.

We begin with what I believe to be an adequate conception of the

[1] *Poetics of Music,* Harvard and Oxford University Presses, 1947, p. 5.

creative process, a conception of it *as process*, and I shall try to avoid the falsity and confusion which arises when one breaks the process at any point and begins to substitute objective analysis of the part for the experienced totality.

I must return to the irrational elements in art, its Dionysian as opposed to its Apollonian elements. It is usually assumed that this opposition underlies the distinction between romantic and classical art, and indeed it does. But it is not a question of their presence or absence. As Stravinsky admits, these distinctions are theoretical in as much as 'we shall always find at the origin of invention an irrational element on which the spirit of submission has no hold and that escapes all constraint'.[1] It is a question of what the artist does with such a necessary force. Stravinsky, who I believe would call himself a classicist, says that 'all the Dionysian elements which set the imagination of the artist in motion and make the life-sap rise must be properly subjugated before they intoxicate us, and must finally be made to submit to the law: Apollo demands it'. Apollo may demand it for the sake of the lucid order which is his ideal: but that, as Yeats would say, is the function of the Creative Mind, and not of the Will. Yeats perhaps confuses the question by associating the word 'creative' with Mind and not with Will, so let us for a moment turn to two or three artists who have not been so partisan in their terminology. I will begin with Kandinsky.

Kandinsky, whose influence on the whole development of modern art has been decisive, had the clearest possible idea of his intentions. He was already forty-two, and had about twelve years of artistic evolution behind him when, in 1908, he made the discovery that it was possible to express an inner feeling, what he called an 'internal' necessity, by means of what he called 'melodic' or 'symphonic' compositions—the musical nature of the terms is significant. He distinguished three different sources of inspiration for such symphonic compositions, the first being a direct impression of nature, the second being a spontaneous expression of inner feeling, which we may call Dionysian, and the third being these same spontaneous expressions 'tested and worked over repeatedly', subjected to rational control and given an Apollonian order. The similarity with Stravinsky's theory of music is close, and there may have been some common source of inspiration in Schönberg, for

[1] Op. cit., p. 79.

Kandinsky had discussions with Schönberg, and refers to them in the book he wrote in 1910.[1]

Stravinsky and Kandinsky have a common aesthetic for painting and music—an identical principle of speculative volition or Will. But what do we mean by the speculative will of the artist—what actually happens when the process of creation is set in motion?

First of all let us note that it is a *movement* that is in question. All becoming, as Paul Klee says, is based on movement, and I shall take Klee's 'Creative Credo', which he wrote in 1920, as the best description of the process known to me.[2] The scene of action, he says, is *time*. The one and only character: *movement*. Klee, too, had been influenced by the metaphysics of the Futurists. 'A certain fire of becoming flares up; it is conducted through the hand, flows to the picture surface and there bursts into a spark, closing the circle whence it came; back into the eye and farther (back to a centre of movement, of volition, of the idea).' And Klee notes that the same temporal activity is repeated in the beholder of the work of art: 'The eye is so organized; it conveys the parts successively into the crucible of vision, and in order to adjust itself to a new fragment it must leave the old. . . . In the work of art ways are laid out for the beholder's eye which gropes like a grazing beast (in music, as everyone knows, there are channels leading to the ear—in drama we have both varieties). The pictorial work springs from movement, it is itself fixated movement, and it is apprehended by movement (eye muscles).'

But what is it that in this manner is depicted or recorded? It used to be things people liked to see or would like to have seen—the Bay of Naples, a storm at sea, a battle or the artist's own features. But now we believe that the phenomenal world present to our vision is only a part of the total reality, and that a far more extensive world lies waiting for revelation. Klee gives some examples:

'A man of antiquity sailing a boat, quite content and enjoying the ingenious comfort of the contrivance. The ancients represented the scene accordingly. And now: what a modern man experiences as he walks across the deck of a steamer: 1. His own movement.

[1] *Ueber das Geistige in der Kunst*, Munich, 1912 (written in 1910). Eng. trans. *Concerning the Spiritual in Art*, New York, Wittenborn, 1947.

[2] Originally published in *Tribuene der Kunst und Zeit*, Berlin, 1920. Reprinted in *Das bildnerische Denken*, ed. Juerg Spiller, Basle–Stuttgart (Benno Schwabe), 1956, pp. 76–80. Eng. trans. by Ralph Manheim, London (Lund Humphries), 1960.

5(a) Pablo Picasso: Bullfight. 1st August 1934
(*Photo: Paul Rosenberg*)

5(b) Jackson Pollock: She-wolf, 1943
(*Museum of Modern Art, New York*)

6(a) Mark Tobey:
Agate World, 1945
(*Seattle Art Museum*)

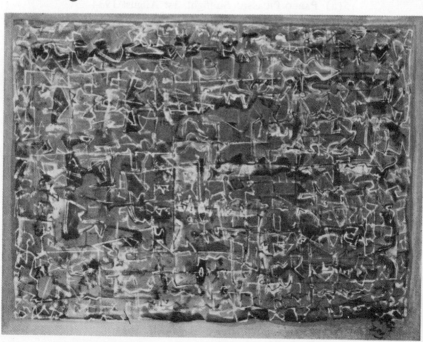

6(b) René Guiette:
Puissance, 1958
(*Collection: the artist*)

7. PIET MONDRIAN: Composition with red, blue, black and yellow-green, 1920
(*Gemeente Musea, Amsterdam*)

8. Kurt Schwitters: The hair-navel, 1920
Cork, wood, sand, cloth, hair, cotton wool
(*Mrs U. M. C. Granville, London*)

2. The movement of the ship which may be in the opposite direction. 3. The direction and the velocity of the current. 4. The rotation of the earth. 5. Its orbit. 6. The orbits of the moons and planets round about.'

'Result: a fabric of movements in the universe, at their centre the I on the ship.'[1]

It will be observed that this fabric depicted by the artist is in no sense irrational: it is a record of events present to the artist's normal consciousness. But Klee gives two more examples which extend the range of the artistic vision. I will omit the second, which depicts what he calls a fabric of states of growth, for again the elements are all present in normal perceptual experience. The third example, however extends the range of perception: 'A sleeping man, the circulation of his blood, the measured breathing of the lungs, the delicate function of the kidneys, in his head a world of dreams, related to the powers of fate. A fabric of functions, united in rest.'

It is obvious that in this third example of the artistic process we are involved in more than a record of normal perceptual experience. We venture into an unknown element, the world of dreams, related to the powers of fate. The first and second processes have as their product works of art that may indeed be abstract, a liberation of the elements, as Klee suggests, 'their grouping into composite subdivisions, dismemberment and rebuilding into a whole on many sides at once, pictorial polyphony, the creation of rest by balance of motion'—all these, as Klee says, 'lofty aspects of the question of form, crucial for formal wisdom'. But they do not yet constitute the highest sphere of art. In that sphere an ultimate secret transcends and transfigures all formal elements, 'and the light of the intellect dies down ignominiously'.

Klee here seems to indicate the possibility of two types of symbolic art. One is an intensification of reality, a symbolic representation of movement and growth, 'imagination borne on the wings of instinctual stimuli', a creation of the Will, therefore. The other 'symbols that console the mind', or, as Kandinsky would say, that express an internal necessity. 'Art plays,' says Klee, 'an ingenious game with ultimate things, and yet it reaches them.' It allows us to shed our human casing, to think that we are God for a moment or two.

[1] Op. cit., p. 79.

It is at this point that we easily fall into theoretical obscurity, which we would vainly dignify with the name of mysticism. Art does not exist unless it is concrete: a symbol only functions if it is precise, of definite form. That is why Stravinsky, Klee and Kandinsky all use the metaphor of crystallization. This necessity is most strongly emphasized by another leader of the modern movement, Piet Mondrian. Plastic art, he says, 'from its origins, shows a progressive determination of relationships, until today relationship can be established only through the elements of form, purified colour and determined space.'[1] Mondrian, too, defines art as an interrelation of the artist's perception to a total reality, as the creation of symbols to depict this total reality. Even the most abstract art, he says, has its origins in the reciprocal action of the individual and the environment, and it is inconceivable without feeling. In spite of all superficial differences, art reveals only one necessity: the expression of the beauty of vitality, which is obscured in life. 'Art is the expression of truth as well as of beauty. We do not know what complete truth is. We only observe many truths, all transient and changing. Plastic art shows us that the purest expression of truth is the purest expression of vitality. . . . As the aesthetic expressions of vitality, pure life, all art is true, but it shows truth in different degrees of clarity.'[2] But art, according to Mondrian, has to struggle for this clarity against self-interest, against subjective factors. The truth is universal, impersonal, and we can only reach it through intuition. In daily life this intuition loses its force, being oppressed by social or intellectual cares, all of which are only partial expressions of vitality.

Mondrian, and indeed all the leading artists of our time, speak of the Modern Movement as a process of liberation, a gradual freeing of the human spirit from 'the oppression of the subject'. Impressionism had begun to emphasize the subjective factor in representation, but gradually it was realized that representation itself was the oppressive burden, and that if art could be freed from this burden, then the plastic elements, planes and volumes, could be used as a dynamic mode of expression, as a means to bring life towards unity, which for Mondrian was the reality to be achieved. The Cubists were the first artists to advance a principle

[1] *Plastic Art and Pure Plastic Art* (1937) *and other Essays*, New York, Wittenborn, 1945, p. 43.

[2] Ibid., pp. 43–44.

of unity independent of representation, but they did not take the final step. 'Gradually,' says Mondrian, 'I became aware that Cubism did not accept the logical consequences of its own discoveries; it was not developing abstraction towards its ultimate goal, the expression of pure reality. In its essential expression, pure plastics is unconditioned by subjective feeling and expression. It took me a long time to discover that particularity of form and natural colour evoke subjective states of feeling, which obscure *pure* reality. The appearance of natural forms changes, but reality remains constant. To create pure reality plastically, it is necessary to reduce natural forms to the *constant elements* of form and natural colour to *primary colour*.'[1] Reality, Mondrian concluded, could be expressed only through the equilibrium of *dynamic movement* of form and colour. In this he agrees with the Russian Constructivists.

Such an ideal of art might be called Platonic, for it is an attempt to create essential Form, and to identify such Form with Reality. Mondrian made an heroic effort to escape from our subjective vision and from our determined position in time, for it is these that make us unhappy, that create tragedy. Reality is a realm beyond our feelings, and it can be reached by vision. Plato believed that this pure timeless realm could be reached by intuition, but the meaning is the same; that time and subjective vision veil the true reality. There is, however, an equivocation in Mondrian's theory, for the elements of art, dynamic movement in equilibrium, can only express 'a clear vision of reality' in human consciousness, and the forms and colours used are present in consciousness as active forces. The very word 'express', which Mondrian constantly uses, implies feeling; Mondrian's ideal of equilibrium, 'of great importance for humanity', as he says, is not to be distinguished from disequilibrium by the exclusion of feeling: it is merely that the feeling inspired by a sense of equilibrium is distinct from the feeling inspired by a sense of disequilibrium. It might be said, therefore, that the aim of this renewal of artistic volition is to purify feeling, to relieve it of irrelevant or confusing images; in other words, to make identical the Form and the Content of the work of art. This is the purpose underlying the Constructivist idea in art, as defined by the sculptor Naum Gabo:

'It [Constructivism] has revealed a universal law that the

[1] *Plastic Art and Pure Plastic Art* (1937) *and other Essays*, p. 10..

elements of a visual art such as lines, colours, shapes, possess their own forces of expression, independent of any association with the external aspects of the world; that their life and their action are self-conditioned psychological phenomena rooted in human nature; that those elements are not chosen by convention for any utilitarian or other reason as words and figures are, they are not merely abstract signs, but they are immediately and organically bound up with human emotions. The revelation of this fundamental law has opened up a vast new field in art giving the possibility of expression to those human impulses and emotions which have been neglected. Heretofore these elements have been abused by being used to express all sorts of associative images which might have been expressed otherwise, for instance, in literature and poetry.'[1]

The arts cannot escape their sensuous basis: their whole purpose is to extract perfection from experience, but they can do this only by using the organs of perception, which convey and communicate human feelings and emotions. A living contemporary art differs from the dead art of the past, not in its exclusion of subjective feeling, but by the concreteness and directness of the means used to express such feeling.

This exposition of a difficult subject would have been simpler if I could have stopped at this point—if the Great Wheel itself had stopped at this point. But since Mondrian and Gabo formulated their clear and logical principles of a renewed art, another and an apparently distinct manifestation of creative renewal has appeared, with its main source of energy in the United States of America. The superficial distinction between this new phase of modern art and the phase we associate with Mondrian and Gabo is a distinction of form—indeed, the new phase is sometimes described as *l'art informel*, art without form. In this respect it has some correspondence with the Dada movement, and like that movement, appeared in the midst of a world war. But it would be a mistake to identify it directly with the second war. Dadaism was anti-art: the Dadaists believed that European civilization had reached a dead-end from which there was no hope of emergence. Art had become irrelevant, and might as well be non-sensical. The new American painting, however, is an art of renewal, and has, not only vitality, but unity. Nevertheless, a clear line of descent can be

[1] Op. cit., p. 163. First published in *Circle*, 1937.

traced from Dada, through Surrealism, and certain surrealists who were resident in the United States during the Second World War, such as André Masson, provide a direct link with the European movement. However, these historical considerations are not our present concern, but rather the aesthetic and philosophical significance of this informal art.

Let us first note that a distinction between a formal and an informal art is not logical. There is a distinction to be drawn between forms that are precise and forms that are irregular, between geometrical and organic forms, between forms determined by calculation and forms automatically projected—calligraphic gestures. But all alike are forms.

It should next be noted that the forms within this informal movement are of the greatest variety. Some are biomorphic, reminiscent of cellular structures as revealed by the microscope; others are calligraphic, equivalent to Chinese pictographs or our own scrawled signatures; others present an abstract image that only differs from the abstract images of earlier painters such as Kandinsky, Gabo and Mondrian by being irregular.

If we turn from the forms to the declared intentions of these artists, then again we find a great variety of expression. Their opinions have been selected and conveniently assembled in the catalogue of an exhibition of New American Painting which has circulated among the principal cities of Europe in 1958 and 1959. The main emphasis in nearly all the statements made by these artists is on the spontaneity of their methods and the spirituality of their aims. First as to their methods: Philip Guston says that 'to paint is a possessing rather than a picturing'—'usually I am on a work for a long stretch, until a moment arrives when the air of the arbitrary vanishes and the paint falls into positions that feel destined'. (Destiny being, as Yeats said, that which comes to us from within.) William Baziotes says that he follows no particular system when he begins a painting—each painting has its own way of evolving. 'Each beginning suggests something. Once I sense the suggestion, I begin to paint intuitively . . . the subject reveals itself.' To James Brooks the painting surface is 'the rendez-vous of what the painter knows with the unknown. . . . An engrossment in the process of changing formal relations is the painter's method of relieving his self-consciousness as he approaches the unknown'. Any procedure is good 'if it permits the unknown to enter the painting almost unnoticed'. Adolph Gottlieb is 'concerned with the problem of projecting intangible and elusive images that seem to me to have a meaning in terms of feeling. The important thing is to transfer the image to the canvas as it appears to me, without distortion'. Barnett Newman declares that 'only an art of no-geometry can be a new beginning'. Clyfford Still says that the artist is 'now committed to an unqualified act, not illustrating outworn myths or contemporary alibis. One must accept total responsibility for what he executes. And the measure of his greatness will be in the depth of his insight and his courage in realizing his own vision'. Finally Jack Tworkov declares that 'his hope is to have no progress and, necessarily then, no preconceived style'.

There is considerable agreement on the quality to be achieved in a work of art—its quality of feeling. Motherwell describes this as 'ethical consciousness', and does not hesitate to quote the anti-aesthetical Kierkegaard. Gottlieb says that 'paint quality is meaningless if it does not express quality of feeling. The idea that a painting is merely an arrangement of lines, colours and forms is boring. Subjective images do not have to have rational association, but the art of painting must be rational, objective and consciously disciplined'. Grace Hartigan bases her art on the vulgarity and vitality of American modern life, but insists that the rawness must be resolved into form and unity—there must be a transcendence into the beautiful. Rothko suggests that 'the progression of a painter's work, as it travels in time from point to point, will be toward clarity: toward the elimination of all obstacles between the painter and the idea, and between the idea and the observer. . . . To achieve this clarity is inevitably, to be understood'. Others speak of 'the new magic of space and colour' (Gorky), of painting as a style of living (de Kooning); of ending the misery of the scientist's space (de Kooning), of 'the static quality of perpetual motion' induced by the tension and complexity of line, the violently interwoven movement so closely knit, of 'the sense that the picture could be continued indefinitely in any direction' (Pollock).

I do not wish to force on these diverse painters a metaphysical unity they do not possess; nor do I wish to accept their own sense of their uniqueness. My whole contention in this chapter is that from the beginnings of Cubism to the present day there has been a consistent development towards a new aesthetic consciousness, which at the same time inevitably implies a new ethical consciousness. It is well described in a passage from Martin Buber's *Between Man and Man* which is quoted by one of these American painters, Jack Tworkov: 'The man who reduces the encounter between the cosmos of history and its eternally new chaos, between Zeus and Dionysos, to the formula of the 'antagonism between fathers and sons', has never beheld it in his spirit. Zeus the Father does not stand for a generation but for a world, for the Olympic, the formed world; the world of history faces a particular generation, which is the world of nature renewed again and again, always without history.'[1] This passage comes from the address which Buber gave to an International Educational Conference at Heidelberg in 1925, the subject of which was 'The Development of the Creative Powers of the Child'. This address contains Buber's important definition of the creative instinct, which he prefers to call the instinct of origination—a definition I have made use of before,[2] and which again is of relevance to this present discussion. Creation, Buber points out, originally meant only the divine summons to the life hidden in non-being, and can only be used metaphorically to describe the human capacity to give form. Everyone, Buber agrees, is elementally endowed with the basic powers of the arts, and these powers have to be developed in education: they are the natural activity of the self upon which education should be built. Buber then proceeds with his definition of this autonomous instinct. 'Man, the child of man, wants to make things. He does not merely find pleasure in seeing a form arise from material that presented itself as formless. What the child desires is its own share in this becoming of things: it wants to be the subject of this event of production. . . . What is important is that by one's own intensely experienced action something arises that was not there before.' Buber then gives the wonderful example of the way children of intellectual passion produce speech, not as something they have taken over, 'but with the headlong powers of utter newness: sound after sound tumbles out of them, rushing from the vibrating throat past the trembling lips into the world's air, and the whole of the

[1] *Between Man and Man*, trans. R. Gregor Smith, London, Kegan Paul, 1947. p. 93.

[2] *Education Through Art*, London, Faber and Faber, revised edition, 1958, Chapter IX.

little vital body vibrates and trembles, too, shaken by a bursting shower of selfhood.'[1]

This would serve as a description of the new painting, the painting that is a possessing rather than a picturing, a projection of intangible and elusive images that seem to have meaning in terms of feeling. There is an instinct, says Buber, which, 'no matter to what power it is raised, never becomes greed, because it is not directed to "having" but only to doing; which alone among the instincts can grow only to passion, not to lust; which alone among the instincts cannot lead its subject away to invade the realm of other lives. Here is pure gesture which does not snatch the world to itself, but expresses itself to the world.'[2]

Pure gesture that does not snatch the world to itself, but expresses itself to the world—what a perfect definition of this latest phase of modern art. But gesture is not enough, Buber goes on to say—and this is the whole point of his address. 'There are two forms, indispensable for the building of true human life, to which the originative instinct, left to itself, does not lead and cannot lead: to sharing in an undertaking and to entering into mutuality.' This raises the whole problem of communication, which is vital to the ethical consciousness; as an originator man is solitary. An education, says Buber (and by implication an art) based on the instinct of origination would prepare a new human solitariness which would be the most painful of all. Art must lead beyond the arts, to an awareness and a share of mutuality.

Buber then goes on to expound his philosophy of dialogue, which is not our immediate concern now, but it is in this connection, and in his further discussion of personal freedom and the responsibility it entails, that he makes the distinction between the 'old' education that was based on the will, more particularly the will to power, and the new education, based on Eros or creative love. Once again we return, it will be realized, to Yeats's distinction between the Will and the Creative Mind, and Buber, too, seems to relate his distinction to the cosmos of history and its eternal renewal of the creative spirit: the world of history facing a particular generation, which is the world of nature renewed again and again, always without history.

When the magical validity of history disappears, as it has done

[1] Op. cit., p. 85.
[2] Op. cit., p. 86.

in our time, then the renewal must come from within the self, from this autonomous instinct of origination. That, I believe, is the spiritual, the metaphysical significance of the modern movement in art. It is the image, the paradigm, of a new reality. But it does not yet constitute a culture—how could it? A culture is a creation of time, of a time in which the icons made by the artist so work on the imagination of man that they precipitate ideas, communicate feelings, establish human bonds. It may seem that a sense of direction is lacking in modern art, but it is already there, obscurely felt as the statements of artists I have quoted make clear. Culture, Buber would say, is finally the coherence given to all individuals by one image; Yeats spoke of 'Those images that yet, Fresh images beget'. Do not let us question the words of the philosopher or the poet: they can speak only in metaphors, as the artist can speak only in images. Buber speaks of the image of God, of the *imitatio Dei absconditi sed non ignoti*. The artist does not speak of God, but of Form or of Vision. But artist, poet and philosopher speak with one meaning, and all would admit, with Buber, that 'Man, the creature, who forms and transforms the creation, cannot create. But he, each man, can expose himself and others to the creative Spirit. And he can call upon the Creator to save and perfect His image.' And that, in this time of nihilism and renewal, is the most we can ask of any man, the most we can ask of the artist.

PART IV

CHAPTER 11

The Creative Nature of Humanism

We do not discover the truth: we create it
SAINT-EXUPÉRY

One book that I read in my youth I have never wholly forgotten. To say that it had a great influence on me would not be correct, for influences are absorbed and become part of one's mind. This book refused to be digested—to use our vivid English metaphor: it stuck in the gizzard, and has been in that uncomfortable position ever since. I refer to Max Stirner's *Der Einzige und sein Eigentum*, or *The Ego and his Own* as it was called in the English translation, published in 1913.

An outrageous book, which subsequent philosophers have somewhat guiltily ignored. Nietzsche undoubtedly stole from it, and our contemporary existentialists are aware of it.[1] I will not delay my present argument to discuss its general significance, but what stood out for me, as a warning at the gateway to life, was Stirner's insistence on the danger of surrendering one's self to an abstraction, to an illusion of any kind. In so far as he was speaking of religious or political illusions, Stirner was merely repeating the warnings of many other philosophers, Feuerbach and Marx in particular. But Stirner went on to suggest that the most dangerous illusion of all was Man himself—the abstraction Man as distinct from the Self. The liberals and freethinkers, he argued, had merely substituted for a *divine* spirit, a *human* spirit, and it was equally tyrannous, equally delusive. Feuerbach in particular thought he had found the truth by humanizing the divine. 'The HUMAN

[1] Cf. Albert Camus, *L'Homme révolté*, Paris, 1951. The passages referring to Stirner do not appear in the English translation.

religion,' declared Stirner, 'is only the last metamorphosis of the Christian religion,' and humanism (or liberalism as he indifferently called it) is a religion 'because it separates my essence from me and sets it above me, because it exalts "Man" to the same extent as any other religion does its God or idol, because it makes what is mine into something other worldly, because in general it makes out of what is mine, out of my qualities and my property, something alien—to wit, an "essence"; in short, because it sets me beneath Man, and thereby creates for me a "vocation".'[1] The human as such, that, concluded Stirner, is an abstraction; but *my* human act is diverse from every other human act, and only by this diversity is it a real act belonging to me.

I shall assume that the Self (with a capital S) is not an essence to which the self (with a small s) must pay homage. There is a mighty difference, as Stirner said, in 'whether I make myself the starting-point or the goal', but we may then ask whether the conception of a Self, as put forward by modern psychology, can be reconciled with the hypothesis of a collective unconscious, and thus provide a sufficient basis for a humanism that is not a vocation nor a tyranny of any kind, but a condition of inner freedom. Man, according to Sartre's notorious dictum, is a useless passion, but he is 'condemned to be free', which means that he is free to make a Self, to make himself the starting-point of an originative and formative activity. The existentialists in general seem to dislike the concept of the Unconscious—it disturbs their conception of the self as a translucent consciousness of being. From their point of view the Jungian archetype would be a limitation of man's freedom, a shadowy threat to his self-creative possibilities. But from another point of view the unconscious constitutes a collective challenge to the self, to ego-consciousness, in virtue of which the highest creative achievements of humanity become possible. The conflict between ego-consciousness or self-will and the predetermined patterns of collective consciousness or social patterns of behaviour is the basis of tragedy, and humanism will remain a shallow conception unless it concerns itself primarily with this conflict which is the conflict inherent in our existence—the basic opposition of good and evil, truth and error, beauty and ugliness, which make up the dialectic of our existence. A scientific philosopher in the pursuit of empirical knowledge may ignore these

[1] Eng. trans. by Steven T. Byington, London and New York, 1913, p. 229.

conflicts on the assumption that they involve judgments of value, but a humanist, even an egoist, if he is to deserve the name, must establish an order of reality,—must, as I shall argue, constitute it by his own creative acts. Even his 'uniqueness' is a value to be established in all its concreteness, that is to say, in objective or material representations of some kind.

The tragic sense of life is represented most directly in literature, and it is perhaps for that reason that the original sense of humanism is not abstract, but has reference to the concrete human activity of writing, *litterae humaniores*. The great humanists of the fifteenth and sixteenth centuries were concerned, not with spiritual questions as such, certainly not with the creation of a new religion of humanity, but rather with the correct use of language. They were scholars first, and became pedants rather than prophets. Their self-appointed task was to elucidate and vulgarize the mysteries of scholasticism, and, incidentally, since scholasticism was based on Aristotelianism, the obscurities of classicism. The work of the Humanists, which we call the Revival of Learning, was essentially a revivification of language and symbolic discourse, first in art and literature, in Giotto and Dante, and then in the *litterae humaniores* of Erasmus and More.

A humanism of this kind is as necessary today as it was in the fifteenth century. Modern psychology may be compared to medieval scholasticism: it is an extensive corpus of expert knowledge for the most part written in a repulsive jargon, and before it can become human, a truth accessible to individual men, it must clarify its imagery and refashion its vocabulary. A science cannot renounce its technical terminology, but the meaning that is inherent in the jargon of psychology—ids, egos, superegos; sublimation, projection, individuation; all this hasty verbalization of an empirical science must be transformed into a humane literature before it can have any wide effect on humanity.

Such a conception of humanism is retrospective: a work of exegesis, perhaps of synthesis. But the conception of humanism which we are to explore is prospective. Warned by Stirner, I for one do not seek an abstracted essence, an illusion to which I give an irrational adherence. What I seek, and what surely we all seek, is a coherent conception of human existence, and an affirmation, as firm as the empirical facts will allow, of any values that give significance to our daily activities.

That we need such a new conception of values is perhaps an arbitrary assumption on my part. There may be Christians or Buddhists among my readers who are satisfied with a traditional solution of the problem of existence. I can only presume to speak for a majority who regard this divided and tragic world we live in as devoid of any compelling image of reconciliation; therefore, absurd. I think I still speak for a majority when I further assume that no compelling image of reconciliation is found in existing religions; or if it does exist there, is distorted by dogma and conventional behaviour—by what Kierkegaard, in his righteous Christian zeal, called 'an impudent indecency'.

I make a further basic assumption: I believe, in the words of one of our profoundest psychologists, that 'the lesion from which man suffers is within the organism of man'.[1] That is to say, a new humanism must look for its foundations, not in the reorganization of man's social and economic activities, but in the structure of his psyche. And that, of course, is where I part company with all who believe that a new humanism would be a direct and inevitable consequence of new economic conditions. Democracy and the welfare state, for example, far from creating a new humanism, are rapidly establishing a vulgar barbarism. Everywhere the spirit of humanism is threatened by the pursuit of technological efficiency and mass amusement: concurrently psychic illnesses multiply and now afflict a terrifying proportion of the world's population.

The conflict between humanism and technology must be examined on another occasion. As for the supposed conflict between humanism and religion, this I believe is due to a verbal confusion. There are various ways in which the fundamental philosophical question—what is the meaning of existence?—can be answered, but in so far as they are all answers given by human beings they are all humanistic; and in so far as they are all answers to questions that cannot be answered positively, they are all transcendental or religious, and Stirner was right in assuming that humanism in this sense is just as much a religion as Buddhism or Christianity; and are we not often told that philosophers like Nietzsche and Heidegger, or poets like Yeats and Rilke, in spite of their specific denials of God, were fundamentally religious? Equally the attempt to equate humanism with romanticism, and religion with classicism,

[1] Burrow, Trigant, 'Emotions and Feelings', *Emotion and the Social Crisis, a Problem in Phylobiology*, ed. Martin L. Reymert, New York, 1950, p. 485.

is a play on words. The humanists of the Enlightenment were essentially classical in mind and manner; and there have been many varieties of religious experience and expression that are essentially romantic. The distinction that we must admit is one between answers that are based on feeling and imagination, and are concretely represented as works of art or literature; and answers that are based on logic and idea (the realism of concepts) and are essentially abstract in the form of their expression. I would agree that religion and humanism are still confusing terms to describe such a contrast; but they are forced on one by the historical terms of the debate. My desire is to redefine humanism in the terms of a sensuous apprehension of being, which apprehension can be as austere, precise and classical as you like; and to distinguish it from those abstract generalizations about truth which take the form of logical or metaphysical statements.

Tragedy, from this point of view, is but one mode of sensuous apprehension of being, and Jaspers is undoubtedly right to claim that 'tragedy is not enough'. But tragic poetry is only one sensuous mode of apprehension, and both before and after the great epochs of the art of tragedy, there were other modes of sensuous apprehension—dance and ritual and the visual arts in the period before the rise of Greek tragedy, and poetry, music and again the visual arts in the post-tragic periods. Tragedy is not enough, not only because as Jaspers says,[1] there is too much that it leaves untouched, forgotten, or unexplained—because it fails 'to grasp the whole terror and insolubility in man's existence'; but equally because it does not attempt to establish an alternative mode of existence, or even of action. It is contemplative, not pragmatic. From this point of view Stoicism is more complete; and above all that serene code of ethics achieved in ancient China—'the feeling of security without the shadow of tragedy, a natural and sublime humanity, a sense of being at home in this world, and a wealth of concrete insights,' to quote Jaspers' own description of pre-tragic knowledge.

A wealth of concrete insights—that is the point: humanism is the creation of a wealth of such concrete insights. We cannot, for reasons I shall give, repeat the solutions of either ancient Greece or ancient China. The situation we have to deal with is indeed tragic; and we tend to accept tragedy as a general characteristic of human

[1] *Tragedy Is Not Enough*. Trans. Harald A. T. Reiche, Harry T. Moore and Karl W. Deutsch, London, 1953, p. 99.

existence. But tragedy in this general sense must be distinguished from any particular solution of the problem of existence such as we find in the Greek or Elizabethan drama. It is possible that completely new art-forms will have to be invented to present the problem of existence effectively to our contemporary sensibility.

The new knowledge of the psyche that is now at our disposal is concerned with human behaviour, human motivation, human sickness and insecurity, and its general tendency, after fifty years of patient research, is to confirm ancient instinctive wisdom. A new humanism, therefore, may turn out to be the old humanism written in a new language, but we must not underestimate the difficulties of the task, for there is no one ready to teach us a new language: poets must be born who will invent its syllables. Moreover, every such invention must be spontaneous. We can endow scholarship, but for art we can only build a nest and pray that a phoenix will adopt it.

We complain that we live in a tragic age, and nevertheless we have no tragedies. But the potential tragic poets among us might retort that we have no tragedies because there is no audience for tragedy. The theatre has been replaced by the television screen; art by entertainment. We live in a tragic age, but we are unable to express ourselves in tragic poetry. We are inarticulate, and our only art is mockery, or self-pity. Our fatalism gives us a stoical appearance, but it is not a genuine stoicism. It is a dull animal endurance of misfortune, unfocused and unexpressed, or expressed in sudden irrational outbreaks of hysteria. There seems to be a direct connection between our inarticulateness, which implies a lack of emotional purgation, and our readiness to respond to mass appeals. Modern war in all its total destructiveness is a dumb acceptance of this anonymous fate. Our armies, as Matthew Arnold said, are ignorant and clash by night.

The problem of our age is not a problem of conscience or commitment—of why people choose to die in wars for or against communism or fascism. The problem is rather why people who have no personal convictions of any kind allow themselves to suffer for indefinite or undefined causes, drifting like shoals of fish into invisible nets. The problem is mass-suffering, mute and absurd: in one word—inhumanism.

I shall ignore explanations of this problem based on a so-called psychology of the masses—the masses are not an organism in the sense that a man is, and we must seek for the sources of man's collective guilt where Jung has found them—in the personal unconscious. A resort to mass psychology is evasive. A collection of individuals may be swayed by hatred, or even by something like love, as when they worship a young queen or a film star. But these are merely personal emotions that gain in intensity by contagion: they do not proceed from a psychic unity with biological foundations. This is not to deny the existence of collective guilt. What Freud called the libidinal structure of the group is an obvious reality, and Max Scheler has explored the workings of social emotions like fellow-feeling, the sense of identity, love and hatred, tracing their relationship to one another and to the collective values with which they are associated. But such social emotions are not moral absolutes,[1] nor are social groups biological entities: they are agglomerations of individuals and the individual remains the only concrete fact in any human situation.

If in war I am the cause, direct or indirect, of the death of another individual, that too is a concrete fact, and I do not dispose of it by any talk of collective guilt or social duty. My motivation is the illusion: the dead man is the reality, and I must not confuse the fact with the idea. Perhaps the line of division between fact and idea, deed and motivation, is not so clear as I have assumed. A dead German or Russian, Englishman or Egyptian, even if he is disguised in a uniform, is clearly a fact, but 'my country right or wrong', or 'democratic freedom'—these are abstractions, and obscure. I have observed that those who take part in the factual business of killing other human beings are not in any way animated by abstractions of this kind (nor are they restrained by moral abstractions of an opposite kind). They leave ideas to the politicians and journalists, and they themselves act or re-act like automata. They have habits, but no conscience. They have faith, but no beliefs. The individual typical of our time is conscious of his ego, and his situation is tragic, but he has no cathartic experience of tragedy to reconcile him to his fate.

Inseparable from the cathartic experience of tragedy is the acceptance of fate as a natural phenomenon. A Greek tragedy is an

[1] Groups are essentially partitive and therefore inhuman. Cf. Freud, *Group Psychology and other Analysis of the Ego*, London, 1922, 1940, p. 51: 'Fundamentally every religion is in this same way a religion of love for all those whom it embraces; while cruelty and intolerance towards those who do not belong to it are natural to every religion.'

exposition of a life that exemplifies the course of a natural phenomenon: tragedy is the unfolding of a preordained fate. This fate is 'encountered', met on the street or the high seas; and there is an event, usually a death, to be explained. The explanation is found in Existence itself, in the preordained scheme of things.[1] Werner Jaeger says of Aeschylus: 'The poet is interested not in a person but in a doom, and . . . the doom need not fall on one individual, but can affect a whole family. In his tragedies man is not the chief problem: man is merely the vehicle of destiny, and that destiny is the real problem.' The problem, that is to say, lies outside the organism of man, and is therefore in no sense a psychological problem.

In archaic Greek tragedy there is a universal order of reality which is absolute, and to human understanding apparently irrational. Greek drama was the poet's attempt to understand this inhuman scheme, to which every man is nevertheless subjected. But as Greek humanism grew in scope and precision, the hero emerged as a man responsible for his own fate, and suffering was then accepted as a retribution for the hero's misdeeds or irreverence. The typically Greek concept of *hybris* is part of this pattern of explanation: man suffers his evil fate because he is overweening, because he oversteps the limits of humane discretion, because he exceeds the measure of man. The idea of a divine justice is then born, but that, we might say, is the original pattern of evasion. An ethical scheme is substituted for the concrete facts, for the divine indifference, for the heaps of corpses on the battlefield.

Greek drama is an attempt to explain catastrophe as a clash between two distinct modes of existence. The more recondite the explanation, the more tragic the drama. The connection between crime and punishment need not be direct—the sins of the fathers are ingeniously visited on the sons, and misfortune is all the more

[1] This would seem to be the interpretation put on Greek tragedy by Professor Kitto. Cf. 'Greek tragedy (Professor Kitto insists) is not, primarily, a tragedy of human character at all. The drama is one in which the real point is not the tragic hero, but the divine background: whereby the tragic action is constantly illuminated by the revelation of the laws at work in it. Aeschylus conceives these laws, embodied in the deities, as in course of evolution; the law of Zeus changes, by a change in Zeus himself. To Sophocles they are eternal. But the underlying "justice" which they evince is not primarily a punishment of the individual for transgression.' Quoted by J. Middleton Murry reviewing *Form and Meaning in Drama*, by H. D. F. Kitto, London, 1956, in *The London Magazine*, Vol. 4, No. 3, March 1957, p. 60.

effective for being undeserved. In this divine dispensation, guilt is transmitted like a disease. Pride and arrogance, which are forms of personal vanity rather than mortal sins, are peculiarly provocative of divine anger. Aeschylus, to quote Werner Jaeger again, 'did not believe that destiny was simply a force which punishes the guilty man to make an example for others. . . . What we call character is not an essential element in Aeschylean tragedy. . . . The guilt of Orestes is not founded on his character. Aeschylus does not consider him to be a man whose nature destines him to commit matricide. He is merely the unfortunate son who is bound to avenge his father: at the moment when he enters manhood, he is faced by the dreadful deed which will destroy him before he even tastes life, and to which the god of Delphi constrains him again and again whenever he shrinks from the fixed end. He bears the burden of an immutable fate.'[1]

This conception of tragedy would seem very absurd, and by our modern standards unjust, were it not an expression of the belief that only through suffering can a knowledge of reality be reached. If Greek drama had confined itself to the theme of retribution, its poetic scope would have been limited. Its universality is due to its convincing demonstration of this 'mighty spiritual unity of suffering and knowledge'. It leads beyond the specifically human tragedy—the conflict within the personal psyche—to a collective sense of predestination. The individual tragedy is merged into the absurdity of existence, the arbitrary death becomes the prototype of the natural death. A solution of the contradiction of death must be a creative act, reconciling all oppositions. The creative act envelops the paradox: becomes the reality we can contemplate. The Greek experience of tragedy ends therefore in aesthetic contemplation, which is a kind of stoicism—not the indifference of ignorance, but an enlightened understanding.

Greek drama, and the tragic philosophy it expresses, were obviously the products of a civilization very different from our own. The family affairs of the Atridae, or even the wars of the Persians or the Trojans, seem to belong to an order of existence totally distinct from the class politics and world wars of our own time. Fate no longer selects princes as prototypes: force strikes against no representative hero, but against the dumb defenceless

[1] Paideia, *The Ideals of Greek Culture*, trans. Gilbert Highet (3 vols.), Oxford 1946–47, Vol. I, pp. 258–60.

masses. Fate as the absurdity to which we must be reconciled has not changed in nature; it differs only in the apparent distribution of its effects.

In our time philosophers and poets have gradually conceived a need for a revival of the tragic conception of life. The disillusion and cynicism of the modern world were a direct consequence of the First World War, which brought to an end not only an era of social optimism, but even of Christian faith. Though the Christian world had for centuries tolerated the irreligious wars of Christian princes and potentates, blaming the evil on the inheritance of original sin, it could not so easily shift the guilt of Christian peoples engaged in mutual extermination. Love itself had turned to hate, and an appeal to a Saviour of Mankind had become a mockery. We found ourselves deprived equally of catharsis and of consolation. I remember my own cynical disillusionment when, marching to some battlefield we passed a church or a wayside crucifix that had been hit by a shell. In one such moment of despair I wrote this short poem:

His body is smashed
Through the belly and chest,
And the head hangs lopsided
From one nailed hand.

Emblem of agony,
We have smashed you!

I meant that we had obliterated the symbol of agony and sacrifice by our own excessive experience of suffering. We had suffered a shock that caused a profound revolution in the most sensitive natures among us. From that same shock emerged the revised beliefs of men like Albert Schweitzer and D. H. Lawrence, the demand for 'some revolutionary renewal of love from some primal, untapped, virgin source'.[1]

Simone Weil, in her beautiful essay on Homer's poem, suggests that one is always conscious in the *Iliad* of fate as force, as impersonal energy—the x that turns anybody who is subjected to it into a *thing*—the bodies on the ground, 'dearer to the vultures than to their wives'. From this first property of force (the ability to turn a human being into a thing by the simple method of killing him)

[1] John Middleton Murry, *Love, Freedom and Civilization*, London, 1957.

flows, says Simone Weil, another property, 'quite prodigious too, in its way, the ability to turn a human being into a thing while he is still alive.' He is alive; he has a soul; and yet—he is a thing. Simone Weil is thinking of the passive victim, about to die. But there is another sense in which force can turn a human being into a thing, and to me this is much more horrible. Suddenly in the excitement of the battle the soldier loses his self, his 'facticity', his consciousness of himself as a human being, and becomes an anonymous machine, a machine that kills, an energy operating the weapon in his hands. Danger no longer exists, or is an abstraction.

The transformation may be defined physiologically as the drenching of the bloodstream with adrenalin, or some other secretion of the glandular system. It is only in a secondary sense a psychological change. The transformation has the suddenness and completeness of an epileptic fit, and is perhaps constitutionally related to it. To go 'berserker' was the old Norse phrase for this condition: a man transformed into a wild animal, a savage bear, without feeling, even without sensation, for in this condition wounds give no pain. When the fit is over the man no longer remembers the animal or thing he has been, or the inhuman things he has done. He grows conscious of what he has been as the wounds begin to hurt.

We can conceive force in this impersonal way, as a wild energy that invades the human body; but force is also used deliberately or consciously by one person against another, or against a whole group of people, even against a nation. The man who uses force in this way we call a tyrant, and we call a slave the man who submits to force and becomes a thing. But it would seem that even if a man begins by using force deliberately, he ends by using it obsessively. To quote Simone Weil again: 'Violence obliterates anybody who feels its touch. It comes to seem just as external to its employer as to its victim. And from this springs the idea of a destiny before which executioner and victim stand equally innocent, before which conquered and conqueror are brothers in the same distress.' From this illusion proceeds the apotheosis or personification of Fate or Destiny. Fate is no longer an impersonal energy; it does not exist apart from its users, or its victims. Destiny, in the sense of a preordained life and death for the individual, does not exist, but serves to explain man's inevitable death through the agency of an external force. It is the blight man was born for.

Death and the idea of force are closely connected. Man does not like to acknowledge the inevitability of his natural death; he prefers to think that life is forcibly taken from him. Hence the primitive personifications of death as a soul-snatcher, a wild horse, etc. Death and resurrection, growth and decay—the whole development of magic and religion, and even of science, centres on the natural cycle of human existence. If the death of the flesh is accepted as inevitable, then the resurrection, if not of the body, then of the independent soul, gives a sense of continuity to personal existence. Sex and generation are seen as aspects of earth's fertility, and the exiled soul of man may take refuge in a tree or a rock. There is no end to the subterfuges to which man resorts in order to preserve his identity. He ends by willingly sacrificing his body in the belief that he will thereby preserve his soul.

Freud's explanation of this whole complex of life and death is by now well known, but I must refer to it because his hypothesis, if true, would explain the modern individual's fatalism—his willing acceptance of unreasonable death. Freud suggests that a characteristic of all organic life is its tendency to return to inorganic inertia—in fact, that this tendency is instinct itself. Earth's diurnal course has left its imprint on the human organism; we return from whence we came. 'It would be counter to the conservative nature of instinct,' says Freud, 'if the goal of life were a state never hitherto reached. It must rather be an ancient starting point, which the living being left long ago, and to which it harks back again by all the circuitous paths of development. If we may assume as an experience admitting of no exception that everything living dies from causes within itself, and returns to the inorganic, we can only say *The goal of all life is death*, and casting back, *The inanimate was there before the animate*!'[1]

There are objections to this conception of instinct—it does not explain how the properties of life were ever awakened in inorganic matter; it is inconsistent with the teleological belief, which seems to be equally instinctive, that such properties are not accidental. To say that 'the inanimate was there before the animate' is a statement that cannot be proved, an unscientific assumption: and though we cannot conceive of animation without matter to be animated, it is perfectly possible to imagine a cosmic isomorphism,

[1] *Beyond the Pleasure Principle*, trans. C. J. M. Hubback, 2nd edition, London, 1942, p. 47.

in which spirit and matter, animate and inanimate, are reciprocally interlocked. The boundaries between the organic and inorganic are not so definite as Freud assumed, and they become less definite as our scientific researches proceed.

But all this is irrelevant to my purpose, except in so far as the death-wish, as Freud called it, is used, as he used it, as an argument to justify the inevitability of war, or of mutual slaughter. If death is preordained, then we might say with equally consistent logic, so is life, so is humanism. What is not preordained, what constitutes our human tragedy, is the ending of life by force or violence.

In the context of our modern experience we do not speak of justice, divine or human, and it is doubtful if indiscriminate suffering brings enlightening knowledge, or is in any way a valuable experience. We are too conscious that this suffering is not inevitable; that it comes, not from gods, but from the neurosis of man. Face to face with their gods the Greeks could create a drama: we have only our newspapers and our pathology. We can speak of the 'sombre tragic power' of the *Oresteia* or *The Seven Against Thebes*, but what kind of language do we use to describe Auschwitz or Hiroshima? A few documents like *The Diary of Anne Frank* reveal the emergence of a beautiful character in the midst of our mass suffering, but the Greeks would not have found material for tragedy in such a document—partly because they lacked the Christian concept of innocence. They could conceive tragedy only as equity, as retribution. We on our part lack this concept of equity. Force in our time has filled the world with anonymous misery, and that situation is the challenge to which our humanism must creatively respond. 'The sense of human misery,' said Simone Weil, 'is a precondition of justice and love. . . . Only he who has measured the dominion of force, and knows how to transcend it, is capable of love and justice.'

Modern culture expresses the dominion of force, but does not measure it. The prevalence of all forms of brutality in contemporary fiction, especially American fiction, in contemporary films and in television, and above all in the popular press, is surely one of the most striking characteristics of our age. Every day, in every so-called civilized country, millions of people stare like fascinated animals at scenes of the utmost brutality—above all scenes in which the human body is subjected to outrage and violence. This characteristic of our culture is not confined to the mass media of entertainment. Writers like Faulkner and Hemingway, both recipients of the Nobel Prize, exult in the description of these same brutalities, and their skill only serves to make their sadistic intention the more effective.

The art and literature of earlier civilizations was full of similar violence: in what respect is our modern indulgence in force any different from the blood-baths of the Elizabethan stage, the gruesome brutalities related with zest in the medieval chronicles, or the actual scenes of slaughter in the Roman amphitheatres? In what sense is Faulkner's *Sanctuary* more brutal than the *Iliad*? If we are to *measure* the dominion of force, must we not in the very process depict it?

It is impossible to conceive drama or poetry, or their modern substitutes such as fiction and film, without action. Not only tragedy, but all art conforms to Aristotle's definition and is an imitation of action. Any avoidance of acts of violence would be arbitrary, and falsify the truthful relation of art to life. The problem is to determine the kind of relationship that should subsist between art and action, or, to make the problem more precise, between art and violence.

Aristotle's consideration of the problem resulted in the doctrine of *Katharsis*, and ambiguous as his exposition of that doctrine is, we still lack a better one. Do not avoid reality in any way, said Aristotle, but impose measure on it. Confine your plot into a reasonable compass, describe it in poetic language and metrical diction, embody it in noble characters, ritualize the action, set it to music, and then, far from being a harmful indulgence in gross passions, these very passions are sublimated, and the spectator is given an immense sense of relief and justification.

Modern psychology has given much support to the Aristotelian theory of Katharsis—has elaborated it without departing from the broad outline of the theory. Terms like transference and sublimation can be adapted for the purposes of poetics, and we can have nothing but wonder for the intuitive way in which Aristotle anticipated our analysis of the dynamics of what we would now call the individuation process. We now have all the essential prerequisites of tragedy—a sense of human misery—and we have a complete understanding of how tragedy should work. All we lack is tragedy—an art-form to effect the necessary purgation of our emotions.

Greek tragedy belongs to the Greek world—to a certain stage in human development, to a particular consciousness of human destiny, and to a people conditioned by particular economic circumstances. We cannot revive Greek drama. But we must seek equivalent forms to contain our violence, to make us capable of love and justice. These forms, these representative symbols, must be popular, must therefore make use of mass media of communication, and they must conform to the general laws of poetics. By that I mean (as Aristotle meant) that their form cannot be arbitrary: they must possess a size or shape which is not a matter of chance, but has the concrete elements that constitute beauty. In other words, these symbolic forms must be the work of poets, who, according to Aristotle, possess either a happy natural capacity or an element of madness. I think we might express this requirement in another way. The dominion of force can be measured only in the individual psyche: tragedy, as an art-form, is a process of reconciliation that takes place within the individual psyche. There are no collective tragedies: only misery is collective. The way is always shown by the creative Self, in measure or in madness.

Tragedy is a man-made toy—not a part of reality, but a conquest of reality, a victory for human consciousness. It is not a blind flight from the misery of our existence, but a deliberate withdrawal to a prepared position. But it does not (as André Malraux would maintain) *substitute* the order of art for the absurdity or chaos of existence. It finds in existence elements from which an order can be created, which order is then a reality for which the poet can feel responsible. The failure of writers like Malraux and Faulkner as humanists is that they describe the cruelty and horror of a tragic situation, but do not create the reconciling symbol. Their art is fundamentally vindictive: art, in Malraux's words, is '. . . man's eternal revenge.'[1]

[1] Cf. the illuminating observations on this subject of Everett W. Knight, *Literature Considered as Philosophy: the French Example*, London, 1957, pp. 157–9.

CHAPTER 12

The Reconciling Image

My 'self', before the modern philosophers and psychologists began to disintegrate the notion, meant the coherent range of my consciousness, my awareness of the external world, the witness of my body as a recording organism in contact with this external world. This neat dichotomy of inner and outer, of stimulus and response, has proved to be too simple as an explanation of the thought and behaviour of a human being. Apart from instincts of whose workings I might not be aware, it was shown that a part of my mental life was not present as consciousness, and though this had always been obvious in brief moments between sleeping and waking, when consciousness overtook the retreating hem of unconsciousness, it was many years before it was possible to give a scientific account of the self in all its depth. When Freud and his associates had at last constructed a reasonable hypothesis, it left the mind attached, as by some umbilical cord, to a deeper source of psychic energy. This source could no longer be called personal; rather it is collective, and Jung was to show what a significant part this collective unconscious plays in our personal development, and in the cultural development of the human race.

The human psyche, Jung has said, 'is made up of processes whose energy springs from the equilibration of all kinds of opposites'—a *complexio oppositorum*. One of the commonest of these formulations is the spirit-instinct antithesis. Psychic processes 'behave like a scale along which consciousness "slides". At one moment it finds itself in the vicinity of instinct, and falls under its influence; at another, it slides along to the other end where spirit predominates and even assimilates the instinctual processes most opposed to it'.[1] It is typical of modern man that he vacillates in this manner—he is either all spirit or intellect, or all passion or instinct. His ineffectuality and his disasters arise from this imbalance, this extremism. The fault is only to be corrected by achieving a conjunction of the two sources of energy—by what Jung calls a 'realization of the shadow'. But Jung is careful to warn us that the shadow is not painlessly reconciled to the spirit, but only as the Greeks believed, by way of suffering and self-surrender.

The instinctual extreme of this fundamental antithesis has been given a new definition by Jung. There is first a distinction to be made between on the one hand collective consciousness, the collectively acceptable dogmas and 'isms' (of religion, race and class) to which the masses give their unreasoning allegiance; and on the other hand those predetermined patterns or archetypes of behaviour which Jung places in the collective unconscious. It is possible, Jung seems to suggest in one place,[2] that the dogmas of collective consciousness were at one time expressions of collective unconsciousness: the symbols of religion, for example, are no longer operative as archetypes because they have lost touch with psychic reality, and must now be consciously inculcated as dogma.

The truth which Jung and other contemporary psychologists have established is that psychic wholeness is achieved by a developmental process that brings the characteristic elements of the unconscious into harmony with consciousness. Jung calls it the 'individuation process', and his description of this process is his greatest contribution to a solution of the cultural problem we are discussing. This individuation process is essentially a reconstruction of the self, and the Self, redefined and deepened in significance, becomes the final ideal of humanism as of Jungian psychology—a new 'totality figure', comprising infinitely more than the ego, but not dominated by whatever unconscious elements it has absorbed.

This reconciliation of individual instincts and universal archetypes is not merely significant for the personal psyche: it is at the same time a socialization of what would otherwise be introspectively unique and isolated. The archetype predicts a social pattern of

[1] 'The Spirit of Psychology', in *Spirit and Nature: Papers from the Eranos Yearbook*, New York and London, 1954, Vol. I, p. 417.

[2] Op. cit., p. 431.

behaviour: it is a predilection to forms of action that are latent in the human organism, and Jung does not hesitate to compare it with the instincts that determine animal behaviour.[1] 'The instinct of the leaf-cutting ant fulfils the image of ant, tree, leaf, cutting, transport, and the little ant garden of fungi. If any one of these conditions is lacking, the instinct does not function, because it cannot exist without its total pattern, without its image. Such an image is an *a priori* type. It is inborn in the ant prior to any activity, for there can be no activity at all unless an instinct of corresponding pattern initiates and makes it possible. This schema holds true of all instincts and is found in identical form in all individuals of the same species.[2] But in the human being these images of instinctual behaviour tend to become separated from their physiological functions, with most important consequences for our present argument. Although in modern man the instincts may be suppressed, or disused, a pattern remains, into which our psychic energy will spontaneously flow. Since the original function of these patterns was, like the instinctive behaviour of the ant, social, the new content is likely to have a social significance. There are many varieties of spontaneous activity with such archetypal significance, but the most effective on the symbolic level is the work of art, because it is essentially a concentrated expression of psychic awareness, a 'concrete insight' into the reality of an existing situation. The mind of a poet in a state of pure consciousness, free from external causality, from preoccupations of any kind, is invisibly guided into archaic moulds. In this way a *Hamlet* or a *Faust* achieves a representative status which was not a conscious intention of the poet.

Whatever may have happened in primitive societies, in the modern world the individuation process must take place by deliberate effort. There must be a conscious engagement of the will—not, of course, the conscious evocation of the unconscious, which would be merely a calling of spirits from the vasty deep, but a conscious will to integration, first in the individual and then in society. And this, as Jung has said, cannot proceed by a process of

[1] At the same time he says: 'The archetype is spirit or pseudo spirit: what it ultimately proves to be depends on the attitude of the human mind. Archetype and instinct are the most polar opposites imaginable, as can easily be seen when one compares a man who is ruled by his instinctual drives with a man who is seized by the spirit.' Op. cit., p. 417.

[2] Op. cit., p. 411.

logical reasoning—'one is dependent on *symbols* which make the irrational union of opposites possible. They are produced spontaneously by the unconscious and are *amplified* by the conscious mind. The central symbols of the process describe the self, which is man's totality, consisting on the one hand of that which is conscious to him, and on the other hand of the contents of the unconscious.'[1] But as Jung proceeds to warn his readers, 'the difference between the "natural" individuation process, which runs its course unconsciously, and the one which is consciously realized, is tremendous. In the first case consciousness nowhere intervenes; the end remains as dark as the beginning. In the second case so much darkness comes to light that the personality is permeated with light, and consciousness necessarily gains in scope and insight.'

A new humanism is precisely such a consciously realized enlightenment, embracing the shadows that threaten our present civilization, which are shadows cast by the unappeased instincts of natural man. We are at the mercy of our instincts because they are not contained in symbolic forms—Pandora's box has been opened, and no effort is being made to recapture the evil spirits that have escaped.

Jung in his later works seems to have reached the conclusion that the appeasing image, which is the archetypal Self, the completed Man, is identical with the God-image. This would seem to be the conclusion of Otto Rank also, as interpreted by Ira Progoff. The religious need is specifically a longing for wholeness, and it therefore 'lays hold of the images of wholeness offered by the unconscious, which, independently of the conscious mind, rise up from the depths of our psychic nature'.[2] *Answer to Job* ends with the picturesque evocation of the person who, though enlightened by God, 'remains what he is, and is never more than his own limited Ego before the One who dwells in him, whose form has no knowable boundaries, who encompasses him on all sides, fathomless as the abysms of the earth and vast as the sky.' This is not perhaps a helpful image: it raises an altar to the Unknown God, and leaves the worshipper incapacitated by his own nescience.

Let us rather agree with Jaspers, that 'since there is no complete truth, our movement towards it is itself the only form in which

[1] *Answer to Job*. Trans. R. F. C. Hull, London, 1954, pp. 175–6.
[2] Op. cit., p. 178.

truth can achieve completion in existence, here and now. In its very process the boundless acquisition of truth experiences that completion which it never reaches as a goal'. This emphasis on Process is in agreement with the conclusions of Bergson and Whitehead, and it is indeed in conformity with Jung's own earlier notion of integration as a process of conscious development, a ceaseless activity involving the creation of symbols of integration. Creativity is of the essence of the process, and every great civilization, seen in historical retrospect, seems to centre on a characteristic symbol of processive integration. The *Iliad* is one such symbol—the reconciliation of force or violence, with love or pity, in a poem depicting the dispensation of divine justice. The *Gita* is another such symbol of processive integration, perhaps the greatest ever conceived by man, the reconciliation of nature and spirit, the attainment of a state of pure consciousness or integral self-knowledge. But though Existence remains forever the same, the phenomenal and spiritual aspects of it in our human experience change or develop, and from time to time the creation of new symbols of reconciliation becomes an acute necessity. We are at such a critical moment of human history, and that is why we can speak hopefully of the possibility of a new humanism.

Nietzsche's *Zarathustra* and Shaw's *Methuselah* are modern attempts to create an integrating symbol of reconciliation on the scale of the *Iliad* or the *Gita*, and they both fail to be effective because they are deliberate constructions. That is to say, they fail as drama, as collective rituals, which brings us again to one of the observations I made in the last chapter, that every revival of the human spirit begins on the linguistic level, as a poetic revolution. This phrase should not be taken too literally—I use 'poetic' in its widest meaning, and it would be possible to use a phrase like 'iconic manifestation' to cover all possible forms of an expanding consciousness.[1]

[1] I have discussed the process historically in *Icon and Idea*, Harvard University Press and London, Faber & Faber, 1955. On this occasion let me call two witnesses to my support. The first is Max Scheler. Towards the end of his book on *The Nature of Sympathy* he discusses certain difficulties we encounter in the perception of other minds, and among them language, which 'intrudes its network of order and articulation between what we see and what we experience'. He continues:

'Anything in our experience which can be put into words is always something which, having been singled out by common language, must also be accessible to others; and such experience presents a quite different appearance in internal per-

Nietzsche is justly regarded as a great renovator of the German language—in his own opinion, he was the first to raise it to the level of the other great poetic languages of mankind, and to make it a worthy vehicle of sublime truth. Nevertheless, neither Zarathustra as a symbolic figure, nor his Song as a coherent myth of reconciliation, has become an integral part of our culture. The reasons for this failure are, I believe, fundamentally imaginative and linguistic (it is impossible to separate these two aspects, for the

ception from anything that is "ineffable". It is given *prior* to the ineffable. For this reason poets, and all makers of language having the "God-given power to tell of what they suffer", fulfil a far higher function than that of giving noble and beautiful expression to their experiences and thereby making them recognizable to the reader, by reference to his own past experience in this kind. For by creating new forms of expression the poets soar above the prevailing network of ideas in which our experience is confined, as it were, by ordinary language; they enable the rest of us to *see*, for the first time, in our own experience something which may answer to these new and richer forms of expression, and by so doing they actually *extend* the scope of our *possible* self-awareness. They effect a real enlargement of the kingdom of the mind and make new discoveries as it were, within that kingdom. It is they who open up new branches and channels in our apprehension of the stream and thereby show us for the first time *what* we are experiencing. That is indeed the mission of all true art: not to reproduce what is already given (which would be superfluous), not to create something in the pure play of subjective fancy (which can only be transitory and must necessarily be a matter of complete indifference to other people), but to press forward into the whole of the external world *and* the soul, to see and communicate those objective realities within it which rule and convention have hitherto concealed.' *The Nature of Sympathy*, trans. by Peter Heath, London, 1954, pp. 252–3.

A less well-known but very intelligent witness to these same truths is an English critic and philosopher, Owen Barfield. In a book on *Poetic Diction* which was published in 1928 he has a chapter on 'The Making of Meaning', and ascribes to the poet, in this same large sense, the same function of expanding the consciousness. He describes the experience of truth as the identification of the self with the meaning of Life, which is both poetry and knowledge, and continues: 'Now although, without the rational principle, neither truth nor knowledge could ever have been, but only Life itself, yet that principle alone cannot add one iota to knowledge. It can clear up obscurities, it can measure and enumerate with greater and ever greater precision, it can preserve us in the dignity and responsibility of our individual existences. But in no sense can it be said to *expand* consciousness. Only the poetic can do this: only poesy, pouring into language its creative intuitions, can preserve its living meaning and prevent it from crystallizing into a kind of algebra. "If it were not for the Poetic or Prophetic character," wrote William Blake, "the philosophic and experimental would soon be at the ratio of all things, and stand still, unable to do other than repeat the same dull round." Like some other of the mystics, he had grasped without much difficulty the essential nature of meaning. For all meaning flows from the creative principle, the τό ποιεῖν, whether it lives on, as given and remembered, or is re-introduced by the individualized creative faculty, the analogy-perceiving, metaphor-making imagination.' *Poetic Diction: A Study in Meaning*, London, 1928, pp. 153–4.

imagination always clothes itself in an appropriate language, according to its intensity). This same failure is all the more evident in Shaw's 'metabiological pentateuch'. The rational principle is there, the knowledge, and the perception of truth, but the concrete poetic insights are lacking, and without these there can be no viable poetic myth.

Jung takes rather a different point of view. *Zarathustra,* he admits, 'brings to light the contents of the collective unconscious of our time'.[1] He concedes that the poem is religious, but nevertheless, since Nietzsche is an introverted thinking type, his standpoint remains aesthetic, pre-eminently intuitive. His symbols are presented for the pleasure they give, without consciousness of their meaning. From this point of view Spitteler's *Prometheus* can seem to be a more significant poem than either *Faust* or *Zarathustra.* These poems are more *beautiful* than *Prometheus,* but the latter, 'as a more or less faithful image of the actual processes of the collective unconscious, has deeper *truth*'.[2]

This may be true, but of one thing we can be certain—Spitteler's poem, which to this day has remained unknown outside the German-speaking peoples, and even among these has created no great stir, will never be effective as a myth. Jung admits that *Prometheus* has defects. 'The abstruse, grotesque, and uncouth quality that always clings to mystical exuberance hinders the flow of sympathy, alienates one's sensibility from the work,' etc. If the truth is made so 'fatiguing and unpalatable', no wonder it has no success with the mass of mankind. But Jung seeks for another explanation and suggests that 'the greatest and most immediately suggestive effect is gained by the poet who knows how to express the most superficial levels of the unconscious'. Should the vision of the creative mind search more deeply, it becomes all the more strange to mankind in the mass, and provokes an ever greater resistance in all those who occupy conspicuous positions in the eyes of the mass. The mass does not understand it although unconsciously living what it expresses; not because the poet proclaims it, but because its life issues from the collective unconscious into which he has peered. The more thoughtful of the nation certainly comprehend something of his message, but, because his utterance corresponds with events already developing among the mass and

[1] *Psychological Types,* trans. H. G. Baynes, London, 1928, p. 237.
[2] Op. cit., p. 240.

also because he anticipates their own aspirations, they hate the creator of such thoughts, not at all viciously, but merely from the instinct of self-protection.[1]

Jung shares with Kierkegaard a deep suspicion of the aesthetic attitude, which he places in opposition to the religious attitude. If the statement I have quoted were universally true, it would mean that Greek tragedy, as an art-form, had no significance for the Greek people except as a comment on their religion; whereas we know that the Greek religion not only developed from a ritualistic drama, but was at all times an aesthetic phenomenon—that was Nietzsche's deep insight into its essential nature, and it has been amply confirmed by later scholarship.

If the aesthetic attitude as such is now ineffectual, the reason is to be found in our conscious and sceptical attitude to works of art. A deep rift divides the poetic consciousness from the collective instincts of mankind. The poet is an outcast, isolated. As a result he has become introspective and analytically self-destructive. The mass does not resist him—it ignores him.

The point I am coming round to is that one can by no means take a short cut to a new culture, or to a new religion. The old myths cannot be reanimated, nor can new myths be created by taking thought. No doubt the new myths will be archetypes of the collective unconscious and therefore of similar structure to the old myths, but they must appear spontaneously in our midst. They can take shape only as icons, as plastic images conceived by the poet and artist. There can be no new mythology until there is a new iconography, a ritual precipitating new symbols.

At this point we come face to face with the real dilemma of our time, which lies in the conflict between any spontaneous manifestations of the unconscious, and our self-awareness—what Sartre calls our 'bad faith'. We must not identify culture with its representative poets and artists, who appear at the stage of consolidation, of summation. Before a Homer or a Dante can appear there has to be a long period of gestation, a slow conquest of reality and the precipitation of many linguistic and plastic images in the consciousness of a people. This process of precipitation is unconscious, and even, at any one phase of the process, insignificant and unobserved. It may consist at the formative stage of small technological changes, new processes of production, new climatic

[1] Op. cit., p. 238.

conditions; or it may consist of small changes in the evolution of a language—the point of ripeness or maturity in a vernacular which then irresistibly aggravates the sensibility of a poet like Dante or Shakespeare. To look for such points in our own cultural wilderness would be to miss them—who can say whether such a subtle fermentation is taking place at the present moment in China or Brazil, in Canada or Siberia. It is against historical probability that it would occur again in exhausted lands like Greece or Italy or England, but there is no law of causality in this realm of culture. Nor is there any guarantee that a new culture will have familiar features. We are speaking of mythological (mythopoeic) phenomena, and their behaviour is dream-like, illogical, or rather pre-logical, prior to the ineffable. One looks in vain for the appearance of any new cultural features in television or film, but we may be looking for what we have lost, instead of waiting on new images, images that emerge spontaneously from the clamouring unconscious of the multitude.

It is difficult to conceive a humanism that is not a literary and retrospective humanism, *litterae humaniores*, and by definition culture implies calm, withdrawal from distractions, leisure, contemplation. A work of art is something we can contemplate, and we contemplate it not to escape from ourselves, nor to escape from the world in the contemplation, as Malraux would have it, of an autonomous or independent world, but to be reconciled with ourselves and with the absurdity of existence. The greatest works of art, as I have already said, have always been images or myths of reconciliation. Can we discern, anywhere in the world today, the emergence of such images of reconciliation?

I believe that there are certain works of contemporary art that constitute such images. Our epoch has seen the rise of a style of art unprecedented in kind, and now universal in its manifestations. I shall be told that much of this non-figurative or abstract art is sophisticated and even consciously academic, but the value of an invention is not destroyed by its being exploited, and no number of ignorant or unscrupulous imitators can take away the significance of the new plastic images that we owe to artists like Kandinsky, Picasso, Klee, Mondrian, Gabo and Moore. All these artists have in common a will to create images that are metaphysical, beyond the limits of the phenomenal world.

These images are of two kinds. Some are geometrical, balanced, harmonious in form and colour. Mandalas, we might call them, images of wholeness and integration, inviting withdrawal from the chaotic distractions of daily perception, inducing contemplation and self-less meditation. Others, though equally abstract in the sense that they do not represent the sense-data of normal modes of perception, are formless and discordant. They are produced by arbitrary methods, often without the intervention of the conscious will, colours tossed onto the canvas very much in the same way as one tosses dice in a game of chance, or the coins in *I Ching* (The Book of Changes). The conscious control of form is eliminated and what is behind consciousness, the impersonal formative processes of the unconscious, is allowed to determine the emergent shape (Gestalt). Of such artists Erich Neumann has remarked that they have one thing in common: 'They have all experienced the creative truth that the spirit blows where it will, and even where they seem to be playing and leaving things to chance, it is not only because the perplexed ego has renounced all hope of knowledge but because they believe profoundly that in and behind chance a greater truth may be at work. Conscious renunciation of form is often falsely interpreted as inability to give form, as incompetence. Actually the breakdown of consciousness, carrying the artist backward to an all-embracing *participation* with the world, contains the constructive, creative elements of a new world vision.'[1]

The paradox which is evident in this new development of the plastic arts is of great significance for my argument, for it shows that the deepest introversion of the creative process in the individual leads to the widest basis for a collective myth: a more than individual force is projected in symbols of strange potency. Only at the beginning of a new epoch in civilization does such an upsurge of symbolic forms take place.

Certain manifestations in literature, such as Proust's *A la recherche du temps perdu*, Joyce's *Ulysses* and T. S. Eliot's later poems, are significant comments on the crisis rather than in themselves reconciling images. Certainly Mr Eliot has been aware of the crisis, no one more so; but he has tried perhaps too deliberately to reanimate ancient symbols rather than create new ones, not wishing to break with the tradition of Christian humanism.

[1] 'Art and Time', in *Man and Time: Papers from the Eranos Yearbooks*, New York and London, 1958, Vol. III, p. 32.

Symbols, since they are archetypal, can be only relatively new; nevertheless, a sophisticated poet can be too consciously traditional and a sophisticated public suspects any poet who has a deliberate design on them.

I was a close observer of the making of a film version of *Murder in the Cathedral*, and Mr Eliot himself devoted much time and thought to this attempt to vulgarize his poetry by means of this new medium. Everything possible was done, without sacrifice of the poetry, to translate the drama of a great traditional poet into the typical art-form of our age, and the attempt failed because the visual symbols thus reanimated had no compelling interest for a public used to the images of Hollywood. The poetry might have been palatable, for a modern audience does not distinguish between poetry and prose unless it becomes conscious of a rhythmical jingle; and perhaps in this matter the audience is right: there is more vital poetry to be found in the prose of their newspapers than in the 'alienated' poetry of a cultural *élite*.

I am not speaking as a social or socialist realist: I do not believe that the masses can have a culture of their own, distinct from the culture of the *élite*: at least, such a culture, like peasant art, would be of minor interest. But the masses are necessary to a culture, as soil is necessary to a flower; and there is no culture unless an intimate relationship, at the level of instinct, exists between a people and its poets. One cannot repeat too often, because it is the distinctive characteristic of any humanism, that the images of wholeness that the poet creates out of his own inner contradictions are at the same time symbols of reconciliation for the conflict of instinct and spirit in a people. Without this intimate correspondence, art remains esoteric and the people remain barbaric.

Modern art, it will be said, is and will remain esoteric. I think it is presumptuous to make such an assertion. For a long time Greek art of the archaic period was esoteric, a tribal art or a magical art, but gradually became the art of a civilization. For a long time the art of the catacombs remained esoteric, until it blossomed into the art of Byzantium and the western world. Even the art of the Renaissance began as an esoteric cult of antiquity.

Artists are essential to a civilization, but do not create it. As Klee suggested in an image which he elaborated with great understanding, the artist stands like the trunk of a tree, gathering and passing on what comes to him from the earth, from roots which are deep in the collective unconscious. The efflorescence of abstract art in our time is not a deliberate creation of the artist: it is a necessary symbol transmitted by the artist from the unconscious, and the intricate crown of this tree is nothing other than the Golden Flower, an oriental emblem of reconciliation. Several of the artists I have mentioned—Kandinsky, Klee and Mondrian in particular—expressed themselves in philosophical terms, and gave verbal as well as pictorial evidence of their awareness of a metaphysical unity, of the *Tao*. They did not use their art to illustrate their metaphysical intuitions; rather they tried to explain the metaphysical intuitions to which they had been led by their creative activity. They found themselves with symbols that had formed beneath their brushes, spontaneously and with insistent urgency.

These symbols we now recognize as symbols of unity or reconciliation, and their proliferation, as Yeats recognized in that curious passage in his mystical treatise, *A Vision*,[1] to which I have already referred, may be 'but the first symptom of our return to the primary tincture'. What Yeats meant by the primary tincture is rather obscure, but he had in mind a new phase of the Creative Mind, a new manifestation of secular culture.

A culture is more than a collection of symbols; a culture expresses itself in the quality of its symbols rather than in their proliferation. It is always finally this intangible sense of quality, this 'Sinn' inherent in the symbol, to which we return.

The quality is in the material of expression, just as the *timbre* is in the voice, the pitch in the tone. It is a question of *style*, but we must not make the mistake of assuming that style is a superficial quality. 'Whereas,' wrote Goethe, '*simple imitation* flourishes under tranquil and satisfying conditions of existence, and whereas *mannerism* calls for a light touch and a fresh individuality, that which I call *style* rests on the deepest foundations of cognition, on the inner essence of things, in so far as this is given to us to comprehend in visible and tangible forms'.[2] What is a question of style is a question of sensibility, indeed, of the senses. But style is also a question of will, of the intention, of faith in the meaning of what is expressed. So finally one cannot separate expression from content, manner from meaning. They interpenetrate dialectically, *complexio*

[1] London, 1937, p. 258. See p. 143 above.

[2] *Simple Imitation of Nature, Mannerism, Style* (1789). Cited by Ludwig Curtius in *Goethe: Wisdom and Experience*, New York and London, 1949, p. 223.

oppositorum. But 'what is expressed'—that is never, in a significant work of art, a subjective phantasy. It is an archetypal image or myth, and fundamentally impersonal or objective.

The question remains whether modern subjectivism is a state of mind compatible with the mythopoeic process, with the creation of the impersonal and collective myth, of poetic tragedy. Have we carried self-awareness to a stage where symbols no longer have any collective force? Symbols should strike directly into the unconscious, but as we are now constituted, they are screened by an introspective and sceptical intelligence. Images, that should please the innocent eye, are received by a consciousness that is already corrupted, confused by guilt and anxiety.

Such was the insight expressed by Yeats in his much quoted poem *The Second Coming*: civilization is falling apart, 'the centre cannot hold'—

Mere anarchy is loosed upon the world,
The blood-dimmed tide is loosed, and everywhere
The ceremony of innocence is drowned;
The best lack all conviction. . . .

Surely, cried Yeats, the Second Coming is at hand, and he sees an image of the Sphinx somewhere in the sands.

. . . moving its slow thighs, while all about it
Reel shadows of the indignant desert birds

and the poet realizes that even after 'twenty centuries of stony sleep', this symbol out of *Spiritus Mundi* had been 'vexed to nightmare' by a rocking cradle in Bethlehem, and he thinks that surely now, in our state of corruption, some revelation is at hand.

I do not wish to end on a vague apocalyptic note. I am too conscious of the concreteness of a culture, of its manifestation in iconic images, in monuments of architecture, in drama and epic poetry, to entertain some vague notion of a spiritual renewal without roots in a pro-creative soil. Even Yeats does not speak of a mystical *logos*, but of a rocking cradle. A new civilization, a secular culture, is expressed in images that move the heart rather than the mind, and if we are in search of one today, let us turn our eyes to the East again, where we may discern, not a cradle, but a spinning-wheel. Culture is expressed in images that move the heart rather than the mind, symbols of sensuous appeal, and I come back to

Tolstoy, who, in spite of much mental confusion and moral denunciation motivated by his own sense of guilt, did have a clear conception of the social significance of art. He realized, for example, that the chief characteristic and great attractive force of art lies in its power of freeing the personality from its separation and isolation, in its fusion of the individual with the group.[1] 'A real work of art,' he said, 'destroys in the consciousness of the recipient the separation between himself and the artist, and not that alone, but also between himself and all whose minds receive this work of art.'[2] He even realized that the evolution of feeling proceeds by means of art, and he might have admitted, if the significance of the admission could have been made clear to him, that the evolution of consciousness itself proceeds by means of art. Art, and only art, he concluded, could cause violence to be set aside and ensure the peaceful co-operation of man. But Tolstoy, like the communists of our own time, had a naïve conception of the process of art: he thought that it worked by contagion on the level of feeling, and though he does occasionally mention the word instinct, it is conceived as an extension of feeling, or perhaps as a somatic basis for it. Tolstoy had no conception of the symbolic function of images, mainly because he had no conception of a dynamic unconscious. He did not realize, as we have had cause to realize since his time, that if the process of art is confined to the level of feeling, it can be an instrument of evil as well as an instrument of good. Art is only secured against such misuse by its recourse to archetypal imagery and symbolism, and the great works which Tolstoy admired, the *Iliad* and the Bible, the Vedas and the story of Sakya Muni, are precisely those works of art that are rich in such imagery and symbolism. The great artist is not the one who unites mankind on a basis of feeling—that is a recipe for the rabble-rouser—but the one who by transcending personal feelings discovers symbols for the universal archetypes of the psyche. These are no doubt residues of the emotional experiences of the human race, forged into shape and significance by mankind's sufferings and longings for peace of mind and immortality.

It will be asked why I avoid the most prevalent archetype of western civilization—the passion of Jesus of Nazareth. I do so

[1] *What is Art?* trans. by Aylmer Maude, Oxford (World's Classics ed.), 1930, Chapter XV, pp. 228–9.

[2] Ibid., Chapter XVI, p. 291.

because I am trying to consider this problem in universal terms, which are the terms of tragic art, and the Christian Church has deprived the Passion of its tragic significance. For the tragedy it substituted the mystery, for relentless fate it substituted damnation and redemption, original sin and salvation. It has often been observed that Christianity and the tragic sense of life are incompatible: there is no tragic art between the end of the Greek civilization and the beginning of the secular civilization in which we now live.[1] It is conceivable that a new conception of Christianity might by drastic revision of its eschatology revitalize the tragedy of Jesus, but of that there is no sign, except perhaps in the speculations of Schweitzer and Jaspers. And where is the poet capable of reshaping such a solid rock of traditional dogma?

The prototype of the artist is the pagan Hephaestus or Vulcan, who was born deformed and lame and cast out of Olympus—the typical outsider. He made the armour of Achilles and golden automata, and even Pandora, the mother of all women, from whose jar the evil instincts escaped to plague the world. For a time he was the cuckold-husband of Venus. He is a genial figure among the Olympians, and it is perhaps significant that the Romans built the Temple of Concord in the grove that was sacred to him. But most significant for our present purpose is the shield he forged for Achilles, for here we have a perfect representation of the artist's capacity to create images of wholeness, symbols of love and reconciliation. According to Homer's account, the shield was forged of four metals—brass, tin, gold and silver, and Chapman, in the dedication of his great translation to the Earl Marshal of England (1598) already pointed out the symbolism inherent in this choice of metals—gold being the equivalent for fire, brass for earth, tin for water and silver for air, the quaternity of elements that symbolize the four functions of the psyche, as Jung has demonstrated. The shield was round, to indicate the roundness of the world, and within it were three circles, to represent the Earth, the Sea, and the Heavens: in which the Sun and Moon and the Stars find their places. Within this circle Homer depicted two cities, one filled 'With sacred nuptialles and with solemne feasts',

[1] Cf. Jaspers, op. cit., p. 38: '. . . Christian salvation opposes tragic knowledge. The chance of being saved destroys the tragic sense of being trapped without a chance of escape. Therefore no genuinely Christian tragedy can exist.'

For an illuminating discussion of this problem see J. Middleton Murry, *Love, Freedom and Civilization*, London, 1957.

with fair brides, 'With golden torches burning by their sides', with dancing and the music of flute and harps.

And all the matrones in their dores appearde
Admiring their enamored bravouries.

Meanwhile, in another part of this city, the citizens are gathered together to witness the Heralds and Judges settle a 'long and costly suit' by arbitration. A city, therefore, of joy, peace and mutual aid.

The other city is a scene of violence and assault. Two hosts besiege it in the hope of dividing the wealthy spoil. The citizens yield to neither, but execute a sally and ambuscade, causing bloody slaughter:

at a river's brinke
Where all their heards had usuall place to drinke.

The two hosts join conflict 'With mutuall force'

betwixt them flew debate
Disordered Tumult and exitial Fate.
Here was one taken with wounds bleeding greene
And here one pale and yeelding, no wound seene:
Another slaine, drawne by the strengthles heeles
From the red slaughter of the ruthless steeles,
And he that slew him on his shoulders wearing
His bloodie weedes as trophies of his daring.
Like men alive they did converse in fight
And tyrde [*fed greedily*] *on death with mutuall appetite.*

It is the same picture of love and violence that is the general theme of the *Iliad*, a theme to which I shall return in the next chapter. But there is still more of symbolical significance in this minor poem of Homer's, for Vulcan then carved images of fertility—

a soft and fruitfull field
Brode and thrice new tild . . .
Where many plowmen turnd up here and there
The earth in furrows . . .
and, every furrow ended,
A bowle of sweetest wine he still extended
To him that first had done . . .

The wonderful description of earth's bounty that follows is too long to quote, but among the reapers and the binders, and the children gleaning,

all silent stood their king
Upon a bulke, his sceptre in his hand,
Glad at his heart to see his yeeldie land.

This scene ends with a ritual dance of youths and maids:

And these sometimes would in a circle meet
Exceeding nimblie and with skilfull feet,
Turning as round as doth a wheel new done,
The wheelwright sitting trying how t'will run

But there is a final symbolic touch:

About this living shielde's circumference
He wrought the Ocean's curled violence,
Arming his work as with a christall wall.

It is the uroboric snake, the primordial ocean ringing the world, the source of creation and of wisdom,[1] familiar to us in the myths of Egypt and Babylon. It is the Great Round whose significance Erich Neumann has elucidated for us: The Archetypal Feminine, 'which is and contains the universe.'

It is not for me to dilate on the significance of this symbol, so lovingly depicted by the world's first and greatest poet. I have merely cited it, at the conclusion of this chapter, as a symbolic colophon to these undogmatic musings. But one dogma is implicit in all I have said. A culture must rise spontaneously from the collective unconscious through the fiery hands of our lame Vulcans. Culture is a created work, not an idea. It is the patient accumulation of many works, and responsible for each work is a Vulcan, beating the constituent metals on his anvil. The instinct that guides his hand is a sure one, the movement not consciously calculated, but responsive to intimations that are beneath all sensations, primordial. Some of our contemporaries, artists of fame and of no fame, have in all innocence been guided by these primordial intimations and have precipitated their experience in symbolic form. These symbols for the moment lie scattered and confused. They can be unified and harmonized only by the silent operation

[1] Cf. E. Neumann, *The Origins and History of Consciousness*, p. 23; *The Great Mother*, pp. 211, 217 *et passim.*

of a collective will such as does not exist in the western world today.

A will to what? The conclusion of both the historical anthropologists and the individual psychologists seems to be that in the past this unifying force has always been a will to immortality. But as Neumann has said such a will today has to overcome the prevailing over-emphasis on consciousness, which again I identify with Sartre's 'bad faith', and I see no possibility of such an event in the terms of traditional symbolism. The new symbols to be created must evade the corroding action of consciousness.

The only symbols capable of this are symbols of reconciliation forged in the unconscious depths of the poet's psyche, works of love that transcend and measure the dominion of force.

On an earlier page I disclaimed any intention of reading into the concept of humanism a new religion, any essence distinct from and superior to the Self. I do not take Stirner's extreme egoistic stand and reject even the Self that I might become, because I have acknowledged the existence within my Self of an archetypal foundation that is common to Man, and this is the possible justification of a new concept of humanism. My self rises like an island from this continuous bedrock of animal instinct. I remain an island —every Self is an island, and that is our tragic fate. We are islands by virtue of the ocean that surrounds us, but its 'curled violence' is the source of all life and of those images of love and unity that constitute our humanism.

CHAPTER 13

Love and Force

The enormous difficulty lies in the fact
that rational *pacifism is based on error*

C. F. VON WEIZSÄCKER
Bulletin of the Atomic Scientists,
May 1958

When Tolstoy had finished his great epic *War and Peace* he added an epilogue of some fifty pages which, since it is not fiction and has apparently nothing to do with the long narrative that precedes it, very few people have read. But this epilogue, which is a consideration of the historical causes of war and peace, is a penetrating essay by a great man who had given the best of his thought and genius to this problem.

Tolstoy dismisses as strange and absurd all previous historical explanations of the subject, and even the view of modern historians, who see history as made either by heroes endowed with extraordinary superhuman capacities, or by men of very various kinds, from monarchs to journalists, who lead, or rather mislead, the masses. This is the historical concept we now call power-politics, and it merely substitutes for the divine intervention, by means of which ancient historians explained war and peace, the intervention of one man or perhaps a complex group of men. As for power itself, this may sometimes be the outcome of events, or, when the historians want to prove something else, the events follow on the exercise of power. Still another class of historians tries to prove that the cause of events lies in intellectual ferment—in the accumulative effect of a book like Rousseau's *Social Contract*.

While not denying that power-politics and political doctrines play a part in shaping events, Tolstoy goes on to show that the historical process is far more complex than this: that the collective will of the people—nationalism as we should now call it—also plays a part; and if he had read Karl Marx he might have admitted economic factors, not as the sole determinant of war and peace, but as one of the forces to be taken into account. But Tolstoy then points out that all these contradictory causes do not justify war, which is the killing of millions of men, and he asks how it is that men can commit these collective crimes. He comes to the conclusion that the conception of a cause is inapplicable to the phenomena we are examining: that there is an infinite chain of cause and effect, and if man were a physical particle, subject to physical laws only, that is all there would be to say about it. But, said Tolstoy—and this is where he put the whole question on a different plane—man is not a material atom and as such governed by forces like gravitation and electricity: man is conscious of self, he knows that as a man he is free, and therefore he is not subject to the general laws that govern inert matter. 'Man's actions proceed from his innate character and the motives acting upon him.' Whence follow these questions: 'What is conscience, and the perception of right and wrong in actions, that follows from the consciousness of freedom?' That, said Tolstoy, is a question for ethics. (Today we might say it is a question for psychology.) But then the further question arises: how should the past life of nations and humanity be regarded—as the result of the free, or as the result of the constrained, activity of man? And that is the question for the historian. 'Whatever presentation of the activity of many men or of an individual we may consider, we always regard it as the result, partly of man's freewill, and partly of the law of inevitability.' Every human action must be seen as a certain combination of freedom and inevitability. 'The proportion of freedom to inevitability decreases and increases according to the point of view from which the action is regarded, but their relation is always one of inverse proportion—to a starving man stealing will have the appearance of inevitability.'[1]

Tolstoy was willing to admit that 'the better we are acquainted with the physiological, psychological and historical laws deduced

[1] My quotations are from the translation of *War and Peace* by Louise and Aylmer Maude, Oxford University Press (World's Classics Edition,) 3 vols., 1933.

by observation and by which man is controlled, and the more correctly we perceive the physiological, psychological, and historical causes of the action, and the simpler the action we are observing and the less complex the character and mind of the man in question, the more subject to inevitability and the less free do our actions and those of others appear'. He had no concept of unconscious motivation, or otherwise he might have recognized that the scope for freedom was even more limited than it would appear; but he concluded, and surely this was a remarkable conclusion in 1869, that freewill represents the unknown vital force in human life. 'In history what is known to us we call inevitability: what is unknown we call freewill,' he says. 'Freewill is for history only an expression for the unknown remainder of what we know about the laws of human life. In order to live a life of reason,' he concluded, 'we must somehow reconcile the mutually exclusive and separately incomprehensible conceptions of freedom and inevitability. Apart from these two concepts which, in their union, mutually define one another as form and content, no conception of life is possible.'

In thus conceiving the problem of war and peace as essentially a problem of reconciliation, Tolstoy was returning to something very like the Greek conception of the problem. For freedom and inevitability we might substitute the more precise words love and force. In an earlier essay (see page 182), I referred to Simone Weil's interpretation of the *Iliad* as 'the Poem of Force', the poem of the might or violence that is opposed to peace or harmony. The discussion of our subject does indeed begin with Homer, is continued in the *Bhagavad Gita* and the Gospels of Jesus, and ends for the present in the writings of Tolstoy and Gandhi. There is a continuity in this great chain of thought to which we might perhaps add another link; we shall not find any other continuous chain, and it would be presumptuous to begin to forge a new one, even although, as I shall presently note, force must now be interpreted as the threat of annihilation, as retribution on the whole of mankind rather than on an individual or a nation.

It is the Greek concept of Nemesis or retribution[1] which seems most alien to our rational modes of thought, but surely such a concept is implicit in our psychology: we lack only a fashionable name

[1] I have in mind Hans Kelsen's interpretation of the idea of retribution in Greek religion and philosophy: *Society and Nature*, London, 1946.

for it. Retribution is simply what happens automatically to the individual or to the race when there is no recognition of the shadow, when we project onto the other person or the other race our own unappeased instincts. 'Where love stops, power begins, and violence, and terror,' Jung has said,[1] and that is the lesson of the *Iliad*, and of Greek tragedy in general. But in this respect, as Simone Weil points out, 'the Gospels are the last and most marvellous expression of Greek genius, as the *Iliad* is the first expression.'[2] Retribution is simply what happens when we cease to love our neighbours as ourselves, when we break faith with our common humanity and condemn those neighbours to slavery, to humiliation or death. 'This retribution,' says Simone Weil, 'of a geometric strictness, which punishes automatically the abuse of strength, became the principal subject of meditation for the Greeks. It constitutes the soul of the Greek epic; under the name of Nemesis it is the mainspring of Aeschylus's tragedies. The Pythagoreans, Socrates, Plato, take this as the point of departure for their thoughts about man and the universe. The notion has become familiar wherever Hellenism has penetrated. It is perhaps this Greek idea which persists, under the name of Kharma, in oriental countries impregnated by Buddhism; but the occident has lost it and has not even in any one of its languages a word to express it; the ideas of limit, of measure, of equilibrium, which should determine the conduct of life, have no more than a servile usage in its technics. We are geometricians only in regard to matter: the Greeks were first of all geometricians in the apprenticeship of virtue.'[3]

The Greeks did not praise war as such, in the spurious manner of Nietzsche and some more recent prophets. War was an occasion for the exercise of divine justice: it was an ordeal, a testing-time for both sides. I remember as a schoolboy being confused by not knowing which side Homer was on—the Trojans seemed just as heroic as the Achaians; the death of Hector just as regrettable as the death of Achilles. And that is what Homer felt about it, too, for Achilles and Hector alike are sacrifices exacted by destiny for the abuse of force, for hybris. It is an external force, an other than

[1] C. G. Jung, *The Undiscovered Self*, London, 1958, p. 106.
[2] *Intimations of Christianity*. Trans. by Elisabeth Chase Geissbühler, London, 1957, p. 52.
[3] Op. cit., p. 35.

human violence, that takes possession of Hector and Achilles, that crushes both heroes. 'So the idea was born,' says Simone Weil, 'of a destiny beneath which the aggressors and their victims are equally innocent, the victors and the vanquished brothers in the same misfortune. The vanquished is a cause of misfortune for the victor as much as the victor is for the vanquished.'[1]

I am anxious to avoid the impatience which this abstract discussion of a war of swords and spears, a toy war, may inspire among people living under the immediate threat of a war of atomic fission, but though the weapons in man's hands have changed, the soul of man has not changed, and it is the same cry for deliverance that echoes through the *Iliad* and in our own hearts. It is a cry for deliverance from the fear of death; for death, absurd, irrational, undeserved, is the substance of our protest.

To witness the death of another being is a universal experience, an experience we suffer with whatever fortitude we possess. If that death is natural, in the fullness of age, we accept it as our common destiny: if it is caused by accident or disease, we can also accept it because such misfortunes are still an organic part of our destiny: we are all animals subject to mischance. But if life is taken from a man, not by age or accident, but by the design of other men, then it is an outrage, a frustration of man's natural destiny, and we have either to justify a sacrifice, or protest against a sacrilege.

One's instinct is to protest. Deep in our nature is a reverence for life, the reverence that Schweitzer would make the basis of human ethics. But we are told that equally deep in our nature is an aggressive instinct, an impulse to take what belongs to other men—their food, their land, their wives; and that this instinct, being active and violent, will always triumph over the reverence for life, which is meek and passive.

It is a curious fact that modern science, which has in general discarded the word 'instinct', has not given an unequivocal dismissal to the notion of an aggressive instinct. Instead of instinct, the scientist will now speak of 'innate behaviour', and he will usually insist that such behaviour is modifiable. Aggression from the scientific point of view can then be explained as learned behaviour (or traditional behaviour), or even as a conditioned reflex. We become aggressive simply because certain events or certain environments produce a secretion of adrenalin which flows

[1] Op. cit., p. 39.

into the blood stream and irritates the brain and nervous system to such effect that we become violent, 'see red', attack the object producing the irritating event.

In our more rational moments, however, we realize that such behaviour is unnatural, unworthy of our common humanity. To be human is to desire to fulfil the natural span of life. 'That men should have death for their future' (again I quote Simone Weil), 'is a denial of nature. As soon as the practice of war has revealed the fact that each moment holds the possibility of death, the mind becomes incapable of moving from one day to the next without passing through the spectre of death. Then the consciousness is under tension such as it can only endure for short intervals. But each new dawn ushers in the same necessity. Such days added to each other make up years. The soul daily suffers violence which every morning must mutilate its aspirations because the mind cannot move through time without meeting death on the way. In this way war wipes out every conception of a goal, even all thoughts concerning the goals of war. To be outside a situation so violent as this is to find it inconceivable; to be inside it is to be unable to conceive its end. Consequently, no one does anything to bring about this end. . . . Always among men, whether war or slavery is in question, intolerable sufferings continue, as it were, by force of their own specific gravity, and therefore, from the outside, they seem easy to bear; they last because they rob the resources required to throw them off.'[1]

This observation can be confirmed by our own personal experiences in modern warfare. When one is engaged in war one loses all capacity for making peace. The mind, as Simone Weil says, is completely occupied in doing *itself* violence, and as we have seen in our time, wars settle nothing: they lead to destruction, to death, but in the minds that survive the death-wish survives, perhaps all the stronger in that it has been frustrated. Our English poet Wilfred Owen, who was killed on the 4th November 1918, expressed this same thought in a poem which he called 'Insensibility':

Happy are these who lose imagination:
They have enough to carry with ammunition.
Their spirit drags no pack.

[1] Op. cit., pp. 41–42.

Their old wounds save with cold can not more ache.
Having seen all things red,
Their eyes are rid
Of the hurt of the colour of blood for ever.
And terror's first constriction over,
Their hearts remain small drawn.
Their senses in some scorching cautery of battle
Now long since ironed,
Can laugh among the dying, unconcerned.[1]

This is Homer's thought, too: man can fight against man, but he cannot fight against war: that would be to fight against the rules of the game, and a game it is. It is best, as Plato said, to regard ourselves as puppets made by the gods, possibly as playthings, possibly for some more serious purpose—that is more than we can tell. But one thing is certain: our impulses, to war or peace, to vice or virtue, are part of the game. The gods pull the strings and pull them with opposite tensions in the direction of opposite actions—at one time peaceable actions, at another time warlike actions. 'It is a current fancy that our serious work should be done for the sake of our play; thus it is held that war is serious work which ought to be well discharged for the sake of peace. But the truth is (says Plato) that in war we do not find, and we never shall find, either any real play or any real education worth the name, and *these* are the things I count supremely serious for such creatures as ourselves. Hence it is peace in which each of us should spend most of his life and spend it best.' Plato proceeds to quote Homer, to the effect that it is all a question of trusting to the favour of the heavenly powers in the needful hour.[2]

The *Iliad* is dominated by the idea of a divine justice ruling over the fate of men. But man does not have the divine knowledge of what is right and wrong: therefore he must submit to the test of war, in which test the gods will reveal their judgment. War is an instrument of divine justice, and if there were no transgressions of law—and the Greeks did not distinguish between divine law and natural law—then there would be no need for war. Peace is the natural condition of men, and the taking of life, the spilling of blood, is an outrage on nature, which man brings about by his pride and folly.

[1] *Poems*, London, 1920, p. 13.
[2] *Laws*, I, 644; VII, 803–4. A. E. Taylor's translation.

At the back of Homer and indeed of all Greek poetry and philosophy is the notion that Strife is a fundamental necessity to the life-process: it is a notion as old as Empedocles, who conceived nature as an eternal cycle governed now by Love, now by Strife. Once there had been a Golden Age, an era of unbroken peace and harmony (the age of Kronos in Plato's myth); but at some point Strife had entered and upset this universal harmony, and now there was a necessary alternation of the two forces:

'There is a double becoming of perishable things and a double passing away. The coming together of all things brings one generation into being and destroys it; the other grows up and is scattered as things become divided. All these things never cease continually changing places, at one time uniting in one through Love, at another each borne in different directions by the repulsion of Strife. Thus, as far as it is their nature to grow into one out of many, and to become many once more when the one is parted asunder, so far they come into being and their life abides not. But, inasmuch as they never cease changing their places continually, so far they are ever immovable as they go round the circle of existence.'[1]

It is a familiar image: the *conjunctio oppositorum* which is found in all philosophies of nature, oriental as well as occidental, and which has in our day been revived by Arnold Toynbee as a theory of Challenge and Response to explain the process of history. But let us be on guard against an illegitimate application of this metaphor to the affairs of men, or at least to the opposition of war and peace. In so far as challenge and response are necessary for the physical and moral health of man, they can be supplied by means less suicidal than the hydrogen bomb. William James once wrote an essay on 'The Moral Equivalents of War',[2] and though it was written before atomic warfare had been conceived, I think it still stands as an adequate answer to those who would defend war as a social prophylactic. He recognized that war (war before 1914, be it noted) promoted the necessary ideals of hardihood and daring, but he thought that the martial spirit could be sublimated. He suggested that 'the whole youthful population' should be conscripted to form for a certain number of years a part of the army enlisted

[1] Empedocles, frag. 17. (Burnet, pp. 207 f.; also Diels, frag. 17. Quoted from Kelsen, op. cit., p. 243.)

[2] In 1910. It was originally published by the Association for International Conciliation. Reprinted in *Memories and Studies*, New York, 1911, pp. 265–96.

against *Nature*, and in this manner 'the military ideals of hardihood and discipline could be wrought into the growing fibre of the people' without the callousness, the cruelty and the spiritual degradation that attend war. 'No one would remain blind, as the luxurious classes now are blind, to man's relations to the globe he lives on, and to the permanently sour and hard foundations of his higher life. To coal and iron mines, to freight trains, to fishing fleets in December, to dishwashing, clothes-washing, and window-washing, to road-building and tunnel-making, to foundries and stoke-holes, and to the frames of skyscrapers, would our gilded youths be drafted off, according to their choice, to get the childishness knocked out of them, and to come back into society with healthier sympathies and soberer ideas. They would have paid their blood-tax, done their own part in the immemorial warfare against nature. . . . Such a conscription, with the state of public opinion that would have required it, and the many moral fruits it would bear, would preserve in the midst of a pacific civilization the manly virtues which the military party is so afraid of seeing disappear in peace.'[1]

The idea of a cosmic opposition of Love and Strife is perhaps merely a projection of our own social conflicts,[2] and all we learn from the Greeks is that a solution of such conflicts can only come about *ab extra*, as an act of divine retribution, as the intervention of divine justice. In any case, the fundamental conflict is not between force and force, which leads merely to the endless perpetuation of Strife, but between force and love. The strife must not end in an unstable victory, but in an everlasting harmony. To quote Empedocles again: 'There [in the cosmic sphere] are distinguished neither the swift limbs of the sun, no, nor the shaggy earth in its might, nor the sea—so fast was the God bound in the close covering of Harmony, spherical and round, rejoicing in its circular solitude.'[3] All things are united in love by Aphrodite.

We reach the conclusion that force cannot be opposed by force, which shows the vanity of all schemes of armed security, of a balance of power. If force meets force it concentrates itself for a greater effort. But if force is evaded, then it expends itself until it is dissipated in empty space.

[1] Op. cit., p. 291.
[2] Cf. Kelsen, op. cit., pp. 243–4.
[3] Frag. 22 (Diels).

Force is counteracted not by force, but by love. This paradox, which was known to Empedocles and to Plato, to Lao-Tze and the Buddha, passed into the teachings of Jesus, but was never wholly comprehended by western Man, who remained the master or the slave of force. Such is the unanswerable condemnation that all oriental religious thinkers bring against the western perversion of the original doctrine of Jesus. Such is the reason why the Christian Church never penetrated into the East, as Buddhism did.[1]

We are not ignorant of love—we all experience it to the degree that we are human. But there is a mystery about the command of Jesus: *Thou shalt love thy neighbour as thyself.* In what is perhaps his greatest work, *Works of Love*, Kierkegaard explored the meaning and the consequences of this command, this 'fulfilling of the law', as St Paul called it.[2] Kierkegaard began by pointing out that a different meaning can be read into the command according to the emphasis we give to different words—

Thou shalt *love thy neighbour*
Thou shalt love thy neighbour
Thou *shalt love thy neighbour*

Kierkegaard explores all the implications of the command, but later writers, such as Martin Buber and Hubert Benoit, have shown that he did not exhaust them. Kierkegaard was concerned to prove what might be called the activist nature of love, and in this respect he returns to the conception of the early Greek philosophers. He goes so far as to say that the poet who sings of earthly love cannot be a Christian, 'for love of one's neighbour is not sung, it is acted'. And there is no partiality in neighbourly love: 'Earthly love and friendship are partiality and the passion of partiality; Christian love is self-denying love.' Love is a matter of conscience, and only

[1] 'It is true that in all times people were guided by violence in arranging their lives. The difference between the Christian nations is only that in the Christian world the law of love was expressed clearly and definitely . . . and that the people of the Christian world have solemnly accepted this law, whilst at the same time they have permitted violence, and built their lives on violence, and that is why the whole life of the Christian peoples is a continuous contradiction between that which they profess and the principles on which they order their lives—a contradiction between love accepted as the law of life and violence which is recognized and praised, acknowledged even as a necessity in different phases of life, such as the powers of the rulers, courts and armies.' Tolstoy, from a letter to Gandhi, 7th September 1910. Quoted in *Selected Writings of Mahatma Gandhi*, ed. by Ronald Duncan, London, 1951, p. 68.

[2] *Rom.* XIII, 8.

when it becomes a matter of conscience is there love from a pure heart and an unfeigned faith. Love works its miracles in stillness. 'Lo, the world raises a tumult just to bring about a little change; it sets heaven and earth in motion for nothing, like the mountain which brought forth a mouse: Christianity in all stillness brings about the change of the infinite as if it were nothing. It is so quiet, quiet as nothing worldly can be; as quiet as only the dead and inwardness can be; and what else is Christianity but inwardness!'[1]

Most of us have no hesitation in speaking of force, of power, of might, but the word 'love' embarrasses us. It does so because it is an ambiguous word, and it was perhaps with a realization of its ambiguity that the English translators of the Authorized Version of the Bible, in certain significant passages, substituted the word 'charity'. But that word, too, has become hopelessly ambiguous in modern English usage, and quite ineffective in our present context —the context of force. We must retain the word 'love' and try to use it realistically. Tolstoy devoted many pages to the effort of redefining the meaning of love in a context of force. He pointed out that true love, universal love, has nothing to do with sentimental or emotional love, which even animals experience. Kierkegaard was clear about that, too. Loving your neighbour, he pointed out, is a matter of equality, but of equality before God. Your neighbour is not the man for whom you have a passionate partiality; he is not your equal in education or social status. Nor is he the man you admire for his distinction, nor the man you pity for his inferiority—partiality or condescension are feelings of selfishness. The neighbour is every man and 'he is your neighbour through equality with you before God, but every man unconditionally has this equality, and has it unconditionally'.[2]

Martin Buber sees a further refinement in this divine command if a more accurate translation is made of the Biblical command, which would then read: 'Love your neighbour as one like yourself' (not 'as I love myself', for, says Buber,[3] in the last reality one does not love oneself, but we should rather learn to love the loving self that we recognize in our neighbour). The neighbour is to be loved as one who has the power to love me. This makes the relationship reciprocal. If we remember Jung's conception of the Self, which is

[1] *Works of Love,* trans. David F. Swenson, Princeton and Oxford, 1946. p. 111.
[2] Ibid., p. 50.
[3] *Between Man and Man,* p. 51.

'not merely the empirical man, but the totality of his being, which is rooted in his animal nature and reaches out beyond the merely human towards the divine', then we might say that we are commanded to love that part of the Self which we hold in common with the Self in others.

These may seem to be unnecessary subtleties, far removed from the human urgency of the problem, but it is very possible that we fail to obey the command to love one another because we do not understand it. But, said Tolstoy, 'it is so simple, so clear. You live; that is, are born, mature, grow old, and then you die. Is it possible that the aim of your life can be in yourself? Certainly not. How then? Man asks himself. What then am I? The only answer is: *I* am something that loves; at first, it seems, something loving only itself; but one need only live a little and think a little to see that to love the self which passes through life and dies, is impossible and purposeless. I feel that I ought to love, and I love myself. But, loving myself, I cannot but think that the object of my love is unworthy of it; yet not to love is impossible for me. In love is life. What is to happen? To love others: one's neighbours, friends, and those who love us? At first it seems that this will satisfy the demands of love; but all these people are in the first place imperfect, and secondly, they change, and, above all, they die. What is one to love? The only answer is: love all, love the source of love, love love, love God. Love, not for the sake of the loved one, nor for oneself, but for love's sake. It is only necessary to understand this, and at once all the evil of human life disappears, and its meaning becomes clear and joyful.'[1]

Kierkegaard, Tolstoy, Buber and Jung are all saying the same thing: Love is God—God is love. But I wish to resist the temptation to make abstract statements about the concrete reality. The love Tolstoy and Kierkegaard, Jung and Buber are discussing is an active love which we must practise in our daily life: 'To live,' as Tolstoy said, 'so as in all things to remember first of all, with every man, thief, drunkard, rough officer, or dependant, not to swerve from love: that is to say, in the business you have with him, to remember his need rather than your own.'

It has been said against Tolstoy, as it will be said against all who believe in the possibility of a new humanism, that he deceived himself because he assumed that virtue is a result of efficient

[1] *Essays from Tula*, London, 1948, p. 289.

reasoning. Berdyaev thought that Tolstoy 'was unable to see the significance of the irrational processes in life that permeate us, get hold of us, imperil us, and thereby transcend our moral and natural aims and ends'.[1] He was certain, not unlike Socrates, that the capacity of the average man to think accurately and to come to the knowledge of truth is a sufficient guarantee for its actualization! Berdyaev admits that 'no one perhaps had experienced the horror of evil, particularly when it parades in the guise of the good, with such intensity as Tolstoy'. Nevertheless, Berdyaev concludes, Tolstoy 'remained blind to the dark, irrational, metaphysical source of evil'. And Berdyaev ingeniously suggests that this peculiar optimism was due to his lack of an awareness of the problem of death: Tolstoy had an animal fear of death and refused to face up to this most profound and significant fact of our human situation.

To return to psycho-analytical terms: the dark, irrational, metaphysical source of evil is that part of the unconscious into which our anti-social wishes are repressed and then lie hidden: with the result that we live a frustrated life, superficially calm, liable to outbreaks of hatred and aggression. The author of *War and Peace* and *Anna Karenina* can hardly be said to have been unaware of the customary manifestations of this condition of psychic insecurity. Nor was the author of *The Death of Iván Ilych* unaware of the *fact* of death. But Berdyaev would argue that to be aware of the fact of death is not necessarily to be aware of the problem of death. Again I would say that the passage about love which I have just quoted from Tolstoy is precisely about the problem of life, and Tolstoy is saying that one problem answers the other—that if we love love, and love life, then we are not afraid of death. At the moment of his death, Iván Ilych 'sought his former accustomed fear of death and did not find it'. 'Where is it? What death?' There was no fear because there was no death.

'In place of death there was light.

' "So that's what it is!" he suddenly exclaimed aloud. "What joy!"

'To him all this happened in a single instant, and the meaning of that instant did not change.'[2]

[1] Preface to *Essays from Tula*.

[2] Trans. Louise and Aylmer Maude, Oxford (World's Classics Edition), 1935, p. 73.

I do not see how we can possibly say, in view of this scene, and many others in Tolstoy's writings, that Tolstoy had not faced up to the problem of death. He had faced the problem straightforwardly, and his solution was that we should live more abundantly, in the light of the principle of human love. Admittedly, there is another solution, and it is the one Berdyaev, like other mystics, would favour—a belief in resurrection, which Berdyaev calls 'the supreme recognition of the reality of death and, at the same time, the affirmation of victory over it'. But Tolstoy, and Freud who is in agreement with Tolstoy on this question, would say that a belief in resurrection is merely a rationalization of the death instinct. It is easy to retort that a belief in the principle of human love is a rationalization of the life instinct, but to favour Eros rather than Thanatos (and these Gods are equally dark, irrational and metaphysical) would seem to be reasonable. Indeed, what Tolstoy is saying, and what I am merely reaffirming under his guidance, is that there is no life without love, as there is no death without hatred. If, as Freud maintained, the death instinct is finally triumphant, because of the inevitable tendency of organic matter to return to a state of inorganic inertia, then there is no escape from an overwhelming pessimism, such as afflicted Freud in his later years. There are reasons for doubting this naïve contrast between organic life and inorganic matter. In any case, the present reality of our consciousness is life, and we animate that consciousness, make it brighter and intenser, by words of love.

Freud recognized that our reason, the Ego, was quite incapable of controlling the unconscious instincts or passions. Indeed, the conscious Ego is essentially dependent on the pull of the unconscious, 'like a rider who is obliged to guide his horse in the direction in which itself wants to go.' Freud never seems to have thought of pitting one instinct against the other, of so strengthening the love instinct that it became the horse with the bit between its teeth and obliged the Ego to go in its direction. Of course if human love is confused with moral values, higher ideals, and all that Freud characterized as the Ego-Ideal, or Super-ego, there would be no chance of this. But as the love we are talking about is also instinctive, dark and metaphysical, there would seem to be no reason why it too should not determine the nature of the Super-ego—that is to say, of the ideals we live by.

There is, we must finally admit, a fundamental dichotomy in our human psyche, a split that divides our being into two irreconcilable realms. We begin our lives because we have a will to live, and we end them because we have a will to die. The psycho-analysts have demonstrated the extent to which these two drives determine all our thoughts and actions, our motives and dreams. The wills or instincts interweave above and below the level of consciousness; become collective passions or inward meditations. We progress towards the Self, the individuated whole personality, to the degree that we become capable of discriminating between spirit and instinct. And to discriminate in such matters is to be capable of making decisions.

If we desire to affirm the life-instinct, then we are immediately involved in actions and decisions that will modify our social consciousness. The difficulty is to become aware of the life-instinct within us, and to recognize its manifestations in so far as they are distinct from our habitual behaviour. Even when we feel that the instinct is alive within us, then there is the temptation, which so many good people do not avoid, of wishing other people to become like us, and from the vanity of this wish we pass easily to forcing other people to become like us, by laws and regulations, police and armies. 'There has long existed among men an illusion,' said Tolstoy in that beautiful farewell addressed to his peasants in 1907 from which I have already quoted, 'to the effect that by good regulations a good life may be arranged for bad people (which is like making good bread out of bad wheat), and this illusion has done much harm, and still does harm. Formerly this illusion was only propagated by the governing classes. They tried, or at least they said they tried, and still try by means of various kinds of coercion, such as taking property, imprisoning and executing, to make a peaceful and good society out of evil people. But now the revolutionaries try to do the same, and call upon you to share in their attempt.

'Dear brothers, do not succumb to this illusion. Let the rulers, czars, ministers, policemen and officials do their evil deeds; but you, who have kept clean from it hitherto, try to remain clean. In just the same way too, try to be clean from participation in those deeds of violence to which the revolutionaries invite you. Your salvation, and that of all men, lies not at all in the sinful, coercive ordering of life, but in the ordering of your soul. Only by that, by ordering his soul, can each man obtain both for himself and for others, the greatest blessing and the best organization of life that men can desire. True blessedness, such as each human heart seeks, will be granted us not in some future organization of life, maintained by violence, but now, to all of us, everywhere, and every moment of life and even of death; and it is obtained by love.'[1]

What are the practical consequences of such an ordering of the soul? Tolstoy told us plainly enough, and Gandhi, who in all these important matters was a disciple of Tolstoy, lived and died in the spirit of this teaching. The consequences are a liberation from the deceit of obedience to human power; in other words—words whose meaning we must not mistake, for at any moment in our lives and the lives of other people they may involve martyrdom—non-violent resistance to force. All our evils can end only by the resolve of each one of us 'not to yield the control of their actions into the hands of others, and become the tools of murder'. It is the way of *Satyagraha* or Civil Disobedience: a way only possible if we are trained to exercise self-control and discipline; the way of courage and humility, of beauty and efficacy.

Satyagraha is a Hindu word invented by Gandhi, and it indicates a mental control or spiritual discipline for which the western psyche is not prepared. It means 'the way of Truth', and the practice of Satyagraha may perhaps be equivalent to the Christian belief: 'He that loveth another hath fulfilled the law.' (Rom., xiii, 8.) The law of love in Hindu is *ahimsa*, and in Gandhi's practical philosophy the way of truth was obedience to the law of love. In western thought love is not legal, but sentimental, or possibly spiritual or mystical. In Gandhi's philosophy the law of love led to the practice of non-violence; but non-violence in the West is not a way of life or a law of love: it is rather a resistance to external laws, civil disobedience. Thoreau, in his essay on 'Civil Disobedience', does not speak of love, but only of his own person and property, and of his refusal to submit his individuality, or his conscience as he alternatively calls it, to the rule of a government that in his opinion has no moral authority. Gandhi's doctrine of non-violence, on the other hand, is a way of life that only incidentally comes into conflict with the State. He claimed that he had put 'a new but natural and logical interpretation upon the whole teaching of the Gita and the Spirit of Hinduism', and the

[1] Op. cit., p. 286.

result was 'a living faith speaking like a mother to her aching child'.[1]

From the dawn of philosophy in the East there has been one light rising and enveloping our human activities, and making it possible for mankind to seek and find the Truth. 'But how is one to realize this truth,' asks Gandhi; and he answers in the words of the Bhagavadgita:

'By single-minded devotion (*abhyasa*) and indifference to every other interest in life (*vairagya*).' That is how one realizes the Truth, which may be likened to the philosopher's stone or the cow of plenty. Truth is the right designation of God—'Hence,' concludes Gandhi, 'there is nothing wrong in every one following Truth according to one's lights. Indeed, it is one's duty to do so. Then if there is a mistake on the part of anyone so following Truth, it will be automatically set right. For the quest of Truth involves *tapas*—self-suffering, sometimes even unto death. There can be no place in it for even a trace of self-interest. In such selfless search for Truth nobody can lose his bearings for long. Directly one takes to the wrong path one stumbles, and is thus redirected to the right path.'[2]

What, in western terms, is meant by a *self*-less search for truth: what is meant by self-suffering? Is it possible that in our search for truth—our scientific search, our search by means of the scientific knowledge of the psyche—we have been led to a similar conception of a Self that surrenders its own immediate interests, a self that suffers, sometimes even unto death?

[1] *Selected Writings*, p. 145.

[2] Extract from *Yeravda Mandir* by M. K. Gandhi. Reprinted in *Selected Writings*, p. 47.

CHAPTER 14

The Flower of Peace

Peace is not the absence of war: it is a virtue born out of the strength of the heart

SPINOZA, *Tr. politicus*, V, 4

Peace may be physical, a state of rest or harmony; or peace may be spiritual or psychic and is then better described as a state of silent growth. We must distinguish an arrest of movement, which in the human psyche would be death, and that harmony which is movement so perfect that it is imperceptible, like the movement of a spinning top. But even this harmonic movement does not represent the full meaning of peace, for the invisible movement of the human psyche is also an unfolding of form, a growth whose perfect analogy is the flower.

This was an image perfected in Hermetic philosophy, and beautifully expressed in a short poem by Henry Vaughan, the English metaphysical poet whose *Silex Scintillans, or Sacred Poems and Private Ejaculations*, was published in London in 1650. I would like to quote this poem, for all that I have to say on this theme of peace is by way of being a commentary on it:

My soul, there is a Countrie
Far beyond the stars,
Where stands a winged Centrie
All skilfull in the wars,
There above noise, and danger
Sweet peace sits crown'd with smiles,
And one born in a Manger
Commands the beauteous files,

He is thy gracious friend,
And (O my soul awake!)
Did in pure love descend
To die here for thy sake.
If thou canst get but thither,
There growes the flowre of peace,
The Rose that cannot wither,
Thy fortresse, and thy ease;
Leave then thy foolish ranges;
For none can thee secure,
But one, who never changes,
Thy God, thy Life, thy Cure.

Peace is here represented as an unwithering flower, growing in a far country, beyond the stars; its possession is security and ease, but it is only to be obtained by the intercession of the healing God, the God who in pure love had sacrificed his life so that man might possess this immortal flower.

Vaughan's master, both in piety and in poetry, was George Herbert, the gravest of our English metaphysical poets, and he also wrote a poem entitled 'Peace' which we might consider at the same time. It was composed at least twenty years earlier than Vaughan's poem, and is twice as long: it is at once simpler in diction and more elaborate in thought—

Sweet Peace, where dost thou dwell? I humbly crave,
Let me once know.
I sought thee in a secret cave,
And ask'd if Peace were there.
A hollow winde did seem to answer. No:
Go seek elsewhere.

I did; and going did a rainbow note:
Surely thought I,
This is the lace of Peace's coat:
I will search out the matter.
But while I lookt, the clouds immediately
Did break and scatter.

Then went I to a garden, and did spy
A gallant flower,

The Crown Imperiall: Sure, said I,
Peace at the root must dwell.
But when I digg'd, I saw a worm devoure
What show'd so well.

At length I met a rev'rend good old man,
Whom when for Peace
I did demand, he thus began:
There was a Prince of old
At Salem dwelt, who liv'd with good increase
Of flock and fold.

He sweetly liv'd; yet sweetness did not save
His life from foes.
But after death out of his grave
There sprang twelve stalks of wheat:
Which many wondring at, got some of those
To plant and set.

It prosper'd strangely, and did soon disperse
Through all the earth:
For they that taste it do rehearse,
That vertue lies therein,
A secret vertue bringing peace and mirth
By flight of sinne.

Take of this grain, which in my garden grows,
And grows for you;
Make bread of it: and that repose
And peace, which ev'ry where
With so much earnestnesse you do pursue,
Is onely there.

Here again we have the discovery of a flower, the Crown Imperial, in a region beyond the clouds; but its 'crown' is deceptive, for as in Blake's poem, 'The Sick Rose':

The invisible worm
That flies in the night,
In the howling storm,

Has found out thy bed
Of crimson joy
And his dark secret love
Does thy life destroy.

Perhaps the worm in George Herbert's poem is not the same worm as Blake's, but we shall see. In Herbert's poem, the flower is apparently abandoned, and a familiar archetypal figure appears, the Wise Old Man, and he directs the seeker for peace to the imaginary city of Salem, where, according to the Bible, Melchisidec, King of Peace, did dwell. But Melchisidec, who had lived at peace for many years, is overrun by foes and killed. From his grave, however, spring twelve stalks of wheat, which increase and multiply until they cover the whole earth. Bread which possesses a secret virtue is then made from this wheat, and those who then partake of it are granted that repose and peace which they have everywhere and so earnestly sought.

It may be that these poets, who were simple and pious men, were only inventing new allegories to illustrate the Christian legend. Melchisidec is the prototype of Christ, and the twelve stalks of wheat are the twelve apostles who spread the gospel of peace throughout the world. Christ as the Prince of Peace is one of his most familiar rôles. But both Herbert and Vaughan were adepts of Hermetic philosophy, and the images they used are archetypal. We have, in these two related poems, at least three such archetypal images: The unwithering flower, the Rose or Crown Imperial; The Wise Old Man and the transubstantiating bread, made from wheat which springs from the grave of the Prince of Peace. In what terms shall we interpret these symbols?

The unwithering flower is the *amaranth* (Gr. ἀμάραντος), sacred to Ephesian Artemis, the many-breasted goddess of fertility, who was served by eunuch priests. In Christian mythology also the amaranth (or amarant as it is more correctly spelt) has a symbolical significance; the crowns of the heavenly angels are inwoven of amarant and gold, and in *Paradise Lost* (III) Milton tells us why:

Immortal Amarant, a Flour which once
In Paradise, fast by the Tree of Life,
Began to bloom, but soon for man's offence
To Heav'n remov'd, where first it grew, there grows.
And flours aloft shading the Fount of Life,

And where the River of Bliss through midst of Heav'n
Rowls over Elisian *Flours her Amber stream;*
With these that never fade the Spirits elect
Bind their resplendent locks inwreath'd with beams,
Now in loose Garlands thick thrown off, the bright
Pavement that like a Sea of Jasper shone
Impurpl'd with Celestial Roses smil'd.

Here again the flower is associated with fertility, with the Tree of Life; it shades the Fount of Life, from which flows the River of Bliss, and with its immortal blossoms the multitude of Angels bind their resplendent locks.

Paradoxically the amarant is also associated with blood. Thus in Spenser's *Faerie Queene* we read (III, 45) of:

Sad Amaranthus, *made a flowre but late,*
Sad Amaranthus, in whose purple gore,
Me seemes I see Amintas wretched fate,
To whom sweete Poets verse hath given endlesse date.

The sweet poet is, of course, Torquato Tasso. I am not certain how the amarant would be represented, if represented it ever was, in Ancient or Renaissance painting; but when Herbert calls the flower of peace a 'Crown Imperial' he is suggesting something round and regular, something like the Golden Flower of the East, the symbol of balanced perfection. It serves well enough as a symbol of peace, as I intend to show.

We could spend a very pleasant hour tracing these archetypal images throughout classical and modern literature, but I am anxious to interpret these images in the terms of our practical need, which is to 'seek peace and ensue it'. This is a Biblical phrase, and it is significant that peace in ancient literature and in the English of the translators of the Bible was always referred to in this active or transitive sense. The people *held* their peace; or they *made* peace; peace was a positive condition that had to be created and maintained. It was not a state of inaction or passivity; rather a precarious balance to be achieved by conscious effort.

This necessity has always been present in the minds of political philosophers and statesmen, and they have therefore designed and even put into execution various systems of control or arbitration. These have usually been based on the rule of law, with sanctions either military or economic, for infringement of the law. Such systems of control have always broken down for the reason I have already mentioned: force cannot be controlled by force. If the passions of mankind remain unruly, no rules will keep them in restraint. We are therefore driven to the logical conclusion that it is the passions themselves that must be subdued, and the only way of doing this is the way of love, or to use a more practical term, the way of education. The way of education, as we know from our knowledge of the human psyche, is the way of integration, and it remains to define this process in the terms of a political philosophy.

This problem was the subject of one of Plato's profoundest and nowadays most topical dialogues, the *Politicus*, which incorporates the myth of the Age of Kronos. The purpose of the *Politicus*, it must be remembered, is to define the Statesman, to prove that statesmanship is an art, not a science, and the myth is introduced to show that the Universe being what it is, the art of the statesman is necessary to save mankind from the bottomless abyss of non-being. The Universe was not always 'what it is'; in the Age of Kronos its affairs were directed by the Shepherd King, who ruled mankind through the agency of divine guardians. Life was supported without labour. There was no war and no politics. Men and beasts shared this paradise and were born, not from physical intercourse, but directly from the earth. They lived from maturity to infancy in the opposite course to us, and disappeared in utmost infancy into the earth to be the seed of future generations of the earth-born. All this was part of one great cycle of time, a God-directed cycle. But at a certain point of time there was a reversal: the Universe began to turn in the opposite direction, and mankind lost the guidance of the Divine Pilot. In this new cycle of time, the so-called Age of Zeus in which we live, the Divine Pilot abandons the helm, and chaos begins to reassert its sway. 'Bereft of the guardian care of the Daemon who had governed and reared us up, we had become weak and helpless, and we began to be ravaged by wild beasts—for the many evil-natured beasts had by now turned savage. Men lacked all tools and all crafts in the early years. The earth no longer supplied their food spontaneously and they did not yet know how to win it for themselves: in the absence of necessity they had never been made to learn this. For all these reasons they were in the direst straits. It was to meet this need that the gifts of the gods famous in ancient story were given, along with such teaching and instruction as was indispensable. Fire was the gift of Prometheus, the secrets of the crafts were made known by Hephaestus and his partner in craftmanship, and seeds and plants were made known by other gods. From these gifts everything has come which has furnished human life since the divine guardianship of men ceased . . . and men had to manage their lives and fend for themselves in the same way as the whole Universe was forced to do.'[1]

Plato's point in relating this myth is to distinguish between the task of the Divine Shepherd, who is all-powerful and whose flock is docile to his wisdom, and the task of the Statesman, who is a man like other men, mortal, who has to discover methods of tending his human herd. 'Tendance of human herds by violent control is the tyrant's art; tendance freely accepted by herds of free bipeds we call statesmanship.' How does the Statesman persuade herds of free bipeds (there is a reason for this somewhat contemptuous description of humanity which has to do with parts of the argument that do not concern us now)—how does the Statesman persuade the common herd to follow in the path of wisdom?

Before we go on to consider Plato's answer to this question, let us note that all present proposals for making and preserving peace either assume that we still live in the Age of Kronos, and that mankind can be governed by a Divine Shepherd, whether the resurrected Christ or, a not less chiliastic proposition, Divine Guardians operating as a World Security Authority; or they assume that since we live in the Age of Zeus, tyranny is the only solution, and we must live forever under the threat of an International Police Force, or some such concentration of power. That was not Plato's conception of statesmanship, or of peace.

Plato suggested that statesmanship should work through what he called the method of Example, or Paradigm. He believed in the existence of certain concrete patterns or forms (the whole idea is an extension of his theory of Forms) which if imitated would establish order in the State. There exist types of activity which if practised stamp in a particular way the actions and experiences of men. 'They are specific forms of activity in imitation of which the human or animal soul may be said to be functioning at a given time. Most important among them are the group of Forms repre-

[1] I quote from Prof. J. B. Skemp's edition: *Plato's Statesman* (a translation of the *Politicus* of Plato with Introductory Essays and Footnotes), London, 1952.

sented by the arts; for they represent the ordering and formative intelligence in a particular way to a particular end. To think of such Forms is to make it easier at once to think of all Forms whatsoever as imposing a Limit upon the Unlimited.'[1]

Behind the Paradigm is the concept of 'due measure', the central ideal of Platonic and indeed of all Greek wisdom. But before examining the methods by means of which this ideal is to be realized in the State, or in mankind generally, let us glance at the extraordinarily elaborate analogy which Plato draws, in *Politicus*, from the craft of Weaving. It has an application to our present problem which even Plato did not fully exploit.

Plato realized that in this Age of Zeus men would always react in one way or another according to the affinities of their own dispositions.[2] 'They favour some forms of action as being akin to their own character, and they recoil from acts arising from opposite tendencies as being foreign to themselves. Thus men come into violent conflict with one another on many issues.' The purpose of his long-drawn-out analogy is to suggest that true statesmanship consists in weaving together the woof and warp of these diverse temperaments to make an enduring fabric. But he assumes a previous stage of carding: the diverse strains of which the fabric is made are good according to their kind: one is gentle, the other brave, and the ideal of the statesman is to avoid the extremes of these qualities, dullness and incapacity for action on the one hand, sheer fury and madness on the other, and by miscegenation produce a citizen of balanced temperament.

But what of the discarded, one might ask; what of the weak and the vicious among the children of Zeus? Plato leaves us in no doubt, at any rate in the *Politicus*, about their fate: they will be 'liquidated', banished or put to death. As for those who are merely mentally or morally deficient, they will serve the community as slaves. They are 'slaves by nature'.

Such inhumanity shocks the modern conscience, but it must be seen against the wider background, not only of a civilization fundamentally different from our own, but of Plato's theory of education. After all, in our much more humane age (or those aspects of it to which we give our passionate allegiance) we, too, banish the mentally deficient to asylums, our criminals to prison,

[1] Skemp, op. cit., p. 77.
[2] *Politicus*, 307d.

and we put the murderers among them to death. As for Greek slavery, that is an old bone of contention, but one may wonder how many Greek slaves would have exchanged their position for the dark coal-pits and monotonous production-lines of modern industry. 'Slavery' is one of those rogue words referred to by Ruskin, and best left out of the discussion unless carefully defined.

The whole point of the *Politicus* is to show that 'law can never issue an injunction on all which really embodies what is best for each; it cannot prescribe with perfect accuracy what is good and right for each member of the community at any one time. The differences of human personality, the variety of man's activities and the inevitable unsettlement attending all human experience make it impossible for any art whatsoever to issue unqualified rules holding good on all questions at all time'.[1] So much for the rule of law, on which modern politicians rely for the maintenance of peace. The only alternative is the rule of wisdom, which we also call the rule of love.

Before passing on to Plato's definition of wisdom, which is also his prescription for peace, I would ask the reader to observe how perfectly his use of the craft of weaving as a metaphor for the art of statesmanship could be used as a metaphor for the process of individuation. Our contrary impulses, our introversive and extraversive tendencies, our rationalism and empiricism, idealism and materialism, our toughmindedness and our tender-mindedness—all these as well as Love and Force are the woof and the warp that have to be woven into the enduring fabric of the personality. And what of our weak and vicious promptings, what of the shadowy Strife that is continually threatening the web of psyche? Can we discard this Shadow, banish aggressive thoughts, put Satan behind us? The modern psychologist bids us recognize the Shadow, come to terms with it, but how? It has never seemed to me that the psychologist is very precise in his prescription of a method of accommodation. I am going to suggest that the effective method is the one recommended by Plato for the Statesman, the method of Paradigm. For an account of this method we must go beyond *Politicus*, indeed, to Plato's last work, *The Laws*.

This method is sometimes called 'the Argument from the Arts', but it is very necessary to be forewarned of a misunderstanding that has bedevilled the whole history of Platonism, until quite

[1] *Politicus*, 294b.

recent times. The Greeks had no word for 'art', and though they drew a distinction between the fine and the applied arts, all arts were conceived as *techne*, as a specialized skill exercised productively on a specific material, whether it was the stone of the sculptor, the leather of the shoemaker or the wool of the weaver. This productive action, once perfected as a skill, implied a certain infallibility. Plato goes so far, through the voice of Thrasymachus in the *Republic*, as to assert that no one who practises a craft makes a mistake. 'A man is mistaken when his knowledge fails him; and at that moment he is no craftsman.'[1] The implication is that there is an inherent rightness in the exercise of a craft, a truth to form, and again Form (with a capital F) is implied. It follows that what is true of the craftsman is true of the Statesman; he is never mistaken so long as he is being true to his craft. Wisdom is the distinguishing characteristic of craftsmanship as such; the Statesman is wise not as a man, but as one who exercises statecraft.

Plato's theory of education—and it is always a theory of education for citizenship—relies on this mystique of craftsmanship. Even primary education, as we may gather from the references to the teaching of spelling in the *Politicus*, was taught visually as a craft. In the *Republic* the primary education of the Guardians is divided into three stages, Grammatic, Music, and Gymnastic, but the intention is the same at every stage: to condition the mind to measure, proportion and harmony. Education is a process of conditioning the malleable sensibility and mind of the child to rhythm and metre, to skilful movements which are always graceful movements, to the visible embodiment of perfection in any and every form. For, says Plato, 'excellence of form and content in discourse and of musical expression and rhythm, and grace of form and movement, all depend on goodness of nature . . . so, if our young men are to do their proper work in life, they must follow after these qualities wherever they may be found. And they are to be found in every sort of craftsmanship, such as painting, weaving, embroidery, architecture, the making of furniture; and also in the human frame and all the works of nature: in all these grace and seemliness may be present or absent. And the absence of grace, rhythm, harmony is nearly allied to baseness of thought and expression and baseness of character; whereas their presence goes with that moral excellence and self-mastery of which they are the

[1] *Republic*, I, 340.

embodiment.' All this is clear and precise enough, but Plato continues to emphasize 'the decisive importance of education in poetry and music: rhythm and harmony sink deep into the recesses of the soul and take the strongest hold there, bringing that grace of body and mind which is only to be found in one brought up in the right way'.[1]

All this is repeated, elaborated and emphasized in the *Laws*, and is there related specifically to the view that the State should be permanently organized with a view to peace, not to war. This topic, familiar to us from its treatment in the third book of the *Republic*, is in the second book of the *Laws* handled, as Professor A. E. Taylor has said,[2] 'with a psychological thoroughness for which the *Republic* affords no parallel . . . we have to lay it down as the foundation of a sound pedagogy that a child's first experiences in life are its feelings of pleasure and pain, and that education itself may very properly be said, at this stage, to be simply "learning to feel pleasure and pain about the right things", a declaration which called forth the unqualified applause of Aristotle.'[3] And Professor Taylor (whom it was my privilege to know and admire for a brief time when we were academic colleagues in Edinburgh) further comments:

'To Plato, as a true Greek, the "ugliness" of conduct which is morally out of place is the most immediate salient fact about it, and "the beauty of holiness", if the scriptural phrase may be permitted, is something much more than a metaphor. To judge by the tone of much of our literature, we are less sensitive on the point; we seem slow to perceive ugliness in wrong-doing as such, or even ready to concede the "artistry" of great wickedness. It may be a wholesome discipline to consider carefully whether this difference of feeling may not be due less to a confusion on Plato's part between the beautiful and the morally good than to a certain aesthetic imperceptiveness on ours.'[4]

The *Laws* go into every aspect of the ideal curriculum in great detail, and I must not disguise the fact that this curriculum includes instruction in the arts of war, and that such instruction applies in all respects to girls as much as to boys. But when we see what such

[1] *Republic*, III, 400–1. Trans. F. M. Cornford, Oxford, 1941.
[2] Introduction to his translation of *The Laws of Plato*, London, 1934, p. xxiv.
[3] E.N. 1104, b. 11.
[4] *The Laws of Plato*, p. xxvi.

instruction amounts to—horsemanship and the use of the bow and arrow—we suddenly realize what a gulf separates us from Plato's world. Indeed, the widest part of the gulf, so to speak, stretches from the present to the immediate past, and if it is now ludicrous to compare a war of atomic missiles with a war of gunpowder and foot-soldiers, how much more unreal Plato's world of bows and arrows! Nevertheless it is the technology of war that has changed and not the eternal forms on which Plato's conception of education is based; and this is visibly demonstrated by the survival through all this accelerated strife, and mutilated though they be, of the still unravished, silent but teasing forms of Greek art. It would not now be possible to reconstitute Greek warfare; but the education envisaged by Plato is still a possibility, if we can still believe in the possibility of peace and goodness.

But I feel that I have not yet sufficiently driven home Plato's main contention, which is that a peaceful world is in itself a work of art—that the peace within a state, and *a fortiori* the peace between states, is a condition of equilibrium attained by the skilful adjustment of human desires to absolute values, specifically to the values revealed to the senses as harmony. One might say universal values, for these harmonic values are visibly embodied in the order of the Cosmos, in so far as science can reveal that order. But Plato does not imply that order and harmony are limited to their embodiments in what already exists. That would be to suggest that man has no formative or creative power—that the mind has no imaginative or creative function. In a difficult passage in the *Politicus* he deals with this point. There is a paradox, he says, which most thinkers have failed to notice: 'Likenesses which the senses can grasp are available in Nature to those real existents which are in themselves easy to understand, so that when someone asks for an account of those existents one has no trouble at all—one can simply indicate the sensible likeness and dispense with any account in words. But to the highest and most important class of existents there are no corresponding visible resemblances, no work of nature clear for all to look upon. In these cases nothing visible can be pointed out to satisfy the inquiring mind: the instructor cannot cause the inquirer to perceive something with one or other of his senses and so make him really satisfied that he understands the thing under discussion. Therefore we must train ourselves to give and to understand a *rational* account of every existent thing.

For the existents which have no visible embodiment, the existents which are of the highest value and chief importance, are demonstrable only by reason and are not to be apprehended by any other means.'

In other words, such existents are essences. Plato, like Whitehead, was all for preserving a principle of novelty in the universe. The experience of art tells us, as Santayana has said, that beauty is 'a positive presence to the spirit and not a vague title conventionally bestowed. In a form felt to be beautiful an obvious complexity composes an obvious unity: a marked intensity and individuality are seen to belong to a reality utterly immaterial and incapable of existing otherwise than speciously.[1] This divine beauty is evident, fugitive, impalpable, and homeless in the world of material fact; yet it is unmistakably individual and sufficient unto itself, and although perhaps soon eclipsed is never really extinguished: for it visits time but belongs to eternity.' I do not think Plato himself ran such a danger, but one must not conceive form in art as inflexible, or the practice of an art as a routine. 'The sense of beauty,' to quote Santayana again, 'is not a feeling separable from some intuition of form; on the other hand, it is a feeling, not a verbal or an intellectual judgment.' Realized beauty 'cannot be preserved mummified in any external object; it can belong to things only by being attributed to them by some living soul'.[2]

In the *Symposium* the experience of beauty is seen as a living experience, *ein Erlebnis*, to use the more expressive German word. It is a process of initiation, which is the word we ought to use instead of education: a heavenly ladder of learning as Plato calls it, leading from bodily beauty, the beauty inculcated by music and dance, to the beauty of institutions; from institutions to the beauty of knowledge, philosophical beauty: and from the beauty of philosophy to the beauty of holiness, the love of beauty itself, essential beauty. The final vision is 'an everlasting loveliness which neither comes nor goes, which neither flowers nor fades . . . Nor will this vision of the beautiful take the form of a face, or of anything that is of the flesh; it will be neither words, nor knowledge, nor a something that exists in something else, such as a living creature, or the earth, or the heavens, or anything that is, but subsisting of itself and by itself in an eternal oneness; which every

[1] Cf. the Latin *speciosus*, meaning good looking, beautiful.
[2] *The Realm of Essence*, London, 1928, pp. 152–4.

lovely thing partakes of it in such sort that, however much the parts may wax and wane, it will be neither more nor less, but still the same inviolable whole.'[1]

Shelley, the reincarnation of Plato in English poetry, said in his *Defence of Poetry* that: 'The great secret of morals is love; or a giving out of our own nature, and an identification of ourselves with the beautiful which exists in thought, action, or person, not our own. A man to be greatly good, must imagine intensely and comprehensively; he must put himself in the place of another and of many others; the pleasures and pains of his species must become his own. The great instrument of moral good is the imagination; and poetry administers to the effect by acting upon the cause. . . . Poetry strengthens the faculty which is the organ of the moral nature of man, in the same manner as exercise strengthens a limb.'[2] It would not be difficult to describe this process in our ugly scientific terminology, but I do not propose to do so. I have given the beautiful and simple words of Plato and Kierkegaard, of Shelley and Tolstoy, and there is not any need to translate them into an obscure jargon. Force, violence, fear on the one side; love, imagination, beauty on the other side. 'Perfect Love,' we are told by St John, 'casteth out fear.'[3] We have heard this a thousand times, and heard many theological interpretations of this profound utterance. Plato, I have been suggesting, gives us a very concrete and practical interpretation; so does Shelley. The creative imagination, conceived actively, as *paideia*, is the only effective instrument of peace.

To return to Herbert's poem, with which I began this phase of my argument. Peace, he said, is not to be found in some secret cave; we cannot find it by searching for it in remote places. It is not an insubstantial mirage, that eludes us; nor is it the gift of idleness and inaction. It is a seed which must be planted and set, brought to flower and fruition, harvested and milled, and then we must make bread of it, and this bread will possess a secret virtue, bringing peace and mirth to all who partake of it. A simple allegory, it may be thought, but I have tried, with the aid of Plato, to give it an application to our present discussion of the problem of

[1] *Symposium*, 211. Trans. Michael Joyce, London (Everyman Library), 1938, pp. 64–65.

[2] *A Defence of Poetry*, 1821.

[3] *John*, IV, 18.

peace. It may be that Plato's conception of the Statesman as the Prince of Peace is far removed from our conception of Christ as the Prince of Peace, but Simone Weil has drawn attention to the 'intimations' of Christianity in Plato, and of course Platonism is one element, and an important one, in the development of Christian mysticism. But I have resorted to Plato, not for a mystical doctrine, but for a practical solution to the problem of peace; and we have found, not moral exhortations, but the outlines of a precise discipline: a discipline combining organic growth and harmonic form, a discipline that is a reconciliation of Strife and Love, of what Tolstoy called the mutually exclusive and separately incomprehensible conceptions of freedom and inevitability; and the image of such a reconciliation is this 'flower of peace, the Rose that cannot wither'.

Index

INDEX

ABOUT THE AUTHOR

SIR HERBERT READ was born in Yorkshire in 1893, the son of a farmer. An early and omnivorous reader, he started to write while yet in his teens. Enrolled at the University of Leeds in 1912, his studies were interrupted by the First World War in which he served for four years, rising to the rank of Captain and receiving the Distinguished Service Order and the Military Cross. During the war, he helped found the magazine *Arts and Letters.* After the Armistice, he worked for a while as an assistant to His Majesty's Treasury, edited T. E. Hulme's papers on literary criticism, and spent ten years at the Victoria and Albert Museum in the department of ceramics, writing definitive works on English pottery and stained glass.

In 1931 he became Watson Gordon Professor of Fine Arts at the University of Edinburgh. He has also been Clark Lecturer, Trinity College, Cambridge, 1929–30, and Sidney Jones Lecturer in Art, University of Liverpool, 1935–36. Lecturing extensively in the United States, he has been Norton Professor of Fine Art at Harvard, 1953–54, and delivered the A. W. Mellon Lectures in Fine Arts for 1954. He is an Hon. D. Litt., University of Leeds. For his remarkable and numerous literary works, he was knighted by Queen Elizabeth in 1953. He is President of the Institute of Contemporary Arts, London.